레전드 **한국어** 필수단어

BASIC
KOREAN
VOCABULARY

English ver.

레전드 한국어 필수단어 English ver.

BASIC KOREAN VOCABULARY

6th Edition published 2025.1.10.
1st Edition published 2019.5.20.

written by	the Calling
supervised by	Colin Moore
edited by	Eunkyung Kim
copy-edited by	Jeeyoung Lee
designed by	IndigoBlue
illustrated by	Jeongim Seo
voice actor	Youme Song / Tina Kim
voice recording by	BRIDGE CODE

publisher	Kyung-a Cho
published by	LanguageBooks (101-90-85278, 2008.7.10.)
address	208 Bellavista, (390-14, Hapjeong-dong) 31, Poeun-ro 2na-gil, Mapo-gu, Seoul, Korea
telephone	+82-2-406-0047
fax	+82-2-406-0042
e-mail	languagebooks@hanmail.net
mp3 free download	blog.naver.com/languagebook

ISBN	979-11-5635-115-3 (13710)
Price	KRW19,000

레전드 한국어 필수단어

BASIC
KOREAN
VOCABULARY

English ver.

Language Books

Begin your adventure in this charming country, Korea, with 'BASIC KOREAN VOCABULARY.'

As Korean culture is becoming more active in the world, people are increasingly interested in Korean language. Korean-wave celebrities too are promoting their nation and the fans are watching and listening. During my travels to foreign countries, my pride in being a Korean grows.

Since Korean is written in Hangeul, which is based on very scientific principles, it is easy to learn the basics. Of course, the system of language as a whole is considered a difficult one to learn because it is so different from Western languages, especially English. However, after teaching Korean to foreigners, I've found that these differences can be overcome with both interest and passion. Language is not just a communication tool but a way to learn and understand the culture and lives of others.

<Basic Korean Vocabulary> is a collection of words that are used frequently, in actual conversation, from those essential "dictionary" words to ones that reflect the rapidly changing times. Since the Korean language was developed with honorifics, it is relatively strict in selecting the appropriate vocabulary depending on the situation and the age or status of the people who are communicating. We have added the necessary tips to prevent mistakes in this area. Confidence in language learning is also a must, and so all Korean words and examples have been Romanized for your convenience. There are also MP3 files so that you may listen and follow the correct pronunciation of native Korean speakers. Do your best!

I thank my wonderful friend Colin for helping me finish this book. I hope for the prosperity of Language Books, which published this book.

Finally, I give all my glory to God, who is always the reason for my life.

the Calling writer Joenghee Kim

매력 가득한 나라 한국,
〈레전드 한국어 필수단어〉로 시작하세요.

한국 문화의 세계 진출이 활발해지면서, 한국어에 대한 관심도 갈수록 높아지고
있습니다. 한류 스타들의 활약으로 한국을 알리고 많은 팬들이 보고 듣고
있습니다. 외국을 여행하는 동안, 한국인이라는 자부심도 점점 더 커집니다.

한국어는 매우 과학적인 원리로 만들어진 한글로 표기되기 때문에, 기본 원리를
배우기는 쉬운 편입니다. 물론 언어의 체계는 서양의 언어, 특히 영어와는
상당히 다른 구조로 되어 있기 때문에 배우기 어려운 언어로 꼽히기도 합니다.
하지만 필자가 외국인에게 한국어를 지도해 본 결과, 이는 한국어와 한국
문화에 대한 관심과 열정으로 충분히 극복할 수 있음을 알게 되었습니다.
언어는 그저 대화의 수단이라는 접근보다는 문화와 생활을 통해 이해하며
익혀야 합니다.

〈레전드 한국어 필수단어〉는 실제 회화에서 자주 사용되는 단어의 모음으로,
사전에 수록된 필수 어휘에서부터 급변하는 시대적 상황을 최대한 반영한
단어들까지 수록하였습니다. 존댓말이 발달된 한국어는 상황이나 나이,
대화하는 사람들과의 신분에 따라 엄격하게 골라 써야 합니다. 이 부분에
대해 실수하지 않도록 필요한 팁을 추가해 놓았습니다. 언어 학습에서 자신감
또한 필수이므로, 학습자 편의를 위해 모든 한국어 단어와 예문을 로마자로
표기하였습니다. 또한 녹음을 듣고 원어민의 정확한 발음을 따라 할 수 있도록
MP3 음원이 있습니다. 최선을 다하세요!

이 책이 완성될 수 있도록 도와준 나의 멋진 친구 Colin에게 감사의 마음을
전합니다. 이 책이 출판될 수 있도록 힘써 준 랭귀지북스의 번창을 빕니다.

마지막으로, 언제나 내 삶의 이유 되시는 하나님께 모든 영광을 돌립니다.

저자 더 콜링_김정희

About this book

We've collected the most commonly used vocabulary in Korea. We're confident that these essentials of daily life will help lay the foundation for your Korean language learning.

1. Nearly 3,200 essential Korean words!

This book contains vocabulary for beginner to intermediate Korean learners. In it, we've included 6 chapters of 24 must-have units or topics, plus an additional 13 topics. Together, the collection amounts to almost 3,200 words.

After learning each of the 24 topics, you can practice with Useful Conversations, dialogues based on real situations. You can then test yourself with review Exercises at the end of each chapter.

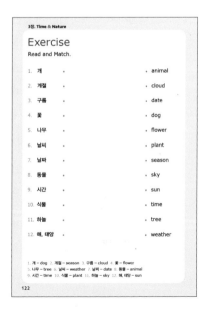

이 책의 특징

한국에서 가장 많이 쓰는 필수 어휘를 엄선하여 모았습니다. 일상생활에 꼭 필요한 어휘 학습을 통해, 다양한 회화 구사를 위한 기본 바탕을 다져 보세요.

1. 한국어 필수 어휘 약 3,200개!

왕초보부터 중급 수준의 한국어 학습자를 위한 필수 어휘를 수록하고 있습니다. 일상생활에서 꼭 필요한 대표 주제 24개를 선정하였고, 13개 주제를 추가하여 약 3,200여 개의 어휘를 담았습니다.

24개 주제별 어휘 학습 후 'Useful Conversation(실전 회화)'의 실제 상황에 입각한 회화에서 어떻게 응용되는지 확인해 보세요. 그리고 각 장의 마지막에는 간단한 'Exercise(연습 문제)'가 있어 테스트도 할 수 있습니다.

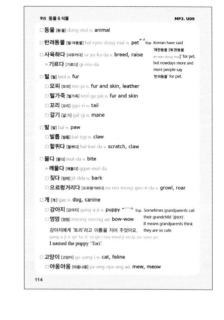

2. Strengthen your basic vocabulary with easy-to-understand pictures!

You can assist your learning with more than 1,000 illustrations. Give yourself a visual boost!

3. Romanized Korean lets you speak Korean immediately!

The easiest way for pure beginners to read Korean is via Romanization. Korean pronunciation by way of the Roman alphabet is not a perfect match but is helpful nonetheless. The contents of this book are Romanized as closely as possible with pronunciation in the Standard Korean Dictionary. Beginners can speak confidently.

4. MP3 audio for intensive speaking training!

This book has audio recordings of the Korean alphabet (consonants and vowels), basic words and more, recorded by a special Korean voice actress.

We provide two recordings for your learning practice: the Korean version and the Korean-English version. Choose the file that meets your level and needs. Listen regularly and repeat loudly and your Korean language skills will strengthen as you become more fluent.

2. 눈에 쏙 들어오는 그림으로 기본 어휘 다지기!

1,000여 컷 이상의 일러스트가 당신의 학습을 도와줄 것입니다. 재미있고 생생한 그림과 함께 학습하는 기본 어휘는 기억이 오래 남습니다.

3. 바로 찾아 즉시 말할 수 있는 로마자로 발음 표기!

기초가 부족한 초보 학습자가 한국어를 읽을 수 있는 가장 쉬운 방법은 바로 로마자로 발음을 표기하는 것입니다. 한국어 발음이 로마자와 일대일로 대응하지 않지만, 여러분의 학습에 편의를 드리고자 표준국어대사전에 있는 표준 발음과 최대한 가깝게 로마자로 표기하였습니다. 초보자도 자신 있게 말할 수 있습니다.

4. 말하기 집중 훈련 MP3!

이 책에는 한글의 자음, 모음부터 기본 단어, 기타 추가 단어까지 한국어 전문 성우의 정확한 발음으로 녹음한 파일이 들어 있습니다.

한국어만으로 구성된 '한국어' K 버전과 한국어와 영어를 이어서 들을 수 있는 '한국어+영어' E 버전, 두 가지 파일을 제공합니다. 학습자 수준과 원하는 구성에 따라 파일을 선택하세요. 꾸준히 듣고 큰 소리로 따라 하면 당신의 한국어 실력이 유창해질 것입니다.

Contents

차례

About

Republic of Korea

The Flag of Republic of Korea
(**태극기** [태극끼] tae-geuk-ggi)

✔ **Name of Country**	Republic of Korea
	(**대한민국** [대:한민국] dae-han-min-guk)
✔ **Location**	Asia (Northeast Asia)
✔ **Capital**	Seoul (**서울** [서울] seo-ul)
✔ **Official Language**	Korean (**한국어** [한:구거] han-gu-geo)
✔ **Population**	51.69 million (2024)
✔ **Area**	100,364㎢
✔ **GDP**	$1.6 trillion (2024)
✔ **Currency**	South Korean Won(KRW) (**원** [원] won)

* source www.korea.net, tradingeconomics.com

Learning the Basics

- About Korean Language and Letters

About Korean Language and Letters
한국어와 한글 han-gu-geo-wa han-geul

Hangeul 한글 han-geul

MP3. U00

Hangeul is the Korean alphabet. This written form of the Korean language was commissioned by King Sejong (1397-1450) during the Joseon Dynasty and made the nation's official script in 1446. Hangeul today is composed of nineteen consonants and twenty-one vowels.

1. Consonants 자음 ja-eum

tip. Consonants in the Korean alphabet may sound differently depending on whether they are the initial or final letter in a syllable. Some consonants only appear in either the initial or final position in a syllable.

• 9 plain consonants

letter	letter's name	sample word		meaning
ㄱ	기역 gi-yeok	가구	[가구] ga-gu	furniture
ㄴ	니은 ni-eun	나비	[나비] na-bi	butterfly
ㄷ	디귿 di-geut	다리미	[다리미] da-ri-mi	iron
ㄹ	리을 ri-eul	라디오	[라디오] ra-di-o	radio
ㅁ	미음 mi-eum	마차	[마:차] ma-cha	carriage, wagon
ㅂ	비읍 bi-eup	바지	[바지] ba-ji	trousers, pants
ㅅ	시옷 si-ot	사탕	[사탕] sa-tang	candy
ㅇ	이응 i-eung	아기	[아기] a-gi	baby
ㅈ	지읒 ji-eut	자유	[자유] ja-yu	freedom

14

• 5 aspirated consonants

letter	letter's name	sample word	meaning
ㅊ	치읓 chi-eut	차표 [차표] cha-pyo	ticket
ㅋ	키읔 ki-euk	카메라 [카메라] ka-me-ra	camera
ㅌ	티읕 ti-eut	타조 [타:조] ta-jo	ostrich
ㅍ	피읖 pi-eup	파도 [파도] pa-do	wave
ㅎ	히읗 hi-eut	하마 [하마] ha-ma	hippopotamus

• 5 tense consonants

letter	letter's name	sample word	meaning
ㄲ	쌍기역 ssang-gi-yeok	까치 [까:치] gga-chi	magpie
ㄸ	쌍디귿 ssang-di-geut	딸기 [딸:기] ddal-gi	strawberry
ㅃ	쌍비읍 ssang-bi-eup	빨래 [빨래] bbal-rae	laundry
ㅆ	쌍시옷 ssang-si-ot	쌍둥이 [쌍둥이] ssang-dung-i	twins
ㅉ	쌍지읒 ssang-ji-eut	짜장면 [짜장면] jja-jang-myeon	black bean sauce noodles

tip. Consonants in the Korean alphabet can be combined into 11 consonant clusters, which always appear in the final position in a syllable.
They are: ㄳ, ㄵ, ㄶ, ㄺ, ㄻ, ㄼ, ㄽ, ㄾ, ㄿ, ㅀ, and ㅄ.

2. Vowels 모음 mo-eum

tip. The vowels 'o [이응 i-eung]' has no sound, just form.

• 6 simple vowels

letter	letter's name	sample word	meaning
ㅏ	아 a	바나나 [바나나] ba-na-na	banana
ㅓ	어 eo	어머니 [어머니] eo-meo-ni	mother
ㅗ	오 o	도로 [도:로] do-ro	road
ㅜ	우 u	구두 [구두] gu-du	shoes
ㅡ	으 eu	드레스 [드레스] deu-re-seu	dress
ㅣ	이 i	기린 [기린] gi-rin	giraffe

• 9 compound vowels

letter	letter's name	sample word	meaning
ㅐ	애 ae	냄새 [냄:새] naem-sae	smell
ㅔ	에 e	세제 [세:제] se-je	detergent
ㅘ	와 wa	과일 [과:일] gwa-il	fruit
ㅙ	왜 wae	돼지 [돼:지] dwae-ji	pig
ㅚ	외 oe	외국 [외:국/웨:국] oe-guk/we-guk	foreign country
ㅝ	워 wo	권투 [권:투] gwon-tu	boxing
ㅞ	웨 we	웨이터 [웨이터] we-i-teo	waiter
ㅟ	위 wi	취미 [취:미] chwi-mi	hobby
ㅢ	의 ui	의자 [의자] ui-ja	chair

16

• 6 iotized vowels

letter	letter's name	sample word		meaning
ㅑ	야 ya	야구	[야:구] ya-gu	baseball
ㅓ	여 yeo	여자	[여자] yeo-ja	woman
ㅛ	요 yo	교수	[교:수] gyo-su	professor
ㅠ	유 yu	유리	[유리] yu-ri	glass
ㅒ	얘 yae	얘기	[얘:기] yae-gi	story
ㅖ	예 ye	예약	[예:약] ye-yak	reservation

System of the Parts of a Speech
Please refer these notations about parts of speech in this book.

n.	명사	v.	동사	a.	형용사	ad.	부사
suf.	접미사	b.n.	의존명사	d.n.	관형명사	num.	수사
d.	관형사	p.	조사				

1장

Greetings

1과 **Introductions**
2과 **Gratitude & Apologies**

Introductions 소개 so-gae

□ **소개** [소개] so-gae
　n. introduction

□ **소개하다** [소개하다] so-gae-ha-da
　v. introduce

□ **이름** [이름] i-reum
　n. name, first name

□ **성명** [성:명] seong-myeong
　n. name

□ **명함** [명함] myeong-ham
　n. business card

□ **성별** [성:별] seong-byeol
　n. sex

□ **남자** [남자] nam-ja
　n. man

□ **남성** [남성] nam-seong
　n. male

□ **아저씨** [아저씨] a-jeo-ssi
　= **아재** [아재] a-jae
　n. sir

□ **여자** [여자] yeo-ja
　n. woman

□ **여성** [여성] yeo-seong
　n. female

□ **아주머니** [아주머니] a-ju-meo-ni
　= **아줌마** [아줌마] a-jum-ma
　n. ma'am

□ **나이** [나이] na-i

　　n. age

□ **생일** [생일] saeng-il

　　n. birthday

□ **국적** [국쩍] guk-jjeok

　　n. nationality

□ **국가** [국까] guk-gga

= **나라** [나라] na-ra

　　n. nation, country

□ **언어** [어너] eo-neo

　　n. language

□ **직업** [지겁] ji-geop

　　n. job, occupation, profession

□ **주소** [주:소] ju-so

　　n. address

□ **전화번호** [전:화번호]

jeon-hwa-beon-ho

　　n. phone number

□ **인사** [인사] in-sa

n. greeting

□ **인사하다** [인사하다] in-sa-ha-da

v. greet

□ **안녕하세요!** an-nyeong-ha-se-yo!

Hello!

□ **안녕!** an-nyeong!

Hi!

□ **반가워(요).** ban-ga-wo(-yo)

Nice to meet you.

□ **안녕히 주무세요. / 잘 자.**

an-nyeong-hi ju-mu-se-yo / jal ja

Good night.

□ **어떻게 지내(요)?**

eo-ddeo-ke ji-nae(-yo)?

How are you?

□ **안녕히 가세요. / 잘 가.**

an-nyeong-hi ga-se-yo / jal ga

Good bye.

□ **또 만나(요).** ddo man-na(-yo)

See you again.

□ **실례합니다.** sil-rye-ham-ni-da
Excuse me.

□ **감사합니다. / 고마워(요).**
gam-sa-ham-ni-da / go-ma-wo(-yo)
Thank you. / Thanks.

□ **미안해(요).** mi-an-hae(-yo)
= **죄송해요.** joe-song-hae-yo/
jwe-song-hae-yo
I'm sorry.

□ **천만에(요).** cheon-ma-ne(-yo)
You're welcome.

□ **괜찮아(요).** gwaen-cha-na(-yo)
It's okay.

□ **환영하다** [환영하다]
hwan-yeong-ha-da
v. welcome

□ **초대하다** [초대하다] cho-dae-ha-da
v. invite

□ **손님** [손님] son-nim
n. guest

□ **친구** [친구] chin-gu
= **벗** [벋ː] beot
n. friend

23

□ **소개** [소개] so-gae n. introduction

　□ **소개하다** [소개하다] so-gae-ha-da v. introduce

　　□ **자기소개** [자기소개] ja-gi-so-gae n. self-introduction

　제 소개를 하겠습니다.
　je so-gae-reul ha-get-sseum-ni-da
　Let me introduce myself.

□ **이름** [이름] i-reum n. name, first name

　□ **성명** [성:명] seong-myeong n. name

　□ **성함** [성:함] seong-ham n. name

　tip. '성함' is the formal of '이름'. Use '성함' is better for elders.

　이름이 뭐예요?
　i-reu-mi mwo-ye-yo?
　May I have your name?

□ **성** [성:] seong n. last name

　'김'은 성입니다.
　gi-meun seong-im-ni-da
　'Kim' is my last name.

□ **별명** [별명] byeol-myeong n. nickname

□ **명함** [명함] myeong-ham n. business card

　명함 한 장 주시겠어요?
　myeong-ham han jang ju-si-ge-sseo-yo?
　May I have your business card?

□ **성별** [성:별] seong-byeol n. sex

□ **남자** [남자] nam-ja n. man

　□ **남성** [남성] nam-seong n. male

□ **사나이** [사나이] sa-na-i n. guy

= **사내** [사내] sa-nae

tip. '사내' is the abbreviation of '사나이'.

그는 멋진 사나이예요.
geu-neun meot-jjin sa-na-i-e-yo
He is a nice guy.

□ **아저씨** [아저씨] a-jeo-ssi n. sir

= **아재** [아재] a-jae

tip. '아재' is the informal abbreviation of '아저씨'.

□ **여자** [여자] yeo-ja n. woman

□ **여성** [여성] yeo-seong n. female

□ **아주머니** [아주머니] a-ju-meo-ni n. ma'am

= **아줌마** [아줌마] a-jum-ma

tip. '아줌마' is the informal abbreviation of '아주머니'.

□ **나이** [나이] na-i n. age

□ **연세** [연세] yeon-se n. age •⎯⎯⎯⎯→ **tip.** '연세' is the formal of '나이'.
Use '연세' is better for elders.

□ **생일** [생일] saeng-il n. birthday

오늘이 내 생일이에요.
o-neu-ri nae saeng-i-ri-e-yo
This is my birthday.

□ **국적** [국쩍] guk-jjeok n. nationality

국적이 어떻게 돼요?
guk-jjeo-gi eo-ddeo-ke dwae-yo?
What's your nationality?

□ **국가** [국까] guk-gga n. nation, country

= **나라** [나라] na-ra

□ **고국** [고:국] go-guk n. one's homeland

□ **언어** [어너] eo-neo n. language

□ **모국어** [모:구거] mo-gu-geo n. mother tongue

□ **외국어** [외:구거/웨:구거] oe-gu-geo/we-gu-geo n. foreign language

몇 가지 언어를 할 수 있어요?
myeot ga-ji eo-neo-reul hal ssu i-sseo-yo?
How many languages do you speak?

□ **한국어** [한:구거] han-gu-geo n. Korean (language)

□ **영어** [영어] yeong-eo n. English

□ **중국어** [중구거] jung-gu-geo n. Chinese

□ **일본어** [일보너] il-bo-neo n. Japanese

□ **독일어** [도기러] do-gi-reo n. German

□ **프랑스어** [프랑스어] peu-rang-seu-eo n. French

□ **스페인어** [스페이너] seu-pe-i-neo n. Spanish

= **에스파냐어** [에스파냐어] e-seu-pa-nya-eo

□ **직업** [지겁] ji-geop n. job, occupation, profession

□ **직장** [직짱] jik-jjang n. workplace

□ **업무** [엄무] eom-mu n. work, task, business

□ **직급** [직끕] jik-ggeup n. position

= **직위** [지뒤] ji-gwi

직업은 무엇입니까?
ji-geo-beun mu-eo-sim-ni-gga?
What's your occupation?

□ **전공** [전공] jeon-gong n. major

   □ **부전공** [부:전공] bu-jeon-gong n. minor

   □ **복수전공** [복쑤전공] bok-ssu-jeon-gong double major

□ **학년** [항년] hang-nyeon n. grade, school year

□ **종교** [종교] jong-gyo n. religion

   □ **기독교** [기독꾜] gi-dok-ggyo n. Christianity

   □ **천주교** [천주교] cheon-ju-gyo n. Catholicism

   □ **불교** [불교] bul-gyo n. Buddhism

   □ **이슬람교** [이슬람교] i-seul-ram-gyo n. Islam

   무슨 종교를 믿어요?
   mu-seun jong-gyo-reul mi-deo-yo?
   What religion do you believe in?

□ **살다** [살:다] sal-da v. live

□ **주소** [주:소] ju-so n. address

   주소를 말해 주실래요?
   ju-so-reul mal-hae ju-sil-rae-yo?
   Would you please tell me your address?

□ **전화번호** [전:화번호] jeon-hwa-beon-ho n. phone number

□ **가족** [가족] ga-jok n. family

   □ **식구** [식꾸] sik-ggu n. family member

□ **안부** [안부] an-bu n. say hello

   가족에게 안부를 전해 주세요.
   ga-jo-ge-ge an-bu-reul jeon-hae ju-se-yo
   Say hello to your family for me.

□ **인사** [인사] in-sa n. greeting

□ **인사하다** [인사하다] in-sa-ha-da v. **greet**

안녕하세요!
an-nyeong-ha-se-yo!
Hello!

안녕!
an-nyeong!
Hi!

반가워(요). ●——→ **tip.** '∼요 [-yo]' and '∼니다 [-ni-da]' are the polite expressions.
ban-ga-wo(-yo)   Korean uses honorific language for elder people.
Nice to meet you.

안녕히 주무세요. / 잘 자.
an-nyeong-hi ju-mu-se-yo / jal ja
Good night.

어떻게 지내(요)?
eo-ddeo-ke ji-nae(-yo)?
How are you?

잘 지내(요).
jal ji-nae(-yo)
I'm doing well.

아니(요), 못 지내(요).
a-ni(-yo), mot ji-nae(-yo)
No, I'm not well.

별로(요).
byeol-ro(-yo)
Not so good.

그럭저럭(요).
geu-reok-jjeo-reok(-yo)
So-so.

식사하셨어요? / 밥 먹었니?
sik-ssa-ha-syeo-sseo-yo? / bap meo-geon-ni?
Did you eat yet?

tip. The other meaning of '식사하셨어요?' is 'How are you?'.
It is a kind of Korean culture.

오랜만이네(요).
o-raen-ma-ni-ne(-yo)
Long time no see.

안녕히 가세요. / 잘 가.
an-nyeong-hi ga-se-yo / jal ga
Good bye.

이따가 만나(요).
i-dda-ga man-na(-yo)
See you later.

또 만나(요).
ddo man-na(-yo)
See you again.

내일 만나(요).
nae-il man-na(-yo)
See you tomorrow.

실례합니다.
sil-rye-ham-ni-da
Excuse me.

좋은 주말 되세요.
jo-eun ju-mal doe-se-yo
Have a nice weekend.

어서 오세요. / 어서 와(요).
eo-seo o-se-yo / eo-seo wa(-yo)
Welcome. / Come on.

감사합니다. / 고마워(요).
gam-sa-ham-ni-da / go-ma-wo(-yo)
Thank you. / Thanks.

천만에(요).
cheon-ma-ne(-yo)
You're welcome.

미안해(요). / 죄송해요. •————————→ **tip.** '죄송해요' is politer than '미안해요'.
mi-an-hae(-yo) / joe-song-hae-yo/jwe-song-hae-yo
I'm sorry.

괜찮아(요).
gwaen-cha-na(-yo)
It's okay.

□ **환영** [환영] hwan-yeong n. **welcome**

  □ **환영하다** [환영하다] hwan-yeong-ha-da v. **welcome**

서울에 오신 걸 환영합니다.
seo-u-re o-sin geol hwan-yeong-ham-ni-da
Welcome to Seoul.

□ **초대** [초대] cho-dae n. **invitation**

  □ **초대하다** [초대하다] cho-dae-ha-da v. **invite**

  □ **초대장** [초대짱] cho-dae-jjang n. **invitation card**

그를 초대하기 싫어요.
geu-reul cho-dae-ha-gi si-reo-yo
I don't want to invite him.

□ **손님** [손님] son-nim n. **guest**

□ **지인** [지인] ji-in n. **acquaintance**

  = **아는 사람** [아는 사람] a-neun sa-ram

□ **친구** [친구] chin-gu **n. friend**

= **벗** [벋ː] beot

그는 제일 친한 친구입니다.
geu-neun je-il chin-han chin-gu-im-ni-da
He is my best friend.

이. 인사

Useful Conversation

김미나   안녕, 헨리. 잘 지냈니?
          an-nyeong, hen-ri. jal ji-naet-ni?
          Hi, Henry. How are you doing?

Henry   잘 지냈어. 주말 어떻게 보냈니?
          jal ji-nae-sseo. ju-mal eo-ddeo-ke bo-naet-ni?
          Pretty good. How's your weekend?

김미나   그럭저럭. 친구들과 나영이네 집에 갔었어.
          geu-reok-jjeo-reok. chin-gu-deul-gwa na-yeong-i-ne ji-be
          ga-sseo-sseo
          Not bad. I went to Nayeong's house with some
          friends.

Henry   나영이는 어때?
          na-yeong-i-neun eo-ddae?
          How's Nayeoung?

김미나   걔는 잘 지내.
          gyae-neun jal ji-nae
          She is fine.

Gratitude & Apologies 감사 & 사과 gam-sa & sa-gwa

□ **감사** [감:사] gam-sa
n. gratitude, appreciation

□ **감사하다** [감:사하다] gam-sa-ha-da
a. thankful v. thank, appreciate

□ **고맙다** [고:맙따] go-map-dda
a. thankful

□ **친절** [친절] chin-jeol
n. kindness

□ **친절하다** [친절하다]
chin-jeol-ha-da
a. kind

□ **도움** [도움] do-um
n. help, assistance

□ **돕다** [돕:따] dop-dda
v. help

□ **혜택** [혜:택/헤:택] hye-taek/he-taek
n. benefit

□ **배려** [배:려] bae-ryeo
n. consideration

□ **신세** [신세] sin-se
n. favor

□ **은혜** [은혜/은헤] eun-hye/eun-he
n. favor

□ **보살피다** [보살피다] bo-sal-pi-da
= **돌보다** [돌:보다] dol-bo-da
v. take care of

□ **이해** [이:해] i-hae

　n. understanding

□ **이해하다** [이:해하다] i-hae-ha-da

　v. understand

□ **기다리다** [기다리다] gi-da-ri-da

　v. wait

□ **기회** [기회/기훼] gi-hoe/gi-hwe

　n. chance

□ **격려** [경녀] gyeong-nyeo

　n. encouragement

□ **격려하다** [경녀하다]

　gyeong-nyeo-ha-da

　v. cheer, encourage

□ **충고** [충고] chung-go

　n. advice

□ **충고하다** [충고하다]

　chung-go-ha-da

　v. advise

□ **칭찬** [칭찬] ching-chan

　n. compliment

□ **칭찬하다** [칭찬하다]

　ching-chan-ha-da

　v. praise

□ **사과** [사:과] sa-gwa
n. apology

□ **사과하다** [사:과하다] sa-gwa-ha-da
v. apologize

□ **미안하다** [미안하다] mi-an-ha-da
= **죄송하다** [죄:송하다/줴:송하다]
joe-song-ha-da/jwe-song-ha-da
a. sorry

□ **용서** [용서] yong-seo
n. forgiveness

□ **용서하다** [용서하다] yong-seo-ha-da
v. forgive

□ **잘못** [잘몯] jal-mot
n. fault
ad. wrongly

□ **잘못하다** [잘모타다] jal-mo-ta-da
v. do wrong

□ **실수** [실쑤] sil-ssu
n. mistake

□ **실수하다** [실쑤하다] sil-ssu-ha-da
v. make a mistake

□ **틀리다** [틀리다] teul-ri-da
v. be wrong

□ **난처하다** [난:처하다] nan-cheo-ha-da
　a. embarrassing, awkward

□ **착각** [착깍] chak-ggak
　n. illusion

□ **착각하다** [착까카다] chak-gga-ka-da
　v. be confused

□ **곤란** [골:란] gol-ran
　n. trouble

□ **곤란하다** [골:란하다] gol-ran-ha-da
　a. difficult, hard

□ **피해** [피:해] pi-hae
　n. harm, damage

□ **손해** [손:해] son-hae
　= **손실** [손:실] son-sil
　n. damage, loss

□ **방해** [방해] bang-hae
　= **훼방** [훼:방] hwe-bang
　n. disturbance, interruption

□ **방해하다** [방해하다]
　bang-hae-ha-da
　v. disturb, interrupt

□ **비난** [비:난] bi-nan
　n. blame

□ **비난하다** [비:난하다] bi-nan-ha-da
　v. blame

□ **지각** [지각] ji-gak
　n. lateness, tardiness

□ **지각하다** [지가카다] ji-ga-ka-da
　v. be late

□ **감사** [감:사] gam-sa n. **gratitude, appreciation**

　□ **감사하다** [감:사하다] gam-sa-ha-da a. **thankful** v. **thank, appreciate**

　감사합니다.
　gam-sa-ham-ni-da
　Thank you.

□ **고마움** [고:마움] go-ma-um n. **gratitude, appreciation**

　□ **고맙다** [고:맙따] go-map-dda a. **thankful**

□ **친절** [친절] chin-jeol n. **kindness**

　□ **친절하다** [친절하다] chin-jeol-ha-da a. **kind**

　당신은 참 친절해요.
　dang-si-neun cham chin-jeol-hae-yo
　You are so kind.

□ **도움** [도움] do-um n. **help, assistance**

　□ **돕다** [돕:따] dop-dda v. **help**

　당신 도움에 감사합니다.
　dang-sin do-u-me gam-sa-ham-ni-da
　Thank you for your help.

□ **베풀다** [베풀다] be-pul-da v. **oblige**

□ **관심** [관심] gwan-sim n. **concern, interest**

□ **기쁨** [기쁨] gi-bbeum n. **pleasure**

□ **혜택** [혜:택/헤:택] hye-taek/he-taek n. **benefit**

□ **자비** [자비] ja-bi n. **mercy**

□ **배려** [배:려] bae-ryeo n. **consideration**

　□ **배려하다** [배:려하다] bae-ryeo-ha-da v. **consider**

□ **신세** [신세] sin-se n. favor

  □ **은혜** [은혜/은헤] eun-hye/eun-he n. favor

  당신에게 신세를 졌습니다.
  dang-si-ne-ge sin-se-reul jeot-sseum-ni-da
  I accepted a favor from you.

□ **걱정** [걱쩡] geok-jjeong n. worry, concern

□ **염려** [염:녀] yeom-nyeo n. worry, anxiety

□ **관대하다** [관:대하다] gwan-dae-ha-da a. generous

  그는 관대해요.
  geu-neun gwan-dae-hae-yo
  He is generous.

□ **대접** [대:접] dae-jeop n. reception, treatment

  = **접대** [접때] jeop-ddae

  □ **한턱** [한턱] han-teok n. treat

  □ **한턱내다** [한텅내다] han-teong-nae-da v. give a treat

□ **보살핌** [보살핌] bo-sal-pim n. care

  □ **보살피다** [보살피다] bo-sal-pi-da v. take care of

  = **돌보다** [돌:보다] dol-bo-da

□ **이해** [이:해] i-hae n. understanding

  □ **이해하다** [이:해하다] i-hae-ha-da v. understand

  □ **양해** [양해] yang-hae n. understanding, excuse

  당신은 그것을 이해할 수 있어요?
  dang-si-neun geu-geo-seul i-hae-hal ssu i-sseo-yo?
  Do you understand it?

□ **기다리다** [기다리다] gi-da-ri-da v. wait

□ **기회** [기회/기훼] gi-hoe/gi-hwe n. chance

기회를 주셔서 감사합니다.
gi-hoe-reul ju-syeo-seo gam-sa-ham-ni-da
Thank you for giving me a chance.

□ **격려** [경녀] gyeong-nyeo n. encouragement

□ **격려하다** [경녀하다] gyeong-nyeo-ha-da v. cheer, encourage

그를 격려해 주세요.
geu-reul gyeong-nyeo-hae ju-se-yo
Encourage him please.

□ **충고** [충고] chung-go n. advice

□ **충고하다** [충고하다] chung-go-ha-da v. advise

□ **타이르다** [타이르다] ta-i-reu-da v. persuade, advise

충고 고마워요.
chung-go go-ma-wo-yo
Thank you for your advice.

□ **칭찬** [칭찬] ching-chan n. compliment

□ **칭찬하다** [칭찬하다] ching-chan-ha-da v. praise

□ **사과** [사:과] sa-gwa n. apology

□ **사과하다** [사:과하다] sa-gwa-ha-da v. apologize

□ **미안하다** [미안하다] mi-an-ha-da a. sorry

= **죄송하다** [죄:송하다/줴:송하다] joe-song-ha-da/jwe-song-ha-da

당신에게 사과합니다.
dang-si-ne-ge sa-gwa-ham-ni-da
I apologize to you.

□ **용서** [용서] yong-seo n. forgiveness

  □ **용서하다** [용서하다] yong-seo-ha-da v. forgive

□ **문제** [문:제] mun-je n. problem

□ **잘못** [잘몯] jal-mot n. fault ad. wrongly

  □ **잘못하다** [잘모타다] jal-mo-ta-da v. do wrong

제 잘못이었어요.
je jal-mo-si-eo-sseo-yo
It was my fault.

□ **실수** [실쑤] sil-ssu n. mistake

  □ **실수하다** [실쑤하다] sil-ssu-ha-da v. make a mistake

  □ **틀리다** [틀리다] teul-ri-da v. be wrong

제가 실수했어요.
je-ga sil-ssu-hae-sseo-yo
I made a mistake.

□ **탓** [탇] tat n. blame, reason

제 탓이었어요.
je ta-si-eo-sseo-yo
I blame no one but myself.

□ **착각** [착깍] chak-ggak n. illusion

  □ **착각하다** [착까카다] chak-gga-ka-da v. be confused

□ **오해** [오해] o-hae n. misunderstanding

  □ **오해하다** [오해하다] o-hae-ha-da v. misunderstand

□ **난처하다** [난:처하다] nan-cheo-ha-da a. embarrassing, awkward

□ **번거롭다** [번거롭따] beon-geo-rop-dda a. inconvenient

□ **방해** [방해] bang-hae n. disturbance, interruption

  = **훼방** [훼:방] hwe-bang

  □ **방해하다** [방해하다] bang-hae-ha-da v. disturb, interrupt

  방해해서 미안해요.
  bang-hae-hae-seo mi-an-hae-yo
  Sorry for disturbing you.

□ **곤란** [골:란] gol-ran n. trouble

  □ **곤란하다** [골:란하다] gol-ran-ha-da a. difficult, hard

  곤란에 빠뜨려서 미안합니다.
  gol-ra-ne bba-ddeu-ryeo-seo mi-an-ham-ni-da
  Sorry for getting you into trouble.

□ **비난** [비:난] bi-nan n. blame

  □ **비난하다** [비:난하다] bi-nan-ha-da v. blame

□ **헐뜯다** [헐:뜯따] heol-ddeut-dda v. speak ill of

  = **흉보다** [흉보다] hyung-bo-da

□ **일부러** [일:부러] il-bu-reo ad. on purpose

  □ **고의** [고:의/고:이] go-ui/go-i n. purpose

  일부러 하지 않았어요.
  il-bu-reo ha-ji a-na-sseo-yo
  I didn't do it on purpose.

□ **의도** [의:도] ui-do n. intention

  □ **선의** [서:늬/서:니] seo-nui/seo-ni n. good intentions

  □ **악의** [아긔/아기] a-gwi/a-gi n. spite

□ **피해** [피:해] pi-hae n. harm, damage

□ **손해** [손:해] son-hae n. damage, loss

= **손실** [손:실] son-sil

이건 나한테 많이 손해예요.
i-geon na-han-te ma-ni son-hae-ye-yo
It is huge loss for me.

□ **지각** [지각] ji-gak n. lateness, tardiness

□ **지각하다** [지가카다] ji-ga-ka-da v. be late

지각해서 죄송합니다.
ji-ga-ke-seo joe-song-ham-ni-da
Excuse me for being late.

02. 감사 인사

Useful Conversation

박종훈   실례지만, 이제 가야겠습니다.
      sil-rye-ji-man, i-je ga-ya-get-sseum-ni-da
      Excuse me, but I must be going now.

강민수   괜찮습니다. 오늘 회의를 함께하게 되어 감사합니다.
      gwaen-chan-sseum-ni-da. o-neul hoe-i-reul ham-gge-ha-ge
      doe-eo gam-sa-ham-ni-da
      That's okay. Thank you for meeting with us today.

박종훈   천만에요. 좋은 하루 되세요.
      cheon-ma-ne-yo. jo-eun ha-ru doe-se-yo
      It was my pleasure. Have a good day.

강민수   당신도요.
      dang-sin-do-yo
      You too.

Exercise

Read and Match.

1. 감사하다 •   • address

2. 국가, 나라 •   • age

3. 나이 •   • fault

4. 돕다 •   • forgive

5. 미안하다 •   • greeting

6. 소개 •   • help

7. 용서하다 •   • introduction

8. 이름 •   • kind

9. 인사 •   • name

10. 잘못 •   • nation, country

11. 주소 •   • sorry

12. 친절하다 •   • thank

1. 감사하다 – thank 2. 국가, 나라 – nation, country 3. 나이 – age 4. 돕다 – help
5. 미안하다 – sorry 6. 소개 – introduction 7. 용서하다 – forgive 8. 이름 – name
9. 인사 – greeting 10. 잘못 – fault 11. 주소 – address 12. 친절하다 – kind

2장

People

The Body 신체 sin-che

□ **신체** [신체] sin-che
= **몸** [몸] mom
n. body

□ **머리** [머리] meo-ri
n. head

□ **목** [목] mok
n. neck

□ **어깨** [어깨] eo-ggae
n. shoulder

□ **등** [등] deung
n. back

□ **가슴** [가슴] ga-seum
n. chest

□ **배** [배] bae
n. stomach

□ **머리카락** [머리카락]
meo-ri-ka-rak
n. hair

□ **팔** [팔] pal
n. arm

□ **팔꿈치** [팔꿈치]
pal-ggum-chi
n. elbow

□ **허리** [허리] heo-ri
n. waist

□ **엉덩이** [엉:덩이]
eong-deong-i
n. hip

□ **다리** [다리] da-ri
n. leg

□ **무릎** [무릅] mu-reup
n. knee

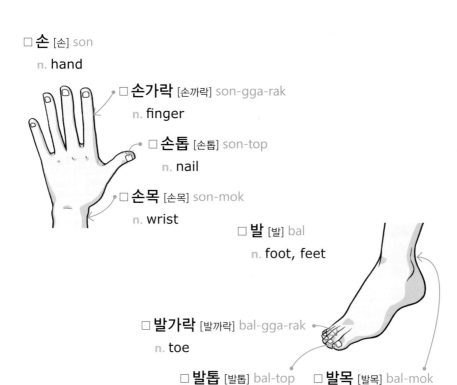

□ **손** [손] son
  n. hand

□ **손가락** [손까락] son-gga-rak
  n. finger

□ **손톱** [손톱] son-top
  n. nail

□ **손목** [손목] son-mok
  n. wrist

□ **발** [발] bal
  n. foot, feet

□ **발가락** [발까락] bal-gga-rak
  n. toe

□ **발톱** [발톱] bal-top
  n. toenail

□ **발목** [발목] bal-mok
  n. ankle

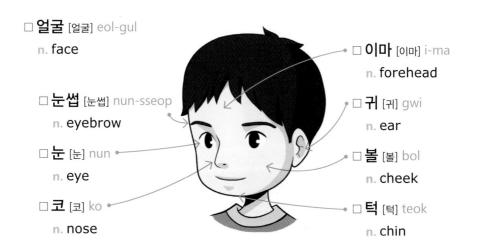

□ **얼굴** [얼굴] eol-gul
  n. face

□ **이마** [이마] i-ma
  n. forehead

□ **눈썹** [눈썹] nun-sseop
  n. eyebrow

□ **귀** [귀] gwi
  n. ear

□ **눈** [눈] nun
  n. eye

□ **볼** [볼] bol
  n. cheek

□ **코** [코] ko
  n. nose

□ **턱** [턱] teok
  n. chin

□ **입** [입] ip

　　n. mouth

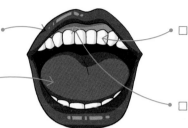

　□ **입술** [입쑬] ip-ssul

　　n. lip

　□ **혀** [혀] hyeo

　　n. tongue

□ **이** [이] i

= **치아** [치아] chi-a

n. tooth, teeth

□ **잇몸** [인몸] in-mom

n. gum

□ **키** [키] ki　　　　□ **크다** [크다] keu-da　　　□ **작다** [작:따] jak-da

　n. height　　　　　a. tall　　　　　　　a. short

□ **몸무게** [몸무게] mom-mu-ge

　n. weight

□ **뚱뚱하다** [뚱뚱하다]　　　　　　□ **날씬하다** [날씬하다]　　

　ddung-ddung-ha-da　　　　　　　　nal-ssin-ha-da

　a. fat　　　　　　　　　　　　a. slender

□ **비만** [비:만] bi-man　　　　　　　□ **홀쭉하다** [홀쭈카다]　　

　n. obesity, corpulence　　　　　　hol-jju-ka-da

　　　　　　　　　　　　　　a. thin

□ **피부** [피부] pi-bu

n. skin

□ **주름** [주름] ju-reum

n. wrinkle

□ **보조개** [보조개]

bo-jo-gae

n. dimple

□ **점** [점] jeom

n. dot

□ **뽀루지** [뽀루지] bbyo-ru-ji

n. pimple, eruption,
rash

□ **모공** [모공] mo-gong

n. pore

□ **외모** [외:모/웨:모]

oe-mo/we-mo

n. appearance

□ **잘생기다** [잘생기다]

jal-saeng-gi-da

v. be handsome

□ **못생기다** [몯:쌩기다]

mot-ssaeng-gi-da

v. be ugly

□ **아름답다** [아름답따]

a-reum-dap-dda

a. beautiful

□ **예쁘다** [예:쁘다]

ye-bbeu-da

a. pretty

□ **귀엽다** [귀:엽따]

gwi-yeop-dda

a. cute

47

☐ **신체** [신체] sin-che n. body

= **몸** [몸] mom

☐ **머리** [머리] meo-ri n. head

☐ **머리카락** [머리카락] meo-ri-ka-rak n. hair

당신의 머리카락은 무슨 색깔이에요?
dang-si-ne meo-ri-ka-ra-geun mu-seun sack gga-ri-e-yo?
What is the color of your hair?

☐ **긴 머리** [긴 머리] gin meo-ri long hair

☐ **짧은 머리** [짤븐 머리] jjal-beun meo-ri short hair

나는 짧은 머리예요.
na-neun jjal-beun meo-ri-ye-yo
I have short hair.

☐ **곱슬머리** [곱쓸머리] gop-sseul-meo-ri n. curly hair

그녀는 곱슬머리에 짧은 금발이에요.
geu-nyeu-neun gop-sseul-meo-ri-e jjal-beun geum-ba-ri-e-yo
She has short, curly blonde hair.

☐ **생머리** [생:머리] saeng-meo-ri n. straight hair

☐ **단발머리** [단:발머리] dan-bal-meo-ri n. bobbed hair

☐ **목** [목] mok n. neck

☐ **어깨** [어깨] eo-ggae n. shoulder

☐ **등** [등] deung n. back

☐ **가슴** [가슴] ga-seum n. chest

☐ **젖가슴** [젇까슴] jeot-gga-seum n. breast

가슴을 펴세요.
ga-seu-meul pyeo-se-yo
Puff your chest out.

□ **배** [배] bae n. stomach ● ────────→ **tip.** '배' has three meanings: stomach, pear and ship.

□ **허리** [허리] heo-ri n. waist

□ **엉덩이** [엉:덩이] eong-deong-i n. hip

□ **팔** [팔] pal n. arm

　□ **팔꿈치** [팔꿈치] pal-ggum-chi n. elbow

　□ **손목** [손목] son-mok n. wrist

□ **손** [손] son n. hand

　□ **손등** [손뜽] son-ddeung n. back of hand

　□ **손바닥** [손빠닥] son-bba-dak n. palm

　손부터 씻으세요.
　son-bu-teo ssi-seu-se-yo
　Wash your hands first.

□ **오른손** [오른손] o-reun-son n. right hand

　= **바른손** [바른손] ba-reun-son

　□ **오른손잡이** [오른손자비] o-reun-son-ja-bi n. right-handed

□ **왼손** [왼:손/웬:손] oen-son/wen-son n. left hand

　□ **왼손잡이** [왼:손자비/웬:손자비] oen-son-ja-bi/wen-son-ja-bi

　n. left-handed

　저는 왼손잡이예요.
　jeo-neun oen-son-ja-bi-ye-yo
　I am left-handed.

□ **손가락** [손까락] son-gga-rak n. finger

  □ **손톱** [손톱] son-top n. nail

□ **다리** [다리] da-ri n. leg

  □ **허벅지** [허벅찌] heo-beok-jji n. thigh

  □ **종아리** [종:아리] jong-a-ri n. calf

□ **무릎** [무릅] mu-reup n. knee

□ **발** [발] bal n. foot, feet

  □ **발바닥** [발빠닥] bal-bba-dak n. sole

  □ **발등** [발뜽] bal-ddeung n. top side of the foot

믿는 도끼에 발등 찍히다.

tip. '믿는 도끼에 발등 찍히다' is a kind of Korean traditional saying.

mit-neun do-ggi-e bal-ddeung jji-ki-da

Trust is the mother of deceit.

□ **발목** [발목] bal-mok n. ankle

발목을 삐었어요.

bal-mo-geul bbi-eo-sseo-yo

I sprained my ankle.

□ **발가락** [발까락] bal-gga-rak n. toe

  □ **발톱** [발톱] bal-top n. toenail

□ **얼굴** [얼굴] eol-gul n. face

  □ **얼굴형** [얼굴형] eol-gul-hyeong n. face shape

  □ **얼굴빛** [얼굴삗] eol-gul-bbit n. complexion

  = **안색** [안색] an-saek

□ **이마** [이마] i-ma n. forehead

그는 이마가 넓어요.
geu-neun i-ma-ga neol-beo-yo
He has a broad forehead.

☐ **귀** [귀] gwi n. ear

☐ **볼** [볼] bol n. cheek

   ☐ **보조개** [보조개] bo-jo-gae n. dimple

나는 양쪽 볼에 보조개가 있어요.
na-neun yang-jjok bo-re bo-jo-gae-ga i-sseo-yo
I have dimples on my cheeks.

☐ **턱** [턱] teok n. chin

☐ **눈썹** [눈썹] nun-sseop n. eyebrow

   ☐ **속눈썹** [송:눈썹] song-nun-sseop n. eyelash

☐ **눈** [눈] nun n. eye •———————→ **tip.** '눈' has two meanings: eye and snow.

   ☐ **눈동자** [눈똥자] nun-ddong-ja n. pupil

   ☐ **쌍꺼풀** [쌍꺼풀] ssang-ggeo-pul n. double eyelid

나는 쌍꺼풀이 있어요.
na-neun ssang-ggeo-pu-ri i-sseo-yo
I have double eyelids.

☐ **코** [코] ko n. nose

   ☐ **콧대** [코때/콛때] ko-ddae/kot-ddae n. the bridge of the nose

   ☐ **콧구멍** [코꾸멍/콛꾸멍] ko-ggu-meong/kot-ggu-meong n. nostril

☐ **입** [입] ip n. mouth

그는 입이 커요.
geu-neun i-bi keo-yo
His mouth is big.

□ **입술** [입쑬] ip-ssul n. lip

□ **혀** [혀] hyeo n. tongue

    □ **혓바닥** [혀빠닥/혇빠닥] hyeo-bba-dak/hyeot-bba-dak

    n. surface of the tongue

□ **이** [이] i n. tooth, teeth

    = **치아** [치아] chi-a

    □ **이빨** [이빨] i-bbal n. tooth, teeth ⌐→ **tip.** '이빨' is used when talking about
                                            an animal's tooth.

□ **잇몸** [인몸] in-mom n. gum

□ **키** [키] ki n. height

키가 얼마입니까?
ki-ga eol-ma-im-ni-gga?
What's your height?

□ **크다** [크다] keu-da a. tall

    □ **키다리** [키다리] ki-da-ri n. beanpole

□ **작다** [작:따] jak-da a. short

    □ **작다리** [작따리] jak-da-ri n. a short person

그는 키가 좀 작아요.
geu-neun ki-ga jom ja-ga-yo
He is a little short.

□ **몸무게** [몸무게] mom-mu-ge n. weight

□ **뚱뚱하다** [뚱뚱하다] ddung-ddung-ha-da a. fat

    □ **통통하다** [통통하다] tong-tong-ha-da a. plump, chubby

    □ **비만** [비:만] bi-man n. obesity, corpulence

□ **날씬하다** [날씬하다] nal-ssin-ha-da a. slender

  □ **홀쭉하다** [홀쭈카다] hol-jju-ka-da a. thin

  그녀는 키가 크고 날씬해요.
  geu-nyeo-neun ki-ga keu-go nal-ssin-hae-yo
  She is tall and slender.

□ **피부** [피부] pi-bu n. skin

□ **주름** [주름] ju-reum n. wrinkle

  당신 얼굴에 주름이 많은데요.
  dang-sin eol-gu-re ju-reu-mi ma-neun-de-yo
  You have a lot of wrinkles on your face.

□ **점** [점] jeom n. dot

□ **여드름** [여드름] yeo-deu-reum n. pimple

  얼굴에 여드름이 났어요.
  eol-gu-re yeo-deu-reu-mi na-sseo-yo
  There are pimples on my face.

□ **뽀루지** [뽀루지] bbyo-ru-ji n. pimple, eruption, rash

□ **주근깨** [주근깨] ju-geun-ggae n. freckle

□ **기미** [기미] gi-mi n. freckle

  경미의 얼굴은 기미투성이예요.
  gyeong-mi-e eol-gu-reun gi-mi-tu-seong-i-ye-yo
  Gyeongmi's face is covered with freckles.

□ **잡티** [잡티] jap-ti n. blemish

□ **모공** [모공] mo-gong n. pore

□ **비듬** [비듬] bi-deum n. dandruff

□ **수염** [수염] su-yeom n. facial hair

　□ **턱수염** [턱쑤염] teok-ssu-yeom n. beard

　□ **콧수염** [코쑤염/콛쑤염] ko-ssu-yeom/kot-ssu-yeom n. moustache

　우리 아빠는 콧수염이 있어요.
　u-ri a-bba-neun kot-ssu-yeo-mi i-sseo-yo
　My daddy has a moustache.

□ **외모** [외:모/웨:모] oe-mo/we-mo n. appearance

　= **모습** [모습] mo-seup

　외모에 속지 말아요.
　ui-mo-e sok-jji ma-ra-yo
　Don't be mislead by appearance.

□ **잘생기다** [잘생기다] jal-saeng-gi-da v. be handsome

　= **잘나다** [잘라다] jal-ra-da

　그는 잘생겼어요.
　geu-neun jal-saeng-gyeo-sseo-yo
　He is a handsome guy.

□ **아름답다** [아름답따] a-reum-dap-dda a. beautiful

□ **예쁘다** [예:쁘다] ye-bbeu-da a. pretty

□ **귀엽다** [귀:엽따] gwi-yeop-dda a. cute

　= **깜찍하다** [깜찌카따] ggam-jji-ka-da

□ **우아하다** [우아하다] u-a-ha-da a. grace

□ **근사하다** [근:사하다] geun-sa-ha-da a. wonderful, fabulous

□ **세련되다** [세:련되다/세:련뒈다] se-ryeon-doe-da/se-ryeon-dwe-da

　a. polished, chic

□ **멋지다** [멋찌다] meot-jji-da a. nice

저 남자 멋지지 않아요?
jeo nam-ja meot-jji-ji a-na-yo?
Isn't he nice?

□ **못생기다** [몯:쌩기다] mot-ssaeng-gi-da v. be ugly

= **못나다** [몬:나다] mon-na-da

□ **추하다** [추하다] chu-ha-da a. ugly

03. 외모

Useful Conversation

이준서   안나는 어머니를 많이 닮았어.
an-na-neun eo-meo-ni-reul ma-ni dal-ma-sseo
Anna looks a lot like her mother.

김미나   그래, 그 애는 자기 어머니처럼 머리가 검은색이잖아.
geu-rae, geo ae-neun ja-gi eo-meo-ni-cheo-reom meo-ri-ga
geo-meun-sae-gi-ja-na
Yes, she has black hair. It's same color as her
mother's.

이준서   그런데 며칠 전에 머리를 노랗게 염색했더라고.
geu-reon-de myeo-chil jeo-ne meo-ri-reul no-ra-ke
yeom-sae-kaet-ddeo-ra-go
But she dyed her hair yellow a few days ago.

김미나   정말? 난 그 애를 지난달 이후로 못 봤어.
jeong-mal? nan geu ae-reul ji-nan-dal i-hu-ro mot bwa-sseo
Really? I haven't seen her since last month.

Feelings & Character 감정 & 성격 gam-jeong & seong-gyeok

□ **기쁘다** [기쁘다] gi-bbeu-da

  a. pleased

□ **즐겁다** [즐겁따] jeul-geop-dda

  a. joyful

□ **재미있다** [재미읻따] jae-mi-it-dda

  a. funny

□ **흥미진진하다** [흥:미진진하다]

  heung-mi-jin-jin-ha-da

  a. interested

□ **흥분하다** [흥분하다] heung-bun-ha-da

  v. be excited

□ **행복하다** [행:보카다]

  haeng-bo-ka-da

  a. happy

□ **만족하다** [만조카다] man-jo-ka-da

  a. satisfied v. satisfy

□ **편하다** [편하다] pyeon-ha-da

  a. convenient

□ **믿다** [믿따] mit-dda

  v. believe

□ **슬프다** [슬프다] seul-peu-da

a. sad

□ **우울하다** [우울하다] u-ul-ha-da

a. gloomy

□ **괴롭다** [괴롭따/궤롭따]

goe-rop-dda/gwe-rop-dda

a. painful

□ **비참하다** [비:참하다]

bi-cham-ha-da

a. miserable

□ **실망하다** [실망하다]

sil-mang-ha-da

v. be disappointed

□ **부끄럽다** [부끄럽따]

bu-ggeu-reop-dda

a. shameful

□ **짜증스럽다** [짜증스럽따]

jja-jeung-seu-reop-dda

a. annoying

□ **화** [화:] hwa n. anger

□ **화나다** [화:나다] hwa-na-da

v. get angry

□ **무섭다** [무섭따] mu-seop-dda
　 a. horrible

□ **두렵다** [두렵따] du-ryeop-dda
　 a. fearful

□ **겁나다** [검나다] geom-na-da
　 v. get scared

□ **불안하다** [불안하다] bu-ran-ha-da
　 a. anxious

□ **긴장하다** [긴장하다] gin-jang-ha-da
　 v. be nervous

□ **초조하다** [초조하다] cho-jo-ha-da
　 a. nervy

□ **착하다** [차카다] cha-ka-da
　 a. good

□ **친절하다** [친절하다] chin-jeol-ha-da
　 a. kind

□ **다정하다** [다정하다] da-jeong-ha-da
　 a. friendly

□ **공손하다** [공손하다] gong-son-ha-da
　 a. polite

□ **정직하다** [정:지카다] jeong-ji-ka-da
　 a. honest

□ **침착하다** [침차카다] chim-cha-ka-da
　 a. calm, composed

58

□ **과묵하다** [과:무카다] gwa-mu-ka-da
　　a. reticent

□ **비관** [비:관] bi-gwan
　　n. pessimism

□ **적극** [적꼭] jeok-ggeuk
　　n. the positive

□ **외향** [외:향/웨:향]
　　oe-hyang/we-hyang
　　n. extroversion

□ **소극** [소극] so-geuk
　　n. the negative

□ **내향** [내:향] nae-hyang
　　n. introversion

□ **나쁘다** [나쁘다] na-bbeu-da
　　a. bad

□ **게으르다** [게으르다] ge-eu-reu-da
　　a. idle, lazy

□ **사납다** [사:납따] sa-nap-dda
　　a. fierce

□ **거만하다** [거:만하다] geo-man-ha-da
= **건방지다** [건방지다] geon-bang-ji-da
　　a. haughty

59

□ **기쁘다** [기쁘다] gi-bbeu-da a. pleased

그 소식을 들으니 기뻐요.
geu so-si-geul deu-reu-ni gi-bbeo-yo
I'm pleased to hear that news.

□ **즐겁다** [즐겁따] jeul-geop-dda a. joyful

□ **유쾌하다** [유쾌하다] yu-kwae-ha-da a. cheerful

□ **흐뭇하다** [흐무타다] heu-mu-ta-da a. delighted

□ **재미있다** [재미읻따] jae-mi-it-dda a. funny

□ **흥미진진하다** [흥:미진진하다] heung-mi-jin-jin-ha-da a. interested

이것은 매우 흥미진진해요.
i-geo-seun mae-u heung-mi-jin-jin-hae-yo
It's very interesting.

□ **흥분하다** [흥분하다] heung-bun-ha-da v. be excited

□ **행복하다** [행:보카다] haeng-bo-ka-da a. happy

나는 아주 행복해요.
na-neun a-ju haeng-bo-kae-yo
I'm so happy.

□ **만족하다** [만조카다] man-jo-ka-da a. satisfied v. satisfy

    □ **흡족하다** [흡쪼카다] heup-jjo-ka-da a. enough

□ **편하다** [편하다] pyeon-ha-da a. convenient

□ **믿다** [믿따] mit-dda v. believe

    □ **신뢰** [실:뢰/실:뤠] sil-roe/sil-rwe n. trust, confidence

    □ **안심** [안심] an-sim n. relief

□ **슬프다** [슬프다] seul-peu-da a. sad

  □ **비통하다** [비:통하다] bi-tong-ha-da a. sorrowful

  □ **우울하다** [우울하다] u-ul-ha-da a. gloomy

    그것은 슬픈 영화예요.
    geu-geo-seun seul-peun yeong-hwa-ye-yo
    It's a sad movie.

□ **괴롭다** [괴롭따/궤롭따] goe-rop-dda/gwe-rop-dda a. painful

  □ **고통스럽다** [고통스럽따] go-tong-seu-reop-dda a. painful

□ **비참하다** [비:참하다] bi-cham-ha-da a. miserable

□ **실망하다** [실망하다] sil-mang-ha-da v. be disappointed

    그거 실망이네요.
    geu-geo sil-mang-i-ne-yo
    That disappointed me.

□ **부끄럽다** [부끄럽따] bu-ggeu-reop-dda a. shameful

  □ **수치스럽다** [수치스럽따] su-chi-seu-reop-dda a. disgraceful

□ **짜증스럽다** [짜증스럽따] jja-jeung-seu-reop-dda a. annoying

□ **불편하다** [불편하다] bul-pyeon-ha-da a. uncomfortable, inconvenient

□ **화** [화:] hwa n. anger

  □ **화나다** [화:나다] hwa-na-da v. get angry

□ **무섭다** [무섭따] mu-seop-dda a. horrible

  □ **두렵다** [두렵따] du-ryeop-dda a. fearful

  □ **겁나다** [검나다] geom-na-da v. get scared

□ **불안하다** [불안하다] bu-ran-ha-da a. anxious

□ **긴장하다** [긴장하다] gin-jang-ha-da v. be nervous

  □ **초조하다** [초조하다] cho-jo-ha-da a. nervy

  □ **조마조마하다** [조마조마하다] jo-ma-jo-ma-ha-da a. afraid, nervous

  나는 매우 긴장했어요.
  na-neun mae-u gin-jang-hae-sseo-yo
  I'm very nervous.

□ **어색하다** [어:새카다] eo-sae-ka-da a. awkward

  = **서먹서먹하다** [서먹써머카다] seo-meok-sseo-meo-ka-da

□ **걱정스럽다** [걱쩡스럽따] geok-jjeong-seu-reop-dda a. worried

  = **근심스럽다** [근심스럽따] geun-sim-seu-reup-dda

  = **염려스럽다** [염:녀스럽따] yeom-nyeo-seu-reop-dda

□ **거북하다** [거:부카다] geo-bu-ka-da a. uncomfortable

  이것은 거북한 상황입니다.
  i-geo-seun geo-bu-kan sang-hwang-im-ni-da
  This is an uncomfortable situation.

□ **예민하다** [예:민하다] ye-min-ha-da a. sensitive

□ **귀찮다** [귀찬타] gwi-chan-ta a. troublesome

  = **성가시다** [성가시다] seong-ga-si-da

  = **번거롭다** [번거롭따] beon-geo-rop-dda

□ **섭섭하다** [섭써파다] seop-sseo-pa-da a. regrettable, sorry

  = **서운하다** [서운하다] seo-un-ha-da

  = **아쉽다** [아쉽따] a-swip-dda

□ **안타깝다** [안타깝따] an-ta-ggap-dda a. pitiful

  = **딱하다** [따카다] dda-ka-da

☐ **착하다** [차카다] cha-ka-da a. good

☐ **친절하다** [친절하다] chin-jeol-ha-da a. kind

그는 친절한 사람입니다.
geu-neun chin-jeol-han sa-ra-mim-ni-da
He is a kind person.

☐ **다정하다** [다정하다] da-jeong-ha-da a. friendly

= **정겹다** [정겹따] jeong-gyeop-dda

☐ **상냥하다** [상냥하다] sang-nyang-ha-da a. gentle, tender

☐ **싹싹하다** [싹싸카다] ssak-ssa-ka-da a. affable, gentle

= **사근사근하다** [사근사근하다] sa-geun-sa-geun-ha-da

우리 며느리는 싹싹해요.
u-ri myeo-neu-ri-neun ssak-ssa-kae-yo
My daughter-in-law is affable.

☐ **공손하다** [공손하다] gong-son-ha-da a. polite

= **정중하다** [정:중하다] jeong-jung-ha-da

☐ **고분고분하다** [고분고분하다] go-bun-go-bun-ha-da a. obedient

☐ **겸손하다** [겸손하다] gyeom-son-ha-da a. humble

☐ **정직하다** [정:지카다] jeong-ji-ka-da a. honest

☐ **세심하다** [세:심하다] se-sim-ha-da a. scrupulous

☐ **침착하다** [침차카다] chim-cha-ka-da a. calm, composed

= **차분하다** [차분하다] cha-bun-ha-da

침착하세요.
chim-cha-ka-se-yo
Calm down.

□ **과묵하다** [과:무카다] gwa-mu-ka-da a. reticent

□ **신중하다** [신:중하다] sin-jung-ha-da a. cautious

□ **대담하다** [대:담하다] dae-dam-ha-da a. daring

□ **적극** [적끅] jeok-ggeuk n. the positive

    □ **외향** [외:향/웨:향] oe-hyang/we-hyang n. extroversion

□ **우호** [우:호] u-ho n. friendship

□ **소극** [소극] so-geuk n. the negative

    □ **내향** [내:향] nae-hyang n. introversion

□ **수동** [수동] su-dong n. the passive

□ **비관** [비:관] bi-gwan n. pessimism

□ **이기** [이:기] i-gi n. self

□ **소심하다** [소:심하다] so-sim-ha-da a. timid

    □ **수줍다** [수줍따] su-jup-dda a. shy

    □ **숫기** [숟끼] sut-ggi n. not shy

    □ **숫기가 없다** [숟끼가 업:따] sut-ggi-ga eop-dda be shy

□ **무뚝뚝하다** [무뚝뚜카다] mu-dduk-ddu-ka-da a. curt

    우리 아빠는 무뚝뚝하셔.
    u-ri a-bba-neun mu-dduk-ddu-ka-syeo
    My father has a curt manner.

□ **나쁘다** [나쁘다] na-bbeu-da a. bad

□ **무례하다** [무례하다] mu-rye-ha-da a. rude

□ **게으르다** [게으르다] ge-eu-reu-da a. idle, lazy

□ **신경질** [신경질] sin-gyeong-jil n. nervousness

□ **사납다** [사:납따] sa-nap-dda a. fierce

□ **심술궂다** [심술굳따] sim-sul-gut-dda a. cantankerous

□ **거만하다** [거:만하다] geo-man-ha-da a. haughty

= **교만하다** [교만하다] gyo-man-ha-da

= **건방지다** [건방지다] geon-bang-ji-da

#04. 교통 체증

Useful Conversation

김미나 나는 서울이 싫어.
na-neun seo-u-ri si-reo
I don't like Seoul.

이준서 왜? 서울의 교통 시스템이 편리하다고 했잖아.
wae? seo-u-re gyo-tong si-seu-te-mi pyeon-ri-ha-da-go
haet-jja-na
Why? You said Seoul's transportation system is
convenient.

김미나 그래. 하지만 오늘 아침 교통 체증 때문에 회사에 지각했거든.
geu-rae. ha-ji-man o-neul a-chim gyo-tong che-jeung
ddae-mu-ne hoe-sa-e ji-ga-kae-ggeo-deun
Yes, I did. But I was late for work because of a
traffic jam.

이준서 그렇구나. 교통 체증 때문에 짜증 나는 거야?
geu-reo-ku-na. gyo-tong che-jeung ddae-mu-ne
jja-jeung na-neun geo-ya?
I see. Do traffic jams make you nervous?

Love 사랑 sa-rang

□ **만나다** [만나다] man-na-da

  v. meet

□ **만남** [만남] man-nam

  n. meeting

□ **데이트** [데이트] de-i-teu

  = **교제** [교제] gyo-je

  n. date

□ **사귀다** [사귀다] sa-gwi-da

  v. make a friend

□ **좋아하다** [조:아하다] jo-a-ha-da

  v. like

□ **사랑하다** [사랑하다] sa-rang-ha-da

  v. love

□ **사랑** [사랑] sa-rang

  n. love

□ **남자 친구** [남자 친구]

  nam-ja chin-gu

  boyfriend

□ **여자 친구** [여자 친구]

  yeo-ja chin-gu

  girlfriend

□ **유혹하다** [유호카다] yu-ho-ka-da

  v. tempt, seduce

□ **꾀다** [꾀:다/꿰:다] ggoe-da/ggwe-da

  v. hit on

□ **반하다** [반:하다] ban-ha-da

  v. have a crush on

□ **뽀뽀** [뽀뽀] bbo-bbo

  n. kiss, peck

□ **키스** [키스] ki-seu

  n. kiss

□ **윙크** [윙크] wing-keu

  n. wink

□ **포옹** [포:옹] po-ong

  n. hug

□ **껴안다** [껴안따] ggyeo-an-dda

  v. hug

□ **그립다** [그립따] geu-rip-dda

  a. missable

□ **질투** [질투] jil-tu

   n. jealousy

□ **갈등** [갈뜽] gal-ddeung

   n. trouble

□ **속이다** [소기다] so-gi-da

   v. trick, cheat

□ **거짓말** [거:진말] geo-jin-mal n. lie

□ **배신** [배:신] bae-sin

   n. betrayal

□ **헤어지다** [헤어지다] he-eo-ji-da

   v. break up

□ **이별** [이:별] i-byeol

   n. farewell

□ **잊다** [읻따] it-dda

   v. forget

□ **청혼** [청혼] cheong-hon

   n. proposal

□ **약혼** [야콘] ya-kon

   n. engagement

□ **결혼** [결혼] gyeol-hon
   n. marriage

□ **결혼식** [결혼식] gyeol-hon-sik
   n. wedding ceremony

□ **청첩장** [청첩짱] cheng-cheop-jjang
   n. wedding invitation

□ **신랑** [실랑] sil-rang
   n. groom

□ **신부** [신부] sin-bu
   n. bride

□ **결혼반지** [결혼반지]
   gyeol-hon-ban-ji
   n. wedding ring

□ **웨딩드레스** [웨딩드레스]
   we-ding-deu-re-seu
   n. wedding dress

□ **남편** [남편] nam-pyeon
   n. husband

□ **아내** [아내] a-nae
   n. wife

☐ **만나다** [만나다] man-na-da v. meet

　☐ **만남** [만남] man-nam n. meeting

☐ **데이트** [데이트] de-i-teu n. date

　= **교제** [교제] gyo-je

　데이트 어땠어요?
　de-i-teu eo-ddae-sseo-yo?
　How was your date?

☐ **소개팅** [소개팅] so-gae-ting n. blind date

　☐ **맞선** [맏썬] mat-sseon

　n. meeting with a prospective marriage partner

　= **선** [선:] seon

　소개팅 주선해 주세요.
　so-gae-ting ju-seon-hae ju-se-yo
　Set me up for a blind date.

☐ **사귀다** [사귀다] sa-gwi-da v. make a friend

☐ **좋아하다** [조:아하다] jo-a-ha-da v. like

☐ **사랑하다** [사랑하다] sa-rang-ha-da v. love

　☐ **사랑** [사랑] sa-rang n. love

　☐ **애정** [애:정] ae-jeong n. love, affection

　당신을 사랑해요.
　dang-si-neul sa-rang-hae-yo
　I love you.

☐ **이상형** [이:상형] i-sang-hyeong n. ideal type

☐ **공감대** [공:감대] gong-gam-dae n. sympathy

□ **애인** [애:인] ae-in n. sweetheart

= **연인** [여:닌] yeo-nin

애인 있어요?
ae-in i-sseo-yo?
Do you have a sweetheart?

□ **친구** [친구] chin-gu n. friend

□ **남자 친구** [남자 친구] nam-ja chin-gu boyfriend

□ **여자 친구** [여자 친구] yeo-ja chin-gu girlfriend ⤸

□ **매력** [매력] mae-ryeok n. charm

tip. These days young people often use '남사친 [nam-sa-chin] and 여사친 [yeo-sa-chin]', they mean 'male friend(s) and female friend(s)'.

그녀는 매력적인 여자죠.
geu-nyeo-neun mae-ryeok-jjeo-gin yeo-ja-jyo
She is a charming woman.

□ **유혹하다** [유호카다] yu-ho-ka-da v. tempt, seduce

□ **꾀다** [꾀:다/꿰:다] ggoe-da/ggwe-da v. hit on

= **꼬시다** [꼬시다] ggo-si-da ⟶ **tip.** '꼬시다' is for a common word of '꾀다'.

□ **반하다** [반:하다] ban-ha-da v. have a crush on

□ **홀리다** [홀리다] hol-ri-da v. be bewitched

나는 민주에게 반했어요.
na-neun min-ju-e-ge ban-hae-sseo-yo
I have a crush on Minju.

□ **뽀뽀** [뽀뽀] bbo-bbo n. kiss, peck

□ **키스** [키스] ki-seu n. kiss

= **입맞춤** [임맏춤] im-mat-chum

□ **윙크** [윙크] wing-keu n. wink

□ **눈짓** [눈찓] nun-jjit n. eye-signal

□ **포옹** [포:옹] po-ong n. hug

    □ **껴안다** [껴안따] ggyeo-an-dda v. hug

□ **그립다** [그립따] geu-rip-dda a. missable

    □ **그리워하다** [그리워하다] geu-ri-wo-ha-da v. miss

□ **질투** [질투] jil-tu n. jealousy

□ **갈등** [갈뜽] gal-ddeung n. trouble

    □ **고민** [고민] go-min n. worry

□ **속이다** [소기다] so-gi-da v. trick, cheat

    □ **거짓말** [거:진말] geo-jin-mal n. lie

    □ **배신** [배:신] bae-sin n. betrayal

□ **헤어지다** [헤어지다] he-eo-ji-da v. break up

    □ **이별** [이:별] i-byeol n. farewell

    그와 헤어졌어요.
    geu-wa he-eo-jeo-sseo-yo
    I broke up with him.

□ **잊다** [읻따] it-dda v. forget

□ **미혼** [미:혼] mi-hon n. single

    □ **독신** [독씬] dok-ssin n. unmarried person

□ **청혼** [청혼] cheong-hon n. proposal

□ **약혼** [야콘] ya-kon n. engagement

    □ **약혼식** [야콘식] ya-kon-sik n. engagement ceremony

    □ **약혼자** [야콘자] ya-kon-ja n. fiancé, fiancée

    □ **약혼녀** [야콘녀] ya-kon-nyeo n. fiancée

□ **결혼** [결혼] gyeol-hon n. marriage

□ **결혼식** [결혼식] gyeol-hon-sik n. wedding ceremony
  = **혼례** [홀례] hol-rye

□ **신랑** [실랑] sil-rang n. groom

□ **신부** [신부] sin-bu n. bride

  신부가 참 아름다워요!
  sin-bu-ga cham a-reum-da-wo-yo!
  What a beautiful bride!

□ **청첩장** [청첩짱] cheng-cheop-jjang n. wedding invitation

□ **결혼반지** [결혼반지] gyeol-hon-ban-ji n. wedding ring

□ **혼례복** [홀례복] hol-rye-bok n. wedding clothes
  = **예복** [예복] ye-bok

□ **웨딩드레스** [웨딩드레스] we-ding-deu-re-seu n. wedding dress

  □ **면사포** [면:사포] myeon-sa-po n. veil

□ **부케** [부케] bu-ke n. bridal bouquet

□ **피로연** [피로연] pi-ro-yeon n. wedding reception

□ **결혼기념일** [결혼기녀밀] gyeol-hon-gi-nyeo-mil n. wedding anniversary

□ **축하** [추카] chu-ka n. celebration

□ **신혼여행** [신혼녀행] sin-hon-nyeo-haeng n. honeymoon

  신혼여행은 어디로 가나요?
  sin-hon-nyeo-haeng-eun eo-di-ro ga-na-yo?
  Where will you go for your honeymoon?

☐ **부부** [부부] bu-bu n. married couple

  ☐ **남편** [남편] nam-pyeon n. husband

  ☐ **아내** [아내] a-nae n. wife

  ☐ **부인** [부인] bu-in n. wife, ma'am •   →   **tip.** '부인' is used for another person's wife. When talking about your wife, just say '아내'.

☐ **배우자** [배:우자] bae-u-ja n. spouse

  ☐ **반려자** [발:려자] bal-ryeo-ja n. life partner

☐ **시부모** [시부모] si-bu-mo n. parents-in-law   → **tip.** '시부모, 시아버지, 시어머니' are used for husband's parents.

  ☐ **시아버지** [시아버지] si-a-beo-ji n. father-in-law

  ☐ **시어머니** [시어머니] si-eo-meo-ni n. mother-in-law

☐ **처부모** [처부모] cheo-bu-mo n. parents-in-law   → **tip.** '처부모, 장인, 장모' are used for wife's parents.

  ☐ **장인** [장:인] jang-in n. father-in-law

  ☐ **장모** [장:모] jang-mo n. mother-in-law

☐ **시아주버니** [시아주버니] si-a-ju-beo-ni n. brother-in-law

  ☐ **시동생** [시동생] si-dong-saeng n. brother-in-law

  ☐ **시누이** [시누이] si-nu-i n. sister-in-law

☐ **동서** [동서] dong-seo n. brother-in-law, sister-in-law

  ☐ **올케** [올케] ol-ke n. sister-in-law

tip. '시아주버니' is used for a husband's elder brother.
    '시동생' is used for a husband's younger brother.
    '시누이' is used for a husband's sister.
    '동서' is for the husband of your wife's sister or the wife of your husband's brother.
    '올케' is used for a brother's wife.

☐ **처남** [처남] cheo-nam n. brother-in-law

  ☐ **처형** [처형] cheo-hyeong n. sister-in-law

  ☐ **처제** [처제] cheo-je n. sister-in-law

□ **매부** [매부] mae-bu n. **brother-in-law**

□ **매형** [매형] mae-hyeong n. **brother-in-law**

□ **제부** [제:부] je-bu n. **brother-in-law**

tip. '처남' is used for a wife's brother. '매부' is used for a sister's husband.
'매형' is used for an elder sister's husband.
'처남, 매부, 매형' are used by male speakers.
'제부' is for a younger sister's husband, used by females.
'처형' is used for a wife's elder sister.
'처제' is used for a wife's younger sister.

tip. There are many titles for family members in Korea. These can be complicated and are influenced by Korean family culture.

＃ 05. 데이트

Useful Conversation

최지훈　어제 경진이라는 애를 만났는데, 내 이상형이야.
eo-je gyeong-ji-ni-ra-neun ae-reul man-nat-neun-de,
nae i-sang-hyeong-i-ya
I met a girl named Gyeongjin yesterday, she's my type of girl.

이준서　이번 주말에 데이트하자고 했어?
i-beon ju-ma-re de-i-teu-ha-ja-go hae-sseo?
Did you ask her out this weekend?

최지훈　아직. 하지만 그러고 싶어.
a-jik. ha-ji-man geu-reo-go si-peo
Not yet. But I want to.

이준서　그러면 데이트하자고 해. 손해 볼 거 없잖아.
geu-reo-myeon de-i-teu-ha-ja-go hae. son-hae bol geo eop-jja-na
Then ask her on a date. You have nothing to lose.

Family 가족 ga-jok

☐ **가족** [가족] ga-jok
n. family

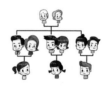

☐ **친척** [친척] chin-cheok
n. relative

  ☐ **부모** [부모] bu-mo
n. parents

☐ **아버지** [아버지] a-beo-ji n. father   ☐ **어머니** [어머니] eo-meo-ni n. mother

☐ **아빠** [아빠] a-bba n. dad   ☐ **엄마** [엄마] eom-ma n. mom

 ☐ **자녀** [자녀] ja-nyeo
= **자식** [자식] ja-sik
n. child

☐ **아들** [아들] a-deul n. son   ☐ **딸** [딸] ddal n. daughter

☐ **형** [형] hyeong n. elder brother   ☐ **누나** [누:나] nu-na n. elder sister

☐ **오빠** [오빠] o-bba n. elder brother   ☐ **언니** [언니] eon-ni n. elder sister

☐ **남동생** [남동생] nam-dong-saeng
n. younger brother   ☐ **여동생** [여동생] yeo-dong-saeng
n. younger sister

□ **남편** [남편] nam-pyeon

n. husband

□ **아내** [아내] a-nae

n. wife

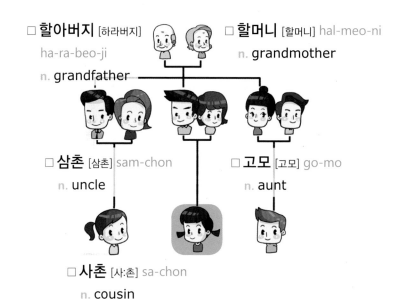

□ **할아버지** [하라버지] ha-ra-beo-ji

n. grandfather

□ **할머니** [할머니] hal-meo-ni

n. grandmother

□ **삼촌** [삼촌] sam-chon

n. uncle

□ **고모** [고모] go-mo

n. aunt

□ **사촌** [사:촌] sa-chon

n. cousin

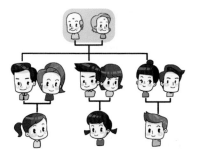

□ **손녀** [손녀] son-nyeo

n. granddaughter

□ **손자** [손자] son-ja

n. grandson

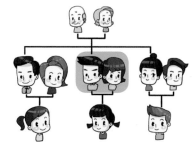

□ **조카** [조카] jo-ka

n. niece

□ **조카** [조카] jo-ka

n. nephew

77

□ **노인** [노:인] no-in
= **늙은이** [늘그니] neul-geu-ni
n. senior, elder

□ **어른** [어:른] eo-reun
= **성인** [성인] seong-in
n. adult

□ **청년** [청년] cheong-nyeon
= **젊은이** [절므니] jeol-meu-ni
n. youth

□ **청소년** [청소년] cheong-so-nyeon
n. youth, teenager

□ **어린이** [어리니] eo-ri-ni
= **아이** [아이] a-i
n. kid, child

□ **아기** [아기] a-gi
n. baby

□ **임신** [임:신] im-sin
n. pregnancy

□ **임산부** [임:산부] im-san-bu
n. expecting mom

□ **출산** [출싼] chul-ssan
n. giving birth to

☐ **수유** [수유] su-yu

　　n. nursing

☐ **분유** [부뉴] bu-nyu

　　n. powdered milk

☐ **모유** [모:유] mo-yu

　　n. breast milk

☐ **젖병** [전뼝] jeot-bbyeong

　　n. nursing bottle

☐ **기저귀** [기저귀] gi-jeo-gwi

　　n. diaper

☐ **유모차** [유모차] yu-mo-cha

　　n. stroller, baby carriage

☐ **기르다** [기르다] gi-reu-da

= **키우다** [키우다] ki-u-da

　v. bring up, raise

☐ **보살피다** [보살피다] bo-sal-pi-da

= **돌보다** [돌:보다] dol-bo-da

　v. take care of

☐ **보모** [보:모] bo-mo n. baby sitter

☐ **유모** [유모] yu-mo n. nanny

☐ **닮다** [담:따] dam-dda

　　v. resemble

☐ **화목** [화목] hwa-mok

　　n. harmony

☐ **불화** [불화] bul-hwa

　　n. discord

79

□ **가족** [가족] ga-jok n. family

   □ **식구** [식꾸] sik-ggu n. family member

   우리 가족은 다섯 식구입니다.
   u-ri ga-jo-geun da-seot sik-ggu-im-ni-da
   There are five people in my family.

□ **부모** [부모] bu-mo n. parents

□ **아버지** [아버지] a-beo-ji n. father

   □ **아빠** [아빠] a-bba n. dad

   이 분은 우리 아버지예요.
   i bu-neun u-ri a-beo-ji-ye-yo
   This is my father.

□ **어머니** [어머니] eo-meo-ni n. mother

   □ **엄마** [엄마] eom-ma n. mom

□ **조부모** [조부모] jo-bu-mo n. grandparents

   □ **할아버지** [하라버지] ha-ra-beo-ji n. grandfather

   □ **할머니** [할머니] hal-meo-ni n. grandmother

□ **외조부모** [외:조부모/웨:조부모] oe-jo-bu-mo/we-jo-bu-mo

   n. mother's parents

   □ **외할아버지** [외:하라버지/웨:하라버지] oe-ha-ra-beo-ji/we-ha-ra-beo-ji

   n. grandfather on one's mother's side

   □ **외할머니** [외:할머니/웨:할머니] oe-hal-meo-ni/we-hal-meo-ni

   n. grandmother on one's mother's side

   나는 우리 외할머니가 좋아요.
   na-neun u-ri oe-hal-meo-ni-ga jo-a-yo
   I like my grandmother on my mother's side.

□ **남매** [남매] nam-mae n. sibling, brother and sister

  □ **형제** [형제] hyeong-je n. sibling, brother

  □ **자매** [자매] ja-mae n. sibling, sister

□ **형** [형] hyeong n. elder brother   **tip.** A male speaker should use '형'.
A female speaker shoud use '오빠'.

  □ **오빠** [오빠] o-bba n. elder brother

□ **누나** [누:나] nu-na n. elder sister   **tip.** A male speaker should use '누나'.
A female speaker should use '언니'.

  □ **언니** [언니] eon-ni n. elder sister

□ **동생** [동생] dong-saeng n. younger brother, younger sister

  □ **남동생** [남동생] nam-dong-saeng n. younger brother

  □ **여동생** [여동생] yeo-dong-saeng n. younger sister

나도 언젠가 동생이 생기면 좋겠어요.
na-do eon-jen-ga dong-saeng-i saeng-gi-myeon jo-ke-sseo-yo
I hope I have a younger brother or sister someday.

□ **부부** [부부] bu-bu n. married couple

  □ **남편** [남편] nam-pyeon n. husband

  □ **아내** [아내] a-nae n. wife

□ **자녀** [자녀] ja-nyeo n. child

  = **자식** [자식] ja-sik

  □ **아들** [아들] a-deul n. son

  □ **딸** [딸] ddal n. daughter

무자식이 상팔자.
mu-ja-si-gi sang-pal-ja
Little goods, little care. (No child, no problem.)

tip. '무자식이 상팔자' is a kind of Korean traditional saying.

□ **사위** [사위] sa-wi n. son-in-law

□ **며느리** [며느리] myeo-neu-ri n. daughter-in-law

□ **손주** [손주] son-ju n. grandchild

  □ **손자** [손자] son-ja n. grandson

  □ **손녀** [손녀] son-nyeo n. granddaughter

□ **친척** [친척] chin-cheok n. relative

□ **삼촌** [삼촌] sam-chon n. uncle

  □ **외삼촌** [외:삼촌/웨:삼촌] oe-sam-chon/we-sam-chon n. uncle

    tip. '삼촌' is for father's brother,
    '외삼촌' is for mother's brother.

□ **고모** [고모] go-mo n. aunt

  □ **이모** [이모] i-mo n. aunt

  □ **숙모** [숭모] sung-mo n. aunt

  □ **외숙모** [외:숭모/웨:숭모] oe-sung-mo/we-sung-mo n. aunt

  tip. '고모' is for father's sister. '이모' is for mother's sister.
  '숙모' is for the wife of '삼촌'. '외숙모' is for the wife of '외삼촌'.

□ **사촌** [사:촌] sa-chon n. cousin

□ **조카** [조카] jo-ka n. nephew, niece

□ **어른** [어:른] eo-reun n. adult

  = **성인** [성인] seong-in

□ **노인** [노:인] no-in n. senior, elder

  = **늙은이** [늘그니] neul-geu-ni

  노인을 공경해야 합니다.
  no-i-neul gong-gyeong-hae-ya ham-ni-da
  We have to respect our elders.

□ **청년** [청년] cheong-nyeon n. youth

= **젊은이** [절므니] jeol-meu-ni

□ **청소년** [청소년] cheong-so-nyeon n. youth, teenager

□ **어린이** [어리니] eo-ri-ni n. kid, child

= **아이** [아이] a-i

tip. '어린이' is the abbreviation of '어린아이 [eo-ri-na-i]'.
'애 [ae]' is the abbreviation of '아이'.

□ **아기** [아기] a-gi n. baby

아기는 내가 돌볼게요.
a-gi-neun nae-ga dol-bol-ge-yo
I will look after the baby.

□ **임신** [임:신] im-sin n. pregnancy

□ **임산부** [임:산부] im-san-bu n. expecting mom

tip. '임산부' means
'임부' and '산부'.

□ **임부** [임:부] im-bu n. pregnant woman

= **임신부** [임:신부] im-sin-bu

□ **산부** [산:부] san-bu n. woman in childbirth

= **산모** [산:모] san-mo

□ **입덧** [입떧] ip-ddeot n. morning sickness

□ **출산** [출싼] chul-ssan n. giving birth to

□ **해산** [해:산] hae-san n. childbirth

□ **수유** [수유] su-yu n. nursing

□ **모유** [모:유] mo-yu n. breast milk

□ **분유** [부뉴] bu-nyu n. powdered milk

□ **젖병** [젇뼝] jeot-bbyeong n. nursing bottle

□ **기저귀** [기저귀] gi-jeo-gwi *n.* **diaper**

기저귀 좀 갈아 줄래요?
gi-jeo-gwi jom ga-ra jul-rae-yo?
Would you mind changing the diaper?

□ **유모차** [유모차] yu-mo-cha *n.* **stroller, baby carriage**

□ **기르다** [기르다] gi-reu-da *v.* **bring up, raise**

= **키우다** [키우다] ki-u-da

= **양육하다** [양:유카다] yang-yu-ka-da

□ **보살피다** [보살피다] bo-sal-pi-da *v.* **take care of**

= **돌보다** [돌:보다] dol-bo-da

아기 돌볼 사람을 찾았어요.
a-gi dol-bol sa-ra-meul cha-ja-sseo-yo
I've found a person to take care of my baby.

□ **보모** [보:모] bo-mo *n.* **baby sitter**

□ **유모** [유모] yu-mo *n.* **nanny**

□ **닮다** [담:따] dam-dda *v.* **resemble**

당신은 어머니를 닮았어요 아버지를 닮았어요?
dang-si-neun eo-meo-ni-reul dal-ma-sseo-yo a-beo-ji-reul dal-ma-sseo-yo?
Do you look more like your mother or your father?

□ **입양** [이뱡] i-byang *n.* **adoption**

□ **입양아** [이뱡아] i-byang-a *n.* **adopted child**

□ **양자** [양:자] yang-ja *n.* **adopted son**

□ **양녀** [양:녀] yang-nyeo *n.* **adopted daughter**

□ **화목** [화목] hwa-mok *n.* **harmony**

□ **불화** [불화] bul-hwa n. discord

□ **동거** [동거] dong-geo n. cohabitation

□ **별거** [별거] byeol-geo n. separation

별거 중입니다.
byeol-geo jung-im-ni-da
I'm separated.

□ **이혼** [이:혼] i-hon n. divorce

□ **재혼** [재:혼] jae-hon n. remarriage

06. 가족 소개

Useful Conversation

김미나 　지훈아, 너는 형제나 자매가 있니?
ji-hu-na, neo-neun hyeong-je-na ja-mae-ga in-ni?
Ji-hun, do you have a brother or a sister?

최지훈 　남동생이 한 명 있어. 나보다 여덟 살이 어려.
nam-dong-saeng-i han myeong i-sseo. na-bo-da yeo-deol sa-ri eo-ryeo
I have one younger brother. He's eight years younger than me.

김미나 　네 남동생과 사이가 좋으니?
ne nam-dong-saeng-gwa sa-i-ga jo-eu-ni?
Do you get along with him?

최지훈 　응, 그런데 그 애는 좀 장난꾸러기야.
eung, geu-reon-de geu ae-neun jom jang-nan-ggu-reo-gi-ya
Yes, but he is a mischievous little boy.

Exercise

Read and Match.

1. 가족 •		• baby
2. 결혼 •		• body
3. 사랑 •		• face
4. 슬프다 •		• family
5. 신체, 몸 •		• father
6. 아기 •		• happy
7. 아버지 •		• like
8. 어머니 •		• love
9. 얼굴 •		• marriage
10. 예쁘다 •		• mother
11. 좋아하다 •		• pretty
12. 행복하다 •		• sad

1. 가족 – family 2. 결혼 – marriage 3. 사랑 – love 4. 슬프다 – sad
5. 신체, 몸 – body 6. 아기 – baby 7. 아버지 – father 8. 어머니 – mother
9. 얼굴 – face 10. 예쁘다 – pretty 11. 좋아하다 – like 12. 행복하다 – happy

3장

Time & Nature

Date & Time 날짜 & 시간 nal-jja & si-gan

□ **시간** [시간] si-gan
n. time, hour

□ **시각** [시각] si-gak
n. time, hour

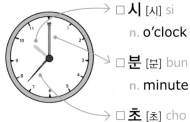

□ **시** [시] si
n. o'clock

□ **분** [분] bun
n. minute

□ **초** [초] cho
n. second

□ **반(半)** [반:] ban
n. half

□ **시계** [시계/시게] si-gye/si-ge
n. clock

□ **손목시계** [손목씨계/손목씨게]
son-mok-ssi-gye/son-mok-ssi-ge
n. watch

□ **새벽** [새벽] sae-byeok
n. dawn

□ **아침** [아침] a-chim
n. morning, breakfast

□ **오전** [오:전] o-jeon
n. morning, a.m.

□ **낮** [낟] nat
n. day time

□ **오후** [오:후] o-hu
n. afternoon, p.m.

□ **점심** [점:심] jeom-sim
n. lunch time, lunch

□ **저녁** [저녁] jeo-nyeok
n. evening, dinner

□ **밤** [밤] bam
n. night

□ **일어나다** [이러나다]
i-reo-na-da
v. get up

□ **깨다** [깨:다] ggae-da
v. wake up

□ **씻다** [씯따] ssit-dda
v. wash

□ **세수** [세:수] se-su
n. washing one's face

□ **양치하다** [양치하다] yang-chi-ha-da
v. brush one's teeth

□ **아침 식사** [아침 식싸]
a-chim sik-ssa
breakfast

□ **점심 식사** [점:심 식싸]
jeom-sim sik-ssa
lunch

□ **저녁 식사** [저녁 식싸]
jeo-nyeok sik-ssa
dinner

□ **자다** [자다] ja-da v. sleep
□ **잠** [잠] jam n. sleep

□ **꿈** [꿈] ggum
n. dream

89

□ **날짜** [날짜] nal-jja n. date　　□ **달력** [달력] dal-ryeok n. calendar

□ **일(日)** [일] il n./b.n. day

□ **요일** [요일] yo-il n. day of week

□ **주(週)** [주] ju n./b.n. week
= **주일** [주일] ju-il

□ **주말** [주말] ju-mal n. weekend

□ **화요일** [화요일]
hwa-yo-il
n. Tuesday

□ **수요일** [수요일]
su-yo-il
n. Wednesday

□ **목요일** [모교일]
mo-gyo-il
n. Thursday

□ **월요일** [워료일]
wo-ryo-il
n. Monday

□ **금요일** [그묘일]
geu-myo-il
n. Friday

□ **일요일** [이료일]
i-ryo-il
n. Sunday

2020　**7월**

일	월	화	수	목	금	토
			1	2	3	4
5	6	7	8	9	10	11
12	13	(14)	15	16	17	18
19	20	21	22	23	24	25
26	27	28	29	30	31	

□ **토요일** [토요일]
to-yo-il
n. Saturday

□ **오늘** [오늘] o-neul
n./ad. today

□ **어제** [어제] eo-je
n./ad. yesterday

□ **내일** [내일] nae-il
n./ad. tomorrow

□ **그저께** [그저께] geu-jeo-gge
n./ad. the day before yesterday

□ **모레** [모:레] mo-re
n./ad. the day after tomorrow

□ **월(月)** [월] wol n./b.n. month
= **달** [달] dal

□ **1월** [이뤌] i-rwol n. January

□ **2월** [이:월] i-wol n. February

□ **3월** [사뭘] sa-mwol n. March

□ **4월** [사:월] sa-wol n. April

□ **5월** [오:월] o-wol n. May

□ **6월** [유월] yu-wol n. June

□ **7월** [치뤌] chi-rwol n. July

□ **8월** [파뤌] pa-rwol n. August

□ **9월** [구월] gu-wol n. September

□ **10월** [시월] si-wol n. October

□ **11월** [시비뤌] si-bi-rwol n. November

□ **12월** [시비월] si-bi-wol n. December

□ **년(年)** [년] nyeon b.n. year
　□ **연** [연] yeon n. year

□ **공휴일** [공휴일] gong-hyu-il
　n. public holiday

□ **국경일** [국껑일] guk-ggyeong-il
　n. national holiday

□ **명절** [명절] myeong-jeol
　n. (national) holiday

□ **설날** [설:랄] seol-ral
　n. Seollal, Korean New Year

□ **추석** [추석] chu-seok
　n. Chuseok,
　Korean Thanksgiving Day

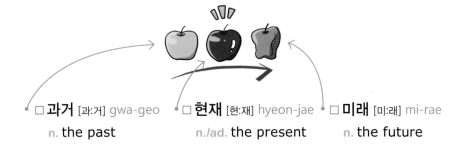

□ **과거** [과:거] gwa-geo
　n. the past

□ **현재** [현:재] hyeon-jae
　n./ad. the present

□ **미래** [미:래] mi-rae
　n. the future

□ **시간** [시간] si-gan n. time, hour

　□ **때** [때] ddae n. the time, the moment

　　(당신 시계로) 몇 시예요?　　　　　　지금은 2시 반이에요.
　　myeot si-ye-yo?　　　　　　　　　　　ji-geu-meun du-si ba-ni-e-yo
　　What time do you have?　　　　　　**It's 2:30 now.**
　　　　　　　　　　　　　　　　　　　　(It's half past two now.)

□ **시각** [시각] si-gak n. time, hour

tip. '시간' means from A (o'clock) to B (o'clock).
　　　'시각' means the point of some time.

　□ **시** [시] si n. o'clock

　□ **분** [분] bun n. minute

　□ **초** [초] cho n. second

　□ **반(半)** [반:] ban n. half

□ **시계** [시계/시게] si-gye/si-ge n. clock

　□ **손목시계** [손목씨계/손목씨게] son-mok-ssi-gye/son-mok-ssi-ge n. watch

□ **새벽** [새벽] sae-byeok n. dawn

□ **아침** [아침] a-chim n. morning, breakfast

□ **오전** [오:전] o-jeon n. morning, a.m.

□ **정오** [정:오] jeong-o n. noon

□ **낮** [낟] nat n. day time

　□ **오후** [오:후] o-hu n. afternoon, p.m.

□ **점심** [점:심] jeom-sim n. lunch time, lunch

□ **저녁** [저녁] jeo-nyeok n. evening, dinner

□ **밤** [밤] bam n. night

□ **일어나다** [이러나다] i-reo-na-da v. get up

　= **기상하다** [기상하다] gi-sang-ha-da

□ **깨다** [깨:다] ggae-da v. wake up

□ **씻다** [씯따] ssit-dda v. wash

  □ **닦다** [닥따] dak-dda v. wipe, dry

□ **세수** [세:수] se-su n. washing one's face

  세수했어요?
  se-su-hae-sseo-yo?
  Did you wash your face?

□ **양치** [양치] yang-chi n. tooth brushing

  = **양치질** [양치질] yang-chi-jil

  □ **양치하다** [양치하다] yang-chi-ha-da v. brush one's teeth

  □ **이를 닦다** [이를 닥따] i-reul dak-dda brush one's teeth

□ **머리를 감다** [머리를 감:따] meo-ri-reul gam-dda wash one's hair

□ **샤워** [샤워] sya-wo n. shower

□ **목욕** [모곡] mo-gyok n. bath

□ **식사** [식싸] sik-ssa n. meal

  □ **식사를 하다** [식싸를 하다] sik-ssa-reul ha-da have a meal

  = **밥을 먹다** [바블 먹따] ba-beul meok-dda

□ **아침 식사** [아침 식싸] a-chim sik-ssa breakfast

  □ **점심 식사** [점:심 식싸] jeom-sim sik-ssa lunch

  □ **저녁 식사** [저녁 식싸] jeo-nyeok sik-ssa dinner

□ **간식** [간:식] gan-sik n. snack

□ **자다** [자다] ja-da v. sleep

  □ **졸다** [졸:다] jol-da v. nap

□ **잠** [잠] jam n. sleep

   = **수면** [수면] su-myeon

   □ **불면증** [불면쯩] bul-myeon-jjeung n. insomnia

   □ **꿈** [꿈] ggum n. dream

□ **낮잠** [낟짬] nat-jjam n. nap

   □ **늦잠** [늗짬] neut-jjam n. oversleeping

□ **날짜** [날짜] nal-jja n. date

□ **그저께** [그저께] geu-jeo-gge n./ad. the day before yesterday

□ **어제** [어제] eo-je n./ad. yesterday

□ **오늘** [오늘] o-neul n./ad. today

□ **내일** [내일] nae-il n./ad. tomorrow

□ **모레** [모:레] mo-re n./ad. the day after tomorrow

□ **글피** [글피] geul-pi n. two days after tomorrow

□ **달력** [달력] dal-ryeok n. calendar

   □ **양력** [양녁] yang-nyeok n. solar calendar

   □ **음력** [음녁] eum-nyeok n. lunar calendar

□ **일(日)** [일] il n./b.n. day

   □ **날** [날] nal n./b.n. day

□ **주(週)** [주] ju n./b.n. week

   = **주일** [주일] ju-il

□ **주말** [주말] ju-mal n. weekend •⟶ **tip.** '주말' means 'Saturday' and 'Sunday'.

□ **요일** [요일] yo-il n. day of week

94

□ **월요일** [워료일] wo-ryo-il n. Monday •⟶ **tip.** In Korea, the week begins on Monday.

□ **화요일** [화요일] hwa-yo-il n. Tuesday

□ **수요일** [수요일] su-yo-il n. Wednesday

□ **목요일** [모교일] mo-gyo-il n. Thursday

□ **금요일** [그묘일] geu-myo-il n. Friday

□ **토요일** [토요일] to-yo-il n. Saturday

□ **일요일** [이료일] i-ryo-il n. Sunday

□ **월(月)** [월] wol n./b.n. month

= **달** [달] dal

□ **1월** [이뤌] i-rwol n. January

= **정월** [정월] jeong-wol •⟶ **tip.** '정월' is the 1st month in the lunar calendar.

□ **2월** [이:월] i-wol n. February

□ **3월** [사뭘] sa-mwol n. March

□ **4월** [사:월] sa-wol n. April

□ **5월** [오:월] o-wol n. May

□ **6월** [유월] yu-wol n. June

□ **7월** [치뤌] chi-rwol n. July

□ **8월** [파뤌] pa-rwol n. August

□ **9월** [구월] gu-wol n. September

□ **10월** [시월] si-wol n. October

□ **11월** [시비뤌] si-bi-rwol n. November

□ **12월** [시비월] si-bi-wol n. December

생일이 몇 월 며칠이에요?
saeng-i-ri myeot wol meo-chi-ri-e-yo?
What date is it your birthday?

□ **년(年)** [년] nyeon **b.n.** year

tip. '년' is a bound noun, so '년' cannot be used alone.

□ **연** [연] yeon **n.** year

□ **세기(世紀)** [세:기] se-gi **n.** century

□ **공휴일** [공휴일] gong-hyu-il **n.** public holiday

□ **국경일** [국꼉일] guk-ggyeong-il **n.** national holiday

□ **명절** [명절] myeong-jeol **n.** (national) holiday

□ **설날** [설:랄] seol-ral **n.** Seollal, Korean New Year

tip. '설날' is the 1st of January in the lunar calendar.

설날은 한국에서 가장 큰 명절이에요.
seol-ra-reun han-gu-ge-seo ga-jang keun myeong-jeo-ri-e-yo
Seollal is the biggest holiday in Korea.

□ **삼일절** [사밀쩔] sa-mil-jjeol **n.** Independence Movement Day

□ **석가탄신일** [석까탄:시닐] seok-gga-tan-si-nil Buddha's Birthday

□ **어린이날** [어리니날] eo-ri-ni-nal **n.** Children's Day

□ **추석** [추석] chu-seok **n.** Chuseok, Korean Thanksgiving Day

tip. '삼일절' is the 1st of March. '석가탄신일' is the 8th of April in the lunar calendar. '어린이날' is the 5th of May. '추석' is the 15th of August in the lunar calendar.

□ **광복절** [광복쩔] gwang-bok-jjeol **n.** National Liberation Day

□ **개천절** [개천절] gae-cheon-jeol **n.** the National foundation Day of Korea

□ **한글날** [한:글랄] han-geul-ral **n.** Hangeul Proclamation Day

tip. '광복절' is the 15th of August. '개천절' is the 3rd of October. '한글날' is the 9th of October.

□ **성탄절** [성:탄절] seong-tan-jeol **n.** Christmas

= **크리스마스** [크리스마스] keu-ri-seu-ma-seu

□ **부활절** [부:활쩔] bu-hwal-jjeol **n.** Easter

□ **추수감사절** [추수감사절] chu-su-gam-sa-jeol Thanksgiving Day

□ **생일** [생일] saeng-il n. birthday

□ **과거** [과:거] gwa-geo n. the past

  □ **옛날** [옌:날] yen-nal n. the old days

  □ **현재** [현:재] hyeon-jae n./ad. the present

  □ **미래** [미:래] mi-rae n. the future

□ **요즈음** [요즈음] yo-jeu-eum n. these days

  = **요즘** [요즘] yo-jeum •———————→ **tip.** '요즘' is short for '요즈음'.

□ **최근** [최:근/췌:근] choe-geun/chwe-geun

  n. the latest

07. 크리스마스

Useful Conversation

이준서   크리스마스에 뭐 하니?

         keu-ri-seu-ma-seu-e mwo ha-ni?

         What will you do on Christmas?

김미나   교회에 예배 드리러 가. 너는?

         gyo-hoe-e ye-bae deu-ri-reo ga. neo-neun?

         I'll go to church to worship. And you?

이준서   집에서 친구들과 크리스마스 파티를 할 거야. 너도 올래?

         ji-be-seo chin-gu-deul-gwa keu-ri-seu-ma-seu pa-ti-reul

         hal ggeo-ya. neo-do ol-rae?

         I'll have a Christmas party with some friends at home. Will you come?

김미나   가고 싶지만, 그날 다른 약속이 있어.

         ga-go sip-jji-man, geu-nal da-reun yak-sso-gi i-sseo

         I'd like to go, but I have other plans that day.

Weather & Seasons 날씨 & 계절 nal-ssi & gye-jeol

□ **날씨** [날씨] nal-ssi
  n. weather

□ **일기예보** [일기예보] il-gi-ye-bo
  weather forecast

□ **맑다** [막따] mak-dda
  a. fine, clear, sunny

□ **따뜻하다** [따뜨타다] dda-ddeu-ta-da
  a. warm

□ **덥다** [덥:따] deop-dda a. hot
□ **더위** [더위] deo-wi n. heat

□ **폭염** [포겸] po-gyeom
= **불볕더위** [불볕떠위] bul-byeot-ddeo-wi
  n. scorching heat

□ **시원하다** [시원하다]
  si-won-ha-da
  a. cool

□ **춥다** [춥따] chup-dda a. cold
□ **추위** [추위] chu-wi n. the cold

□ **하늘** [하늘] ha-neul
n. sky

□ **해** [해] hae
= **태양** [태양] tae-yang
n. sun

□ **구름** [구름] gu-reum
n. cloud

□ **바람** [바람] ba-ram
n. wind

□ **가뭄** [가뭄] ga-mum
n. drought

□ **안개** [안:개] an-gae
n. fog

□ **비** [비] bi
n. rain

□ **소나기** [소나기] so-na-gi
n. shower

□ **홍수** [홍수] hong-su
n. flood

□ **태풍** [태풍] tae-pung
n. typhoon

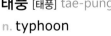

□ **폭풍** [폭풍] pok-pung
n. storm

□ **천둥** [천둥] cheon-dung
n. thunder

□ **번개** [번개] beon-gae
n. lightning

□ **얼음** [어름] eo-reum
n. ice

99

□ **계절** [계:절/게:절] gye-jeol/ge-jeol

　n. season

□ **봄** [봄] bom

　n. spring

□ **무지개** [무지개] mu-ji-gae

　n. rainbow

□ **여름** [여름] yeo-reum

　n. summer

□ **열대야** [열때야] yeol-ddae-ya

　n. tropical night

□ **습하다** [스파다] seu-pa-da

　a. humid, soggy

□ **우산** [우:산] u-san

　n. umbrella

□ **가을** [가을] ga-eul

　n. fall, autumn

□ **단풍** [단풍] dan-pung

　n. autumnal tints

□ **낙엽** [나겹] na-gyeop
n. fallen leaves

□ **추수** [추수] chu-su
= **수확** [수확] su-hwak
n. harvest

□ **겨울** [겨울] gyeo-ul
n. winter

□ **눈** [눈:] nun
n. snow

□ **눈송이** [눈:쏭이] nun-ssong-i
n. snowflake

□ **눈사람** [눈:싸람] nun-ssa-ram
n. snowman

□ **온도** [온도] on-do
= **기온** [기온] gi-on
n. temperature

□ **기후** [기후] gi-hu
n. climate

□ **날씨** [날씨] nal-ssi n. weather

　　오늘 날씨가 어때요?
　　o-neul nal-ssi-ga eo-ddae-yo?
　　How's the weather today?

□ **일기예보** [일기예보] il-gi-ye-bo weather forecast

□ **맑다** [막따] mak-dda a. fine, clear, sunny

　　□ **맑아지다** [말가지다] mal-ga-ji-da v. brighten

　　□ **맑은 날씨** [말근 날씨] mal-geun nal-ssi fine day

　　□ **개다** [개:다] gae-da v. clear up

□ **따뜻하다** [따뜨타다] dda-ddeu-ta-da a. warm

□ **덥다** [덥:따] deop-dda a. hot

　　□ **더위** [더위] deo-wi n. heat

□ **무덥다** [무덥따] mu-deop-dda a. sweltering

　　□ **무더위** [무더위] mu-deo-wi n. sweltering heat

□ **폭염** [포겸] po-gyeom n. scorching heat

　　= **불볕더위** [불볃떠위] bul-byeot-ddeo-wi

□ **시원하다** [시원하다] si-won-ha-da a. cool

　　□ **서늘하다** [서늘하다] seo-neul-ha-da a. cool, chilly

　　□ **쌀쌀하다** [쌀쌀하다] ssal-ssal-ha-da a. chilly

　　□ **썰렁하다** [썰렁하다] sseol-reong-ha-da a. chilly, cold without heat

□ **춥다** [춥따] chup-dda a. cold

　　□ **추위** [추위] chu-wi n. the cold

　　□ **꽃샘추위** [꼳쌤추위] ggot-ssaem-chu-wi n. the last cold snap

□ **하늘** [하늘] ha-neul n. sky

□ **해** [해] hae n. sun

   = **태양** [태양] tae-yang

□ **햇빛** [해삗/핻삗] hae-bbit/haet-bbit n. sunshine

   = **햇볕** [해뼌/핻뼌] hae-bbyeot/haet-bbyeot

□ **구름** [구름] gu-reum n. cloud

   □ **먹구름** [먹꾸름] meok-ggu-reum n. dark clouds

   □ **흐리다** [흐리다] heu-ri-da a. cloudy

□ **궂다** [굳따] gut-dda a. (the weather is) bad

□ **바람** [바람] ba-ram n. wind

□ **산들바람** [산들바람] san-deul-ba-ram n. breeze

□ **강풍** [강풍] gang-pung n. strong wind

   = **센바람** [센:바람] sen-ba-ram

□ **가뭄** [가뭄] ga-mum n. drought

□ **건조하다** [건조하다] geon-jo-ha-da a./v. dry

□ **안개** [안:개] an-gae n. fog

□ **비** [비] bi n. rain

   □ **빗방울** [비빵울/빋빵울] bi-bbang-ul/bit-bbang-ul n. raindrop

   지금 비가 와요.
   ji-geum bi-ga wa-yo
   It's raining now.

□ **강수량** [강:수량] gang-su-ryang n. rainfall

□ **소나기** [소나기] so-na-gi n. shower

   □ **이슬비** [이슬비] i-seul-bi n. drizzle •——→ **tip.** Actually '이슬비' is lighter than

   □ **가랑비** [가랑비] ga-rang-bi n. drizzle   '가랑비'. They are not same.

□ **장마** [장마] jang-ma n. rainy season •——→ **tip.** '장마' is a long period of rain

                                          during the summer season.

□ **홍수** [홍수] hong-su n. flood

□ **우산** [우:산] u-san n. umbrella

   □ **양산** [양산] yang-san n. parasol

비가 올 것 같으니 우산을 가지고 가세요.
bi-ga ol geot ga-teu-ni u-sa-neul ga-ji-go ga-se-yo
Since it looks like rain, take your umbrella.

□ **태풍** [태풍] tae-pung n. typhoon

□ **허리케인** [허리케인] heo-ri-ke-in n. hurricane

□ **폭풍** [폭풍] pok-pung n. storm

□ **천둥** [천둥] cheon-dung n. thunder

□ **벼락** [벼락] byeo-rak n. thunderbolt

□ **번개** [번개] beon-gae n. lightning

□ **이슬** [이슬] i-seul n. dew

□ **우박** [우:박] u-bak n. hail

□ **서리** [서리] seo-ri n. frost

□ **동상** [동:상] dong-sang n. frostbite

□ **얼음** [어름] eo-reum n. ice

□ **공기** [공기] gong-gi n. **air**

 = **대기** [대:기] dae-gi

□ **계절** [계:절/게:절] gye-jeol/ge-jeol n. **season**

□ **봄** [봄] bom n. **spring**

□ **황사** [황사] hwang-sa n. **yellow dust**

 □ **미세먼지** [미세먼지] mi-se-meon-ji **fine dust**

□ **무지개** [무지개] mu-ji-gae n. **rainbow**

□ **씨** [씨] ssi n. **seed**

 = **씨앗** [씨앋] ssi-at

 □ **싹트다** [싹트다] ssak-teu-da v. **sprout, shoot**

 □ **꽃봉오리** [꼳뽕오리] ggot-bbong-o-ri n. **flower bud**

□ **여름** [여름] yeo-reum n. **summer**

□ **눅눅하다** [눙누카다] nung-nu-ka-da a. **humid, damp**

 □ **습하다** [스파다] seu-pa-da a. **humid, soggy**

 □ **습기** [습끼] seup-ggi n. **moisture, humidity**

□ **열사병** [열싸뼝] yeol-ssa-bbyeong n. **heatstroke**

□ **열대야** [열때야] yeol-ddae-ya n. **tropical night**

 tip. '열대야' means the nighttime temperature stay above 25℃.

□ **가을** [가을] ga-eul n. **fall, autumn**

□ **단풍** [단풍] dan-pung n. **autumnal tints**

 □ **단풍나무** [단풍나무] dan-pung-na-mu n. **maple**

 □ **은행나무** [은행나무] eun-haeng-na-mu n. **ginkgo**

□ **낙엽** [나겹] na-gyeop n. **fallen leaves**

□ **추수** [추수] chu-su n. harvest

　= **수확** [수확] su-hwak

□ **겨울** [겨울] gyeo-ul n. winter

　나는 겨울에 추위를 많이 타요.
　na-neun gyeo-u-re chu-wi-reul ma-ni ta-yo
　I feel the cold badly in winter.

□ **눈** [눈:] nun n. snow

　□ **눈송이** [눈:쏭이] nun-ssong-i n. snowflake
　□ **눈사람** [눈:싸람] nun-ssa-ram n. snowman
　□ **눈싸움** [눈:싸움] nun-ssa-um n. snowball fight

□ **온도** [온도] on-do n. temperature

　= **기온** [기온] gi-on

　오늘 몇 도예요?
　o-neul myeot do-ye-yo?
　What's the temperature today?

□ **섭씨** [섭씨] seop-ssi n. Celsius, centigrade

□ **화씨** [화씨] hwa-ssi n. Fahrenheit

□ **영상** [영상] yeong-sang n. above zero

□ **영하** [영하] yeong-ha n. below zero

□ **기후** [기후] gi-hu n. climate

□ **기압** [기압] gi-ap n. atmospheric pressure

　□ **고기압** [고기압] go-gi-ap n. high atmospheric pressure
　□ **저기압** [저:기압] jeo-gi-ap n. low atmospheric pressure

□ **지구온난화** [지구온난화] ji-gu-on-nan-hwa global warming

지구온난화 때문에, 날씨가 더워지고 있어요.
ji-gu-on-nan-hwa ddae-mu-ne, nal-ssi-ga deo-wo-ji-go i-sseo-yo
Due to global warming, the weather is getting hotter.

□ **자외선** [자:외선/자:웨선] ja-oe-seon/ja-we-seon n. ultraviolet rays

□ **적외선** [저괴선/저궤선] jeo-goe-seon/jeo-gwe-seon n. infrared rays

08. 열대야

Useful Conversation

최지훈   더위 때문에 지난밤에 한숨도 못 잤어.
deo-wi ddae-mu-ne ji-nan-ba-me han-sum-do mot ja-sseo
It was so hot I couldn't sleep a wink last night.

이준서   나도 그래. 더워서 죽을 것 같아.
na-do geu-rae. deo-wo-seo ju-geul geot ga-ta
Me too. I can't stand the heat.

최지훈   언제까지 이 더위가 계속 될까?
eon-je-gga-ji i deo-wi-ga gye-sok doel-gga?
How long will the heat last?

이준서   그게 바로 내가 알고 싶은 거야.
geu-ge ba-ro nae-ga al-go si-peun geo-ya
That's what I want to know.

Animals & Plants 동물 & 식물 dong-mul & sing-mul

□ **동물** [동:물] dong-mul

n. animal

□ **반려동물** [발:려동물]

bal-ryeo-dong-mul

n. pet

□ **꼬리** [꼬리] ggo-ri

n. tail

□ **발** [발] bal

n. paw

□ **물다** [물다] mul-da

v. bite

□ **짖다** [짇따] jit-dda

v. bark

□ **개** [개:] gae

n. dog, canine

□ **고양이** [고양이] go-yang-i

n. cat, feline

□ **소** [소] so

n. cattle

□ **염소** [염소] yeom-so

n. goat

□ **돼지** [돼:지] dwae-ji

n. pig

□ **토끼** [토끼] to-ggi

n. rabbit

□ **양** [양] yang

n. lamb, sheep

□ **말** [말] mal

n. horse

□ **얼룩말** [얼룽말]

eol-rung-mal

n. zebra

□ **사자** [사자] sa-ja

n. lion

□ **호랑이** [호:랑이]

ho-rang-i

n. tiger

□ **곰** [곰:] gom

n. bear

□ **여우** [여우] yeo-u

n. fox

□ **늑대** [늑때]

neuk-ddae

n. wolf

□ **원숭이** [원:숭이]

won-sung-i

n. monkey

□ **코끼리** [코끼리] ko-ggi-ri

n. elephant

□ **기린** [기린] gi-rin

n. giraffe

□ **하마** [하마] ha-ma

n. hippopotamus

□ **사슴** [사슴] sa-seum

n. deer

□ **너구리** [너구리]

neo-gu-ri

n. raccoon

□ **다람쥐** [다람쥐]

da-ram-jwi

n. squirrel, chipmunk

□ **쥐** [쥐] jwi

n. mouse, rat

□ **박쥐** [박:쮜] bak-jjwi

n. bat

□ **고래** [고래] go-rae

n. whale

□ 새 [새:] sae

n. bird

□ 날개 [날개] nal-gae

n. wing

□ 부리 [부리] bu-ri

n. bill, beak

□ 닭 [닥] dak

n. chicken

□ 오리 [오:리] o-ri

n. duck

□ 참새 [참새] cham-sae

n. sparrow

□ 비둘기 [비둘기]

bi-dul-gi

n. dove, pigeon

□ 까마귀 [까마귀]

gga-ma-gwi

n. crow

□ 독수리 [독쑤리]

dok-ssu-ri

n. eagle

□ 갈매기 [갈매기]

gal-mae-gi

n. seagull

□ 제비 [제:비] je-bi

n. swallow

□ 칠면조 [칠면조]

chil-myeon-jo

n. turkey

□ 타조 [타:조] ta-jo

n. ostrich

□ 올빼미 [올빼미]

ol-bbae-mi

n. owl

□ 펭귄 [펭귄]

peng-gwin

n. penguin

□ **물고기** [물꼬기]
mul-ggo-gi
n. fish

□ **아가미** [아가미]
a-ga-mi
n. gill

□ **지느러미** [지느러미]
ji-neu-reo-mi
n. fin

□ **열대어** [열때어]
yeol-ddae-eo
n. tropical fish

□ **금붕어** [금붕어]
geum-bung-eo
n. goldfish

□ **어항** [어항] eo-hang
n. fish bowl

□ **상어** [상어] sang-eo
n. shark

□ **문어** [무너] mu-neo
n. octopus

□ **오징어** [오징어] o-jing-eo
n. squid

□ **가오리** [가오리] ga-o-ri
n. ray

□ **거북** [거북] geo-buk
n. turtle

□ **악어** [아거] a-geo
n. crocodile, alligator

□ **용** [용] yong
n. dragon

□ **뱀** [뱀:] baem
n. snake

□ **개구리** [개구리] gae-gu-ri
n. frog

□ **곤충** [곤충] gon-chung
n. insect, bug

□ **벌** [벌:] beol n. bee

□ **꿀벌** [꿀벌] ggul-beol
n. honeybee

□ **나비** [나비] na-bi
n. butterfly

□ **잠자리** [잠자리] jam-ja-ri
n. dragonfly

□ **개미** [개:미] gae-mi
n. ant

□ **파리** [파:리] pa-ri
n. fly

□ **모기** [모:기] mo-gi
n. mosquito

□ **바퀴벌레** [바퀴벌레]
ba-kwi-beol-re
n. cockroach

□ **거미** [거미] geo-mi
n. spider

□ **식물** [싱물] sing-mul
n. plant

□ **심다** [심:따] sim-dda
v. plant

□ **나무** [나무] na-mu
n. tree

□ **가지** [가지] ga-ji

n. branch

□ **잎** [입] ip

n. leaf

□ **뿌리** [뿌리] bbu-ri

n. root

□ **풀** [풀] pul n. **grass**

□ **잔디** [잔디] jan-di

n. **lawn, grass**

□ **꽃** [꼳] ggot

n. **flower**

□ **피다** [피다] pi-da

v. **bloom**

□ **열매** [열매] yeol-mae

n. **fruit**

□ **장미** [장미] jang-mi

n. **rose**

□ **무궁화** [무궁화]

mu-gung-hwa

n. **rose of Sharon**

□ **해바라기** [해바라기]

hae-ba-ra-gi

n. **sunflower**

□ **벚꽃** [벋꼳] beot-ggot

n. **cherry blossom**

□ **난** [난] nan

= **난초** [난초] nan-cho

n. **orchid**

113

□ **동물** [동:물] dong-mul n. **animal**

□ **반려동물** [발:려동물] bal-ryeo-dong-mul n. **pet**

> **tip.** Korean have said
> '애완동물 [애:완동물
> ae-wan-dong-mul]' for pet,
> but nowdays more and
> more people say
> '반려동물' for pet.

□ **사육하다** [사유카다] sa-yu-ka-da v. **breed, raise**
　= **기르다** [기르다] gi-reu-da

□ **털** [털] teol n. **fur**

　□ **모피** [모피] mo-pi n. **fur and skin, leather**

　□ **털가죽** [털가죽] teol-ga-juk n. **fur and skin**

　□ **꼬리** [꼬리] ggo-ri n. **tail**

　□ **갈기** [갈:기] gal-gi n. **mane**

□ **발** [발] bal n. **paw**

　□ **발톱** [발톱] bal-top n. **claw**

　□ **할퀴다** [할퀴다] hal-kwi-da v. **scratch, claw**

□ **물다** [물다] mul-da v. **bite**
　= **깨물다** [깨물다] ggae-mul-da

　□ **짖다** [짇따] jit-dda v. **bark**

　□ **으르렁거리다** [으르렁거리다] eu-reu-reong-geo-ri-da v. **growl, roar**

□ **개** [개:] gae n. **dog, canine**

　□ **강아지** [강아지] gang-a-ji n. **puppy**

> **tip.** Sometimes grandparents call
> their grandchild '강아지'.
> It means grandparents think
> they are so cute.

　□ **멍멍** [멍멍] meong-meong ad. **bow-wow**

　강아지에게 '토리'라고 이름을 지어 주었어요.
　gang-a-ji-e-ge 'to-ri'-ra-go i-reu-meul ji-eo ju-eo-sseo-yo
　I named the puppy 'Tori'.

□ **고양이** [고양이] go-yang-i n. **cat, feline**

　□ **야옹야옹** [야옹냐옹] ya-ong-nya-ong ad. **mew, meow**

□ **소** [소] so n. cattle

  □ **송아지** [송아지] song-a-ji n. calf

  □ **황소** [황소] hwang-so n. bull, ox

  □ **암소** [암소] am-so n. cow

  □ **젖소** [젇쏘] jeot-sso n. milk cow

  □ **한우** [하:누] ha-nu n. Korean native cattle

tip. If an animal does not have a special word for its baby (such as 강아지, 송아지, 망아지), just add '새끼 [sae-ggi]'. For example, '새끼 고양이 [sae-ggi go-yang-i]', which means 'kitten'.

□ **염소** [염소] yeom-so n. goat

□ **돼지** [돼:지] dwae-ji n. pig

□ **토끼** [토끼] to-ggi n. rabbit

□ **양** [양] yang n. lamb, sheep

□ **말** [말] mal n. horse

  □ **망아지** [망아지] mang-a-ji n. foal

□ **조랑말** [조랑말] jo-rang-mal n. pony

□ **얼룩말** [얼룽말] eol-rung-mal n. zebra

□ **사자** [사자] sa-ja n. lion

□ **호랑이** [호:랑이] ho-rang-i n. tiger

□ **곰** [곰:] gom n. bear

□ **여우** [여우] yeo-u n. fox

□ **늑대** [늑때] neuk-ddae n. wolf

  = **이리** [이리] i-ri

□ **원숭이** [원:숭이] won-sung-i n. monkey

□ **침팬지** [침팬지] chim-paen-ji n. chimpanzee

□ **고릴라** [고릴라] go-ril-ra n. gorilla

□ **오랑우탄** [오랑우탄] o-rang-u-tan n. orangutan

□ **코끼리** [코끼리] ko-ggi-ri n. elephant

□ **기린** [기린] gi-rin n. giraffe

□ **하마** [하마] ha-ma n. hippopotamus

□ **사슴** [사슴] sa-seum n. deer

　　□ **꽃사슴** [꼳싸슴] ggot-ssa-seum n. Formosan deer

　　□ **순록** [술록] sul-rok n. reindeer

□ **코뿔소** [코뿔쏘] ko-bbul-sso n. rhinoceros

□ **너구리** [너구리] neo-gu-ri n. raccoon

□ **두더지** [두더지] du-deo-ji n. mole

□ **쥐** [쥐] jwi n. mouse, rat

　　□ **생쥐** [생:쥐] saeng-jwi n. mouse

□ **햄스터** [햄스터] haem-seu-teo n. hamster

　　내 햄스터는 양배추를 즐겨 먹어요.
　　nae haem-seu-teo-neun yang-bae-chu-reul jeul-gyeo meo-geo-yo
　　My hamster likes to eat cabbage.

□ **다람쥐** [다람쥐] da-ram-jwi n. squirrel, chipmunk

□ **박쥐** [박:쮜] bak-jjwi n. bat

□ **고래** [고래] go-rae n. whale

　　□ **돌고래** [돌고래] dol-go-rae n. dolphin

☐ **새** [새:] sae n. bird

  ☐ **날개** [날개] nal-gae n. wing

  ☐ **깃털** [긷털] git-teol n. feather

  ☐ **부리** [부리] bu-ri n. bill, beak

  ☐ **날다** [날다] nal-da v. fly

☐ **알** [알] al n. egg

  ☐ **품다** [품:따] pum-dda v. incubate

  ☐ **둥지** [둥지] dung-ji n. nest

  = **보금자리** [보금자리] bo-geum-ja-ri

☐ **닭** [닥] dak n. chicken

  ☐ **암탉** [암탁] am-tak n. hen

  ☐ **수탉** [수탁] su-tak n. rooster, cock

  ☐ **병아리** [병아리] byeong-a-ri n. chick

☐ **오리** [오:리] o-ri n. duck

☐ **거위** [거위] geo-wi n. goose

☐ **참새** [참새] cham-sae n. sparrow

☐ **비둘기** [비둘기] bi-dul-gi n. dove, pigeon

☐ **까마귀** [까마귀] gga-ma-gwi n. crow

☐ **독수리** [독쑤리] dok-ssu-ri n. eagle

☐ **매** [매:] mae n. hawk, falcon

☐ **갈매기** [갈매기] gal-mae-gi n. seagull

☐ **제비** [제:비] je-bi n. swallow

□ **칠면조** [칠면조] chil-myeon-jo n. turkey

□ **공작** [공:작] gong-jak n. peacock

□ **타조** [타:조] ta-jo n. ostrich

□ **부엉이** [부엉이] bu-eong-i n. owl

□ **올빼미** [올빼미] ol-bbae-mi n. owl

    tip. Although '부엉이' and '올빼미' are the 'owl' in English, but actually not same kind.

□ **펭귄** [펭귄] peng-gwin n. penguin

□ **물고기** [물꼬기] mul-ggo-gi n. fish

    □ **아가미** [아가미] a-ga-mi n. gill

    □ **지느러미** [지느러미] ji-neu-reo-mi n. fin

    □ **비늘** [비늘] bi-neul n. scale

    □ **헤엄치다** [헤엄치다] he-eom-chi-da v. swim

□ **열대어** [열때어] yeol-ddae-eo n. tropical fish

    □ **금붕어** [금붕어] geum-bung-eo n. goldfish

    □ **어항** [어항] eo-hang n. fish bowl

□ **상어** [상어] sang-eo n. shark

□ **문어** [무너] mu-neo n. octopus

□ **오징어** [오징어] o-jing-eo n. squid

□ **가오리** [가오리] ga-o-ri n. ray

□ **뱀장어** [뱀:장어] baem-jang-eo n. eel

    = **장어** [장어] jang-eo

□ **거북** [거북] geo-buk n. turtle

□ **악어** [아거] a-geo n. crocodile, alligator

□ **용** [용] yong n. dragon

□ **뱀** [뱀ː] baem n. snake

□ **도마뱀** [도마뱀] do-ma-baem n. lizard

□ **개구리** [개구리] gae-gu-ri n. frog

　□ **올챙이** [올챙이] ol-chaeng-i n. tadpole

□ **곤충** [곤충] gon-chung n. insect, bug

　□ **벌레** [벌레] beol-re n. worm

　□ **더듬이** [더드미] deo-deu-mi n. antenna

□ **벌** [벌ː] beol n. bee

　□ **꿀벌** [꿀벌] ggul-beol n. honeybee

　□ **말벌** [말벌] mal-beol n. hornet

□ **나비** [나비] na-bi n. butterfly

□ **잠자리** [잠자리] jam-ja-ri n. dragonfly

□ **개미** [개ː미] gae-mi n. ant

□ **파리** [파ː리] pa-ri n. fly

□ **모기** [모ː기] mo-gi n. mosquito

□ **바퀴벌레** [바퀴벌레] ba-kwi-beol-re n. cockroach

□ **딱정벌레** [딱쩡벌레] ddak-jjeong-beol-re n. beetle

□ **거미** [거미] geo-mi n. spider

□ **식물** [싱물] sing-mul n. plant

   □ **심다** [심:따] sim-dda v. plant

□ **가지** [가지] ga-ji n. branch •————————→ **tip.** '가지' has two meanings: branch and eggplant.

   □ **줄기** [줄기] jul-gi n. stem

   □ **잎** [입] ip n. leaf

   □ **뿌리** [뿌리] bbu-ri n. root

□ **나무** [나무] na-mu n. tree

□ **풀** [풀] pul n. grass

   □ **잔디** [잔디] jan-di n. lawn, grass

   □ **잡초** [잡초] jap-cho n. weed

□ **꽃** [꼳] ggot n. flower

   □ **꽃잎** [꼰닙] ggon-nip n. petal

   □ **피다** [피다] pi-da v. bloom

□ **열매** [열매] yeol-mae n. fruit

   □ **맺다** [맫따] maet-dda v. bear

□ **장미** [장미] jang-mi n. rose

□ **무궁화** [무궁화] mu-gung-hwa n. rose of Sharon **tip.** '무궁화' is the national flower of Korea.

□ **튤립** [튤립] tyul-rip n. tulip

□ **해바라기** [해바라기] hae-ba-ra-gi n. sunflower

□ **민들레** [민들레] min-deul-re n. dandelion

□ **백합** [배캅] bae-kap n. lily

□ **데이지** [데이지] de-i-ji n. daisy

□ **붓꽃** [붇꼳] but-ggot n. iris

□ **벚꽃** [벋꼳] beot-ggot n. cherry blossom

□ **수선화** [수선화] su-seon-hwa n. narcissus

□ **난** [난] nan n. orchid

  = **난초** [난초] nan-cho

□ **나팔꽃** [나팔꼳] na-pal-ggot n. morning-glory

□ **개나리** [개:나리] gae-na-ri n. forsythia

□ **진달래** [진달래] jin-dal-rae n. azalea

\# 09. 반려동물

Useful Conversation

김미나   **반려동물 있니?**
           bal-reo-dong-mul in-ni?
           Do you have a pet?

송하영   **응, 개를 키운 지 3년 됐어.**
           eung, gae-reul ki-un ji sam-nyeon dwae-sseo
           Yes, I've had a dog for 3 years.

김미나   **집에 개가 있는 게 편하니?**
           ji-be gae-ga in-neun ge pyeon-ha-ni?
           Is it easy to have a dog at home?

송하영   **물론이지, 우리 개는 교육이 잘 되어 있지.**
           햄스터 두 마리도 있어.
           mul-ro-ni-ji, u-ri gae-neun gyo-yu-gi jal doe-eo i-jji.
           haem-seu-teo du ma-ri-do i-sseo
           Sure, I trained the dog to be good.
           I have two hamsters too.

Exercise

Read and Match.

1. 개 •	• animal
2. 계절 •	• cloud
3. 구름 •	• date
4. 꽃 •	• dog
5. 나무 •	• flower
6. 날씨 •	• plant
7. 날짜 •	• season
8. 동물 •	• sky
9. 시간 •	• sun
10. 식물 •	• time
11. 하늘 •	• tree
12. 해, 태양 •	• weather

1. 개 – dog 2. 계절 – season 3. 구름 – cloud 4. 꽃 – flower
5. 나무 – tree 6. 날씨 – weather 7. 날짜 – date 8. 동물 – animal
9. 시간 – time 10. 식물 – plant 11. 하늘 – sky 12. 해, 태양 – sun

4장

Daily Life

The Home 집 jip

□ **집** [집] jip
  n. house, home

□ **가정** [가정] ga-jeong
  n. home

□ **방** [방] bang
  n. room

□ **침실** [침:실] chim-sil
  n. bed room

□ **서재** [서재] seo-jae
  n. study (room), den

□ **거실** [거실] geo-sil
  n. living room

□ **부엌** [부억] bu-eok
= **주방** [주방] ju-bang
  n. kitchen

□ **욕실** [욕씰] yok-ssil
  n. bathroom

□ **화장실** [화장실]
  hwa-jang-sil
  n. toilet, restroom

□ **문** [문] mun
  n. door

□ **창문** [창문] chang-mun
  n. window

□ **마당** [마당] ma-dang
  n. yard

□ **정원** [정원] jeong-won
  n. garden

□ **현관** [현관] hyeon-gwan
  n. entrance

□ **천장** [천장] cheon-jang
n. ceiling

□ **벽** [벽] byeok
n. wall

□ **바닥** [바닥] ba-dak
= **마루** [마루] ma-ru
n. floor

□ **다락** [다락] da-rak
n. attic

□ **창고** [창고] chang-go
n. strorage

□ **지하실** [지하실] ji-ha-sil
n. basement

□ **차고** [차고] cha-go
n. garage

□ **계단** [계단/게단]
gye-dan/ge-dan
n. stair

□ **엘리베이터** [엘리베이터]
el-ri-be-i-teo
n. elevator

□ **가구** [가구] ga-gu
n. furniture

□ **침대** [침:대] chim-dae
n. bed

□ **옷장** [옫짱] ot-jjang
n. wardrobe

□ **의자** [의자] ui-ja
n. chair

□ **소파** [소파] so-pa
n. sofa

□ **탁자** [탁짜] tak-jja
n. table

□ **텔레비전** [텔레비전]
tel-re-bi-jeon
n. television, TV

□ **책상** [책쌍]
chaek-ssang
n. desk

□ **책장** [책짱]
chaek-jjang
n. bookcase

□ **전기 레인지** [전기 레인지]
jeon-gi re-in-ji
electric range

□ **전자레인지** [전자레인지]
jeon-ja-re-in-ji
n. microwave oven

□ **오븐** [오븐] o-beun
n. oven

□ **냉장고** [냉:장고]
naeng-jang-go
n. refrigerator

□ **믹서** [믹써] mik-sseo
n. blender

□ **토스터** [토스터]
to-seu-teo
n. toaster

☐ **싱크대** [싱크대]

sing-keu-dae

n. sink

☐ **식기세척기** [식끼세척끼]

sik-ggi-se-cheok-ggi

n. dishwasher

☐ **세면대** [세:면대]

se-myeon-dae

n. washstand

☐ **욕조** [욕쪼] yok-jjo

n. bathtub

☐ **샤워기** [샤워기]

sya-wo-gi

n. shower

☐ **수도꼭지** [수도꼭찌]

su-do-ggok-jji

n. tap

☐ **변기** [변기] byeon-gi

n. toilet bowl

☐ **쓰레기통** [쓰레기통] sseu-re-gi-tong

= **휴지통** [휴지통] hyu-ji-tong

n. wastebasket, trashcan

☐ **청소** [청소]

cheong-so

n. cleaning

☐ **청소기** [청소기]

cheong-so-gi

n. cleaner

☐ **세탁기** [세:탁끼]

se-tak-ggi

n. washing machine

127

□ **집** [집] jip n. house, home

  □ **가정** [가정] ga-jeong n. home

  집 청소하는 것 좀 도와줘요.
  jip cheong-so-ha-neun geot jom do-wa-jwo-yo
  Help me clean the house.

□ **방** [방] bang n. room

  □ **안방** [안빵] an-bbang n. main room

  □ **작은방** [자근방] ja-geun-bang n. second room, small room

  □ **침실** [침:실] chim-sil n. bed room

□ **서재** [서재] seo-jae n. study (room), den

□ **거실** [거실] geo-sil n. living room

□ **부엌** [부억] bu-eok n. kitchen

  = **주방** [주방] ju-bang

□ **식당** [식땅] sik-ddang n. dining room

□ **욕실** [욕씰] yok-ssil n. bathroom

  □ **화장실** [화장실] hwa-jang-sil n. toilet, restroom

  화장실이 어디죠?
  hwa-jang-si-ri eo-di-jyo?
  Where is the toilet?

□ **문** [문] mun n. door

  □ **열다** [열:다] yeol-da v. open

  □ **닫다** [닫따] dat-dda v. close

  문을 열어 주세요.
  mu-neul yeo-reo ju-se-yo
  Open the door please.

□ **창문** [창문] chang-mun n. window

   □ **커튼** [커튼] keo-teun n. curtain

□ **발코니** [발코니] bal-ko-ni n. balcony

   □ **베란다** [베란다] be-ran-da n. veranda, porch

□ **마당** [마당] ma-dang n. yard

□ **정원** [정원] jeong-won n. garden

   = **뜰** [뜰] ddeul

   □ **텃밭** [터빧/텃빧] teo-bbat/tteot-bbat n. vegetable garden

□ **울타리** [울타리] ul-ta-ri n. fence

□ **현관** [현관] hyeon-gwan n. entrance

   □ **초인종** [초인종] cho-in-jong n. doorbell

□ **열쇠** [열ː쐬/열ː쒜] yeol-ssoe/yeol-sswe n. key

   □ **자물쇠** [자물쐬/자물쒜] ja-mul-ssoe/ja-mul-sswe n. lock

   내 열쇠가 어디 있어요?
   nae yeol-ssoe-ga eo-di i-sseo-yo?
   Where is my key?

□ **천장** [천장] cheon-jang n. ceiling

□ **벽** [벽] byeok n. wall

□ **바닥** [바닥] ba-dak n. floor

   = **마루** [마루] ma-ru

   □ **온돌** [온돌] on-dol n. Korean floor heating system

□ **다락** [다락] da-rak n. attic

□ **창고** [창고] chang-go n. strorage

　□ **지하실** [지하실] ji-ha-sil n. basement

□ **차고** [차고] cha-go n. garage

　□ **주차장** [주:차장] ju-cha-jang n. parking lot, car park

□ **층** [층] cheung n. floor, story

□ **계단** [계단/게단] gye-dan/ge-dan n. stair

□ **엘리베이터** [엘리베이터] el-ri-be-i-teo n. elevator

　= **승강기** [승강기] seung-gang-gi

□ **지붕** [지붕] ji-bung n. roof

　□ **굴뚝** [굴:뚝] gul-dduk n. chimney

□ **가구** [가구] ga-gu n. furniture

□ **침대** [침:대] chim-dae n. bed

□ **옷장** [옫짱] ot-jjang n. wardrobe

　□ **벽장** [벽짱] byeok-jjang n. closet

　□ **붙박이장** [붇빠기장] but-bba-gi-jang n. built-in wardrobe

　□ **옷걸이** [옫꺼리] ot-ggeo-ri n. hanger

□ **서랍장** [서랍짱] seo-rap-jjang n. bureau, chest of drawers

　□ **서랍** [서랍] seo-rap n. drawer

□ **의자** [의자] ui-ja n. chair

　□ **안락의자** [알라긔자/알라기자] al-ra-gui-ja/al-ra-gi-ja n. easy chair

　□ **흔들의자** [흔드릐자/흔드리자] heun-deu-rui-ja/heun-deu-ri-ja
　n. rocking chair

□ **소파** [소파] so-pa n. sofa

　소파에 앉으세요.
　so-pa-e an-jeu-se-yo
　Sit down on the sofa please.

□ **탁자** [탁짜] tak-jja n. table

　= **테이블** [테이블] te-i-beul

　□ **식탁** [식탁] sik-tak n. dining table

□ **화장대** [화장대] hwa-jang-dae n. dressing table, vanity

□ **거울** [거울] geo-ul n. mirror

□ **전등** [전:등] jeon-deung n. electric light

□ **텔레비전** [텔레비전] tel-re-bi-jeon n. television, TV

　= **티브이** [티브이] ti-beu-i

　이제 티브이를 꺼요.
　i-je ti-beu-i-reul ggeo-yo
　Turn off the TV now.

□ **책상** [책쌍] chaek-ssang n. desk

　□ **책장** [책짱] chaek-jjang n. bookcase

　□ **책꽂이** [책꼬지] chaek-ggo-ji n. bookshelves

□ **장식장** [장식짱] jang-sik-jjang n. cabinet

　□ **진열장** [지:녈짱] ji-nyeol-jjang n. showcase

　□ **선반** [선반] seon-ban n. shelf

□ **전기 레인지** [전기 레인지] jeon-gi re-in-ji electric range

　□ **가스레인지** [가스레인지] ga-seu-re-in-ji n. gas range

　□ **전자레인지** [전자레인지] jeon-ja-re-in-ji n. microwave oven

□ **오븐** [오븐] o-beun n. oven

□ **냉장고** [냉:장고] naeng-jang-go n. refrigerator

   □ **김치냉장고** [김치냉:장고] gim-chi-naeng-jang-go n. kimchi refrigerator

   □ **냉동고** [냉:동고] naeng-dong-go n. freezer

□ **믹서** [믹써] mik-sseo n. blender

□ **토스터** [토스터] to-seu-teo n. toaster

□ **싱크대** [싱크대] sing-keu-dae n. sink

   = **개수대** [개수대] gae-su-dae

   □ **수세미** [수세미] su-se-mi n. loofah sponge

   □ **행주** [행주] haeng-ju n. dishtowel, tea towel

□ **식기세척기** [식끼세척끼] sik-ggi-se-cheok-ggi n. dishwasher

□ **욕조** [욕쪼] yok-jjo n. bathtub

   □ **샤워기** [샤워기] sya-wo-gi n. shower

   □ **세면대** [세:면대] se-myeon-dae n. washstand

   □ **수도꼭지** [수도꼭찌] su-do-ggok-jji n. tap

□ **변기** [변기] byeon-gi n. toilet bowl

□ **쓰레기통** [쓰레기통] sseu-re-gi-tong n. wastebasket, trashcan

   = **휴지통** [휴지통] hyu-ji-tong

□ **청소** [청소] cheong-so n. cleaning

   □ **청소기** [청소기] cheong-so-gi n. cleaner

   □ **진공청소기** [진공청소기] jin-gong-cheong-so-gi n. vaccuum cleaner

□ **빗자루** [비짜루/빋짜루] bi-jja-ru/bit-jja-ru n. broom

   = **비** [비] bi

□ **쓰레받기** [쓰레받끼] sseu-re-bat-ggi n. dustpan

□ **걸레** [걸레] geol-re n. rag

　□ **걸레질** [걸레질] geol-re-jil n. mopping

□ **빨래** [빨래] bbal-rae n. laundry, doing the clothes

　= **세탁** [세:탁] se-tak

　□ **세탁기** [세:탁끼] se-tak-ggi n. washing machine

□ **의류 건조기** [의류 건조기]
ui-ryu geon-jo-gi clothes dryer

□ **공기청정기** [공기청정기]
gong-gi-cheong-jeong-gi air cleaner

10. 설거지

Useful Conversation

김미나　준서야, 설거지 좀 해 줄 수 있어?
jun-seo-ya, seol-geo-ji jom hae jul su i-sseo?
Junseo, could you help me wash the dishes?

이준서　싫은데! 오늘 내가 방 전체랑 화장실 청소했다고.
si-reun-de! o-neul nae-ga bang jeon-che-rang hwa-jang-sil cheong-so-haet-dda-go.
No! I cleaned all the bedrooms and the bathroom.

김미나　그런데, 내가 지금 나가야 되거든.
geu-reon-de, nae-ga ji-geum na-ga-ya doe-geo-deun.
Yes, but I have to go out now.

이준서　알겠어, 하지만 이번 한 번뿐이야.
al-ge-sseo, ha-ji-man i-beon han beon-bbu-ni-ya.
Okay, but just this once.

Clothes 옷 ot

□ **옷** [옫] ot

n. clothes

□ **입다** [입따] ip-dda

v. wear, put on

□ **쓰다** [쓰다] sseu-da

v. wear, put on

□ **한복** [한:복] han-bok

n. Hanbok, Korean traditional clothes

□ **양복** [양복] yang-bok

n. suit

□ **바지** [바지] ba-ji

n. pants, trousers

□ **반바지** [반:바지] ban-ba-ji

n. shorts

□ **청바지** [청바지] cheong-ba-ji

n. jeans

□ **치마** [치마] chi-ma

n. skirt

□ **셔츠** [셔츠] syeo-cheu

n. shirt

□ **티셔츠** [티셔츠] ti-syeo-cheu

n. T-shirt

□ **와이셔츠** [와이셔츠] wa-i-syeo-cheu

n. dress shirt

□ **블라우스** [블라우스]

beul-ra-u-seu

n. blouse

□ **스웨터** [스웨터]

seu-we-teo

n. sweater

□ **카디건** [카디건]

ka-di-geon

n. cardigan

□ **조끼** [조끼] jo-ggi

n. vest

□ **재킷** [재킫] jae-kit

n. jacket

□ **점퍼** [점퍼] jeom-peo

n. jumper

□ **패딩 점퍼** [패딩 점퍼]

pae-ding jeom-peo

padded jumper

□ **외투** [외:투/웨:투]

oe-tu/we-tu

n. overcoat

□ **속옷** [소:곧] so-got

n. underwear

□ **잠옷** [자몯] ja-mot

n. pajamas

□ **비옷** [비옫] bi-ot

n. raincoat

□ **운동복** [운:동복]

un-dong-bok

n. sportswear

135

□ **목도리** [목또리]

mok-ddo-ri

n. muffler

□ **스카프** [스카프]

seu-ka-peu

n. scarf

□ **숄** [숄] syol

n. shawl

□ **멜빵** [멜·빵]

mel-bbang

n. suspenders

□ **허리띠** [허리띠]

heo-ri-ddi

n. belt

□ **장갑** [장:갑] jang-gap

n. gloves

□ **모자** [모자] mo-ja

n. cap, hat

□ **넥타이** [넥타이] nek-ta-i

n. necktie

□ **양말** [양말] yang-mal

n. socks

□ **신발** [신발] sin-bal

n. shoes

□ **구두** [구두] gu-du

n. dress shoes

□ **운동화** [운:동화]

un-dong-hwa

n. sneakers

□ **부츠** [부츠] bu-cheu

n. boots

□ **샌들** [샌들] saen-deul

n. sandals

□ **슬리퍼** [슬리퍼]

seul-ri-peo

n. slippers

□ **실내화** [실래화]

sil-rae-hwa

n. shoes for inside

□ **안경** [안:경] an-gyeong

n. glasses

□ **가방** [가방] ga-bang

n. bag

□ **핸드백** [핸드백]

haen-deu-baek

n. handbag

□ **배낭** [배:낭] bae-nang

n. backpack

□ **트렁크** [트렁크]

teu-reong-keu

n. suitcase, trunk

□ **지갑** [지갑] ji-gap

n. wallet, purse

□ **목걸이** [목꺼리]

mok-ggeo-ri

n. necklace

□ **반지** [반지] ban-ji

n. ring

137

□ **옷** [옫] ot n. clothes

   □ **의류** [의류] ui-ryu n. clothing

   그는 검은색 옷만 입어요.
   geu-neun geo-meun-saek on-man i-beo-yo
   He always wears black clothes.

□ **입다** [입따] ip-dda v. wear, put on •——→   **tip.** '입다' and '걸치다' are

   □ **걸치다** [걸치다] geol-chi-da v. wear, slip on   used for clothes.

   □ **쓰다** [쓰다] sseu-da v. wear, put on   '쓰다' is used for glasses, hat and accessories.

   □ **신다** [신:따] sin-dda v. wear, put on   '신다' is used for shoes and socks.

   오늘 뭐 입어야 하죠?
   o-neul mwo i-beo-ya ha-jyo?
   What should I wear today?

□ **한복** [한:복] han-bok n. Hanbok, Korean traditional clothes

   □ **저고리** [저고리] jeo-go-ri n. Jeogori, Korean traditional jacket

   □ **두루마기** [두루마기] du-ru-ma-gi n. Durumagi,

   Korean traditional coat

   □ **마고자** [마고자] ma-go-ja n. Magoja,

   Korean traditional outerwear for men

   □ **배자** [배:자] bae-ja n. Korean traditional vest for women

   tip. The '한복' for men is made up of '바지' and '저고리'. For women, it's made up of '치마' and '저고리'. The men's '저고리' is longer than the women's '저고리'. For cold weather, add '마고자', '배자' or '두루마기'.

□ **양복** [양복] yang-bok n. suit

   그는 양복을 거의 입지 않아요.
   geu-neun yang-bo-geul geo-i ip-jji a-na-yo
   He rarely wears a suit.

□ **바지** [바지] ba-ji n. **pants, trousers**

  □ **반바지** [반:바지] ban-ba-ji n. **shorts**

□ **청바지** [청바지] cheong-ba-ji n. **jeans**

□ **치마** [치마] chi-ma n. **skirt**

  = **스커트** [스커트] seu-keo-teu

□ **미니스커트** [미니스커트] mi-ni-seu-keo-teu n. **miniskirt**

  = **짧은 치마** [짤븐 치마] jjal-beun chi-ma

□ **원피스** [원피스] won-pi-seu n. **dress**

□ **투피스** [투피스] tu-pi-seu n. **two-piece suit (for women's clothes)**

□ **셔츠** [셔츠] syeo-cheu n. **shirt**

  □ **와이셔츠** [와이셔츠] wa-i-syeo-cheu n. **dress shirt**

  □ **티셔츠** [티셔츠] ti-syeo-cheu n. **T-shirt**

  □ **폴로셔츠** [폴로셔츠] pol-ro-syeo-cheu n. **polo shirt**

□ **블라우스** [블라우스] beul-ra-u-seu n. **blouse**

□ **스웨터** [스웨터] seu-we-teo n. **sweater**

  □ **니트** [니트] ni-teu n. **knit**

□ **카디건** [카디건] ka-di-geon n. **cardigan**

□ **조끼** [조끼] jo-ggi n. **vest**

□ **재킷** [재킫] jae-kit n. **jacket**

□ **점퍼** [점퍼] jeom-peo n. **jumper**

  = **잠바** [잠바] jam-ba

  □ **패딩 점퍼** [패딩 점퍼] pae-ding jeom-peo **padded jumper**

□ **외투** [외:투/웨:투] oe-tu/we-tu n. overcoat

= **코트** [코트] ko-teu

= **겉옷** [거돋] geo-dot

□ **반코트** [반:코트] ban-ko-teu n. half-length coat

겨울을 맞아 코트를 한 벌 샀어요.
gyeo-u-reul ma-ja ko-teu-reul han beol sa-sseo-yo
I bought an overcoat for winter.

□ **속옷** [소:곧] so-got n. underwear

= **내의** [내:의/내:이] nae-ui/nae-i

= **내복** [내:복] nae-bok

□ **팬티** [팬티] paen-ti n. briefs, underpants

□ **러닝셔츠** [러닝셔츠] reo-ning-syeo-cheu n. undershirt

= **러닝** [러닝] reo-ning

= **런닝** [런닝] reon-ning

tip. Some people say '난닝구 [nan-ning-gu]',
but it is a kind of dialect of Gyeongsang-do.

□ **란제리** [란제리] ran-je-ri n. lingerie

□ **브래지어** [브래지어] beu-rae-ji-eo n. brassiere

□ **잠옷** [자몯] ja-mot n. pajamas

□ **우비** [우:비] u-bi n. things for rain: raincoat, umbrella and so on

□ **비옷** [비옫] bi-ot n. raincoat

= **우의** [우:의/우:이] u-ui/u-i

= **레인코트** [레인코트] re-in-ko-teu

비옷 챙기는 거 잊지 마세요. 오늘 비가 올 거예요.
bi-ot chaeng-gi-neun geo it-jji ma-se-yo. o-neul bi-ga ol geo-ye-yo
Don't forget to bring your raincoat. It's going to rain today.

□ **운동복** [운:동복] un-dong-bok n. sportswear

  = **체육복** [체육뽁] che-yuk-bbok

  = **추리닝** [추리닝] chu-ri-ning

□ **수영복** [수영복] su-yeong-bok n. swimsuit

  □ **비키니** [비키니] bi-ki-ni n. bikini

□ **장화** [장화] jang-hwa n. rubber boots

□ **목도리** [목또리] mok-ddo-ri n. muffler

  = **머플러** [머플러] meo-peul-reo

□ **스카프** [스카프] seu-ka-peu n. scarf

□ **숄** [숄] syol n. shawl

□ **멜빵** [멜:빵] mel-bbang n. suspenders

□ **허리띠** [허리띠] heo-ri-ddi n. belt

  = **벨트** [벨트] bel-teu

□ **장갑** [장:갑] jang-gap n. gloves

  □ **벙어리장갑** [벙어리장갑] beong-eo-ri-jang-gap n. mittens

□ **모자** [모자] mo-ja n. cap, hat

□ **귀마개** [귀마개] gwi-ma-gae n. earmuffs

□ **넥타이** [넥타이] nek-ta-i n. necktie

  □ **나비넥타이** [나비넥타이] na-bi-nek-ta-i n. bow tie

□ **양말** [양말] yang-mal n. socks

□ **스타킹** [스타킹] seu-ta-king n. stocking

  □ **레깅스** [레깅스] re-ging-seu n. leggings

□ **신발** [신발] sin-bal n. shoes

   = **신** [신] sin

□ **구두** [구두] gu-du n. dress shoes

□ **운동화** [운ː동화] un-dong-hwa n. sneakers

□ **부츠** [부츠] bu-cheu n. boots

□ **하이힐** [하이힐] ha-i-hil n. high heels

□ **단화** [단ː화] dan-hwa n. loafers

□ **샌들** [샌들] saen-deul n. sandals

□ **가락 신** [가락 신] ga-rak sin flip-flops

tip. Actually, Koreans don't use '가락 신', say '쪼리 [jjo-ri]' as usual. It is the informal word.

□ **슬리퍼** [슬리퍼] seul-ri-peo n. slippers

□ **실내화** [실래화] sil-rae-hwa n. shoes for inside

□ **고무신** [고무신] go-mu-sin n. rubber shoes

□ **안경** [안ː경] an-gyeong n. glasses

   □ **선글라스** [선글라스] seon-geul-ra-seu n. sunglasses

   = **색안경** [새간경] sae-gan-gyeong

□ **가방** [가방] ga-bang n. bag

□ **핸드백** [핸드백] haen-deu-baek n. handbag

□ **숄더백** [숄더백] syol-deo-baek n. shoulder bag

□ **배낭** [배ː낭] bae-nang n. backpack

   □ **책가방** [책까방] chak-gga-bang n. school bag

□ **트렁크** [트렁크] teu-reong-keu n. suitcase, trunk

tip. '트렁크' means a square box for travel and also the back part of a car.

□ **지갑** [지갑] ji-gap n. wallet, purse

최근에 지갑을 잃어버렸어요.
choe-geu-ne ji-ga-beul i-reo-beo-ryeo-sseo-yo
I lost my wallet recently.

□ **액세서리** [액세서리] aek-se-seo-ri n. accessory

= **장식물** [장싱물] jang-sing-mul

□ **장신구** [장신구] jang-sin-gu n. jewel

　□ **목걸이** [목꺼리] mok-ggeo-ri n. necklace

　□ **팔찌** [팔찌] pal-jji n. bracelet

　□ **귀걸이** [귀거리] gwi-geo-ri n. earrings

　□ **반지** [반지] ban-ji n. ring

　□ **브로치** [브로치] beu-ro-chi n. brooch

□ **머리핀** [머리핀] meo-ri-pin n. hairpin

　□ **머리띠** [머리띠] meo-ri-ddi n. hairband

□ **옷깃** [옫낃] ot-ggit n. collar

= **칼라** [칼라] kal-ra

□ **터틀넥** [터틀넥] teo-teul-nek n. turtleneck

　□ **브이넥** [브이넥] beu-i-nek n. V-neck

□ **소매** [소매] so-mae n. sleeve

　□ **긴소매** [긴:소매] gin-so-mae n. long sleeves

　= **긴팔** [긴:팔] gin-pal

　□ **반소매** [반:소매] ban-so-mae n. short sleeves

　= **반팔** [반:팔] ban-pal

　□ **민소매** [민소매] min-so-mae n. sleeveless

□ **호주머니** [호주머니] ho-ju-meo-ni n. pocket

= **주머니** [주머니] ju-meo-ni

□ **지퍼** [지퍼] ji-peo n. zipper

□ **단추** [단추] dan-chu n. button

□ **단춧구멍** [단추꾸멍/단춛꾸멍] dan-chu-ggu-meong/dan-chut-ggu-meong

n. button hole

단추를 달아 주시겠어요?
dan-chu-reul da-ra ju-si-ge-sseo-yo?
Can you put on button?

□ **천** [천ː] cheon n. cloth, fabric

= **옷감** [옫깜] ot-ggam

□ **면** [면] myeon n. cotton

□ **비단** [비ː단] bi-dan n. silk

= **실크** [실크] sil-keu

□ **삼베** [삼베] sam-be n. hemp cloth

□ **모시** [모시] mo-si n. ramie cloth

□ **모직** [모직] mo-jik n. wool

□ **가죽** [가죽] ga-juk n. leather

□ **합성 섬유** [합썽 서뮤] hap-sseong seo-myu synthetic fiber

□ **줄무늬** [줄무니] jul-mu-ni n. stripes

□ **체크무늬** [체크무니] che-keu-mu-ni n. checkers

□ **격자무늬** [격짜무니] gyeok-jja-mu-ni n. plaid

□ **꽃무늬** [꼰무니] ggon-mu-ni n. flower-print

□ **물방울무늬** [물빵울무니] mul-bbang-ul-mu-ni n. polka dots

□ **민무늬** [민무니] min-mu-ni n. plain

144

□ **유행** [유행] yu-haeng n. fashion, trend, vogue

그녀는 최신 유행 옷만 입어요.
geu-nyeo-neun choe-sin yu-haeng on-man i-beo-yo
She only wears the latest fashions.

□ **세련되다** [세:련되다/세:련돼다] se-ryeon-doe-da/se-ryeon-dwe-da

a. polished, chic

세련되어 보이는데.
se-ryeon-doe-eo bo-i-neun-de
You look so chic.

□ **촌스럽다** [촌:쓰럽따] chon-sseu-reop-dda

a. countrified

11. 장갑

Useful Conversation

이준서   생일 선물로 뭐 받고 싶어?
saeng-il seon-mul-ro mwo bat-ggo si-peo?
What do you want for your birthday present?

최지훈   장갑이 필요해. 내 걸 잃어버렸거든.
jang-ga-bi pi-ryo-hae. nae geol i-reo-beo-ryeo-ggeo-deun
I need a pair of gloves. I've lost mine.

이준서   좋아. 지금 쇼핑하러 가자.
jo-a. ji-geum syo-ping-ha-reo ga-ja
Okay. Let's go shopping now.

최지훈   정말? 그럼 스웨터도 사야겠네.
jeong-mal? geu-reom seu-we-teo-do sa-ya-get-ne
Really? Then I should get a sweater, too.

Food 음식 eum-sik

□ **음식** [음:식] eum-sik

n. food

□ **고기** [고기] go-gi

n. meat

□ **소고기** [소고기] so-go-gi

n. beef

□ **돼지고기** [돼:지고기]

dwae-ji-go-gi

n. pork

□ **닭고기** [닥꼬기]

dak-ggo-gi

n. chicken

□ **양고기** [양고기]

yang-go-gi

n. lamb, mutton

□ **해산물** [해:산물]

hae-san-mul

= **해물** [해:물] hae-mul

n. seafood

□ **생선** [생선]

saeng-seon

n. fish

□ **오징어** [오징어]

o-jing-eo

n. squid

□ **새우** [새우] sae-u

n. shrimp, prawn

□ **전복** [전복] jeon-bok

n. abalone

□ **김** [김:] gim

n. seeweed

□ 쌀 [쌀] ssal n. rice

□ 밥 [밥] bap n. rice

□ 콩 [콩] kong

n. bean

□ 옥수수 [옥쑤수]

ok-ssu-su

n. corn

□ 채소 [채:소] chae-so

= 야채 [야:채] ya-chae

n. vegetable

□ 오이 [오이] o-i

n. cucumber

□ 당근 [당근] dang-geun

n. carrot

□ 감자 [감자] gam-ja

n. potato

□ 배추 [배:추] bae-chu

n. Chinese cabbage

□ 양배추 [양배추]

yang-bae-chu

n. cabbage

□ 상추 [상추] sang-chu

n. lettuce

□ 무 [무:] mu

n. white radish

□ 고추 [고추] go-chu

n. chili (pepper)

□ 파 [파] pa

n. green onion

□ 양파 [양파] yang-pa

n. onion

□ 마늘 [마늘] ma-neul

n. garlic

147

□ **과일** [과:일] gwa-il
n. fruit

□ **딸기** [딸:기] ddal-gi
n. strawberry

□ **사과** [사과] sa-gwa
n. apple

□ **배** [배] bae
n. pear

□ **오렌지** [오렌지] o-ren-ji
n. orange

□ **귤** [귤] gyul
n. tangerine,
mandarin

□ **레몬** [레몬] re-mon
n. lemon

□ **포도** [포도] po-do
n. grape

□ **바나나** [바나나]
ba-na-na
n. banana

□ **수박** [수:박] su-bak
n. watermelon

□ **파인애플** [파이내플]
pa-i-nae-peul
n. pineapple

□ **복숭아** [복쑹아]
bok-ssung-a
n. peach

□ **음료** [음:뇨] eum-nyo
n. drink, beverage

□ **물** [물] mul n. water

□ **식수** [식쑤] sik-ssu
n. drinking water

□ **우유** [우유] u-yu
n. milk

□ **양념** [양념] yang-nyeom

n. seasoning

□ **소스** [소스] so-seu

n. sauce, gravy

□ **소금** [소금] so-geum

n. salt

□ **설탕** [설탕] seol-tang

n. sugar

□ **후추** [후추] hu-chu

n. (black) pepper

□ **간장** [간장] gan-jang

n. soy sauce

□ **된장** [된:장/뒌:장]

doen-jang/dwen-jang

n. soybean paste

□ **고추장** [고추장]

go-chu-jang

n. red pepper paste

□ **식용유** [시굥뉴]

si-gyong-nyu

n. cooking oil

□ **볶다** [복따] bok-dda

v. stir-fry

□ **튀기다** [튀기다] twi-gi-da

v. deep fry

□ **굽다** [굽:따] gup-dda

v. roast, grill

□ **냄비** [냄비] naem-bi

n. pot, saucepan

□ **프라이팬** [프라이팬]

peu-ra-i-paen

n. frying pan

□ **그릇** [그륻] geu-reut

= **사발** [사발] sa-bal

n. bowl

149

☐ **음식** [음:식] eum-sik n. food

☐ **요리** [요리] yo-ri n. dish, cooking

☐ **식사** [식싸] sik-ssa n. meal

= **끼니** [끼니] ggi-ni

간단하게 식사하고 싶은데요.
gan-dan-ha-ge sik-ssa-ha-go si-peun-de-yo
I'd like to have a light meal.

☐ **먹다** [먹따] meok-dda v. eat, have

☐ **요리하다** [요리하다] yo-ri-ha-da v. cook

= **조리하다** [조리하다] jo-ri-ha-da

나는 요리하는 것을 좋아해요.
na-neun yo-ri-ha-neun geo-seul jo-a-hae-yo
I like to cook.

☐ **고기** [고기] go-gi n. meat

  ☐ **소고기** [소고기] so-go-gi n. beef

  ☐ **돼지고기** [돼:지고기] dwae-ji-go-gi n. pork

  ☐ **닭고기** [닥꼬기] dak-ggo-gi n. chicken

  ☐ **양고기** [양고기] yang-go-gi n. lamb, mutton

  ☐ **오리고기** [오:리고기] o-ri-go-gi n. duck meat

☐ **해산물** [해:산물] hae-san-mul n. seafood

= **해물** [해:물] hae-mul

☐ **생선** [생선] saeng-seon n. fish

tip. '생선' is the fish for food,
'물고기 [물꼬기 mul-ggo-gi]' is
the fish as animals.

식사는 소고기와 생선 중 무엇으로 하시겠어요?
sik-ssa-neun so-go-gi-wa saeng-seon jung mu-e-seu-ro ha-si-ge-sseo-yo?
Would you like beef or fish for dinner?

□ **멸치** [멸치] myeol-chi n. anchovy

□ **연어** [여너] yeo-neo n. **salmon**

□ **참다랑어** [참다랑어] cham-da-rang-eo n. **tuna**

= **참치** [참치] cham-chi

□ **고등어** [고등어] go-deung-eo n. **mackerel**

□ **갈치** [갈치] gal-chi n. **hairtail, cutlassfish**

□ **대구** [대구] dae-gu n. **cod**

□ **도미** [도:미] do-mi n. **snapper**

□ **오징어** [오징어] o-jing-eo n. **squid**

□ **문어** [무너] mu-neo n. **octopus**

□ **새우** [새우] sae-u n. **shrimp, prawn**

□ **게** [게:] ge n. **crab**

□ **꽃게** [꼳께] ggot-gge n. **blue crab**

□ **가재** [가:재] ga-jae n. **crawfish, crayfish**

□ **바닷가재** [바다까재/바닫까재] ba-da-gga-jae/ba-dat-gga-jae n. **lobster**

= **랍스터** [랍쓰터] rap-sseu-teo

□ **조개** [조개] jo-gae n. **clam**

□ **굴** [굴] gul n. **oyster**

□ **전복** [전복] jeon-bok n. **abalone**

□ **홍합** [홍합] hong-hap n. **mussel**

□ **꼬막** [꼬막] ggo-mak n. **cockle**

□ **김** [김:] gim n. seeweed

□ **곡물** [공물] gong-mul n. grain

□ **쌀** [쌀] ssal n. rice

    □ **밥** [밥] bap n. rice •⸻⸻⸻➔ **tip.** '밥' is the staple food of Koreans, '밥' is boiled '쌀'.

    밥 더 줄까요?
    bap deo jul-gga-yo?
    Do you want some more rice?

□ **찹쌀** [찹쌀] chap-ssal n. glutinous rice

□ **보리** [보리] bo-ri n. barley

□ **콩** [콩] kong n. bean

    □ **대두** [대:두] dae-du n. soybean

    □ **완두콩** [완두콩] wan-du-kong n. pea

    □ **강낭콩** [강낭콩] gang-nang-kong n. kidney bean

□ **팥** [팥] pat n. adzuki bean

□ **옥수수** [옥쑤수] ok-ssu-su n. corn

□ **채소** [채:소] chae-so n. vegetable
    = **야채** [야:채] ya-chae

□ **시금치** [시금치] si-geum-chi n. spinach

□ **오이** [오이] o-i n. cucumber

□ **당근** [당근] dang-geun n. carrot

□ **감자** [감자] gam-ja n. potato

    □ **고구마** [고:구마] go-gu-ma n. sweet potato

□ **배추** [배:추] bae-chu n. Chinese cabbage

□ **양배추** [양배추] yang-bae-chu n. cabbage

□ **상추** [상추] sang-chu n. lettuce

□ **깻잎** [깬닙] ggaen-nip n. perilla leaf

□ **무** [무:] mu n. white radish

□ **고추** [고추] go-chu n. chili (pepper)

□ **피망** [피망] pi-mang n. bell pepper, capsicum

□ **파프리카** [파프리카] pa-peu-ri-ka n. paprika

□ **가지** [가지] ga-ji n. eggplant

□ **호박** [호:박] ho-bak n. pumpkin

　　□ **애호박** [애호박] ae-ho-bak n. zucchini

□ **토마토** [토마토] to-ma-to n. tomato

□ **브로콜리** [브로콜리] beu-ro-kol-ri n. broccoli

□ **콩나물** [콩나물] kong-na-mul n. soybean sprouts

　　□ **숙주나물** [숙쭈나물] suk-jju-na-mul n. mungbean sprouts

□ **고사리** [고사리] go-sa-ri n. bracken, brake fern

□ **파** [파] pa n. green onion

□ **양파** [양파] yang-pa n. onion

□ **마늘** [마늘] ma-neul n. garlic

□ **생강** [생강] saeng-gang n. ginger

□ **과일** [과:일] gwa-il **n.** fruit

□ **딸기** [딸:기] ddal-gi **n.** strawberry

   □ **산딸기** [산딸기] san-ddal-gi **n.** raspberry

   □ **블루베리** [블루베리] beul-ru-be-ri **n.** blueberry

□ **사과** [사과] sa-gwa **n.** apple

□ **배** [배] bae **n.** pear

□ **오렌지** [오렌지] o-ren-ji **n.** orange

□ **귤** [귤] gyul **n.** tangerine, mandarin

   = **밀감** [밀감] mil-gam

□ **감** [감:] gam **n.** persimmon

   □ **홍시** [홍시] hong-si **n.** ripe persimmon, soft persimmon

□ **레몬** [레몬] re-mon **n.** lemon

□ **포도** [포도] po-do **n.** grape

□ **바나나** [바나나] ba-na-na **n.** banana

□ **수박** [수:박] su-bak **n.** watermelon

□ **참외** [차뫼/차붸] cha-moe/cha-mwe **n.** oriental melon

□ **멜론** [멜론] mel-ron **n.** melon

□ **파인애플** [파이내플] pa-i-nae-peul **n.** pineapple

□ **복숭아** [복쑹아] bok-ssung-a **n.** peach

   □ **천도복숭아** [천도복쑹아] cheon-do-bok-ssung-a **n.** nectarine

□ **자두** [자두] ja-du **n.** plum

☐ **살구** [살구] sal-gu n. apricot

☐ **앵두** [앵두] aeng-du n. cherry

　= **체리** [체리] che-ri

☐ **망고** [망고] mang-go n. mango

☐ **리치** [리치] ri-chi n. lychee

☐ **무화과** [무화과] mu-hwa-gwa n. fig

☐ **아보카도** [아보카도] a-bo-ka-do n. avocado

☐ **음료** [음ː뇨] eum-nyo n. beverage, drink

　= **음료수** [음ː뇨수] eum-nyo-su

☐ **마시다** [마시다] ma-si-da v. drink

☐ **물** [물] mul n. water

　☐ **식수** [식쑤] sik-ssu n. drinking water

　물 좀 더 주시겠어요?
　mul jom deo ju-si-ge-sseo-yo?
　May I have more water?

☐ **우유** [우유] u-yu n. milk

　☐ **두유** [두유] du-yu n. soybean milk

☐ **포도주** [포도주] po-do-ju n. wine

　= **와인** [와인] wa-in

☐ **맥주** [맥쭈] maek-jju n. beer

☐ **소주** [소주] so-ju n. Korean distilled spirits

☐ **막걸리** [막껄리] mak-ggeol-ri n. white rice wine ↗

tip. '막걸리' is a kind of Korean traditional alcohol, made of rice.

□ **탄산음료** [탄:사늠뇨] tan-sa-neum-nyo n. soda

  □ **콜라** [콜라] kol-ra n. Coke

  □ **사이다** [사이다] sa-i-da n. Sprite, 7UP ↝ **tip.** '사이다' doesn't mean cider,
                                                     a kind of alcohol as usual.

□ **커피** [커피] keo-pi n. coffee

  커피는 나중에 갖다주세요.
  keo-pi-neun na-jung-e gat-dda-ju-se-yo
  Bring me the coffee later, please.

□ **홍차** [홍차] hong-cha n. (black) tea

  □ **녹차** [녹차] nok-cha n. green tea

□ **후식** [후:식] hu-sik n. dessert

  = **디저트** [디저트] di-jeo-teu

□ **양념** [양념] yang-nyeom n. seasoning

  □ **소스** [소스] so-seu n. sauce, gravy

  □ **드레싱** [드레싱] deu-re-sing n. dressing

□ **간장** [간장] gan-jang n. soy sauce

  □ **된장** [된:장/뒌:장] doen-jang/dwen-jang n. soybean paste

  □ **고추장** [고추장] go-chu-jang n. red pepper paste

  된장은 콩으로 만든 것이에요. ●⟶ **tip.** '간장', '된장' and '고추장'
  doen-jang-eun kong-eu-ro man-deun geo-si-e-yo   are made from beans.
  Korean soybean paste is made from soybeans.   They are the Korean
                                                 traditional pastes.

□ **소금** [소금] so-geum n. salt

□ **설탕** [설탕] seol-tang n. sugar

□ **후추** [후추] hu-chu n. (black) pepper

□ **깨소금** [깨소금] ggae-so-geum n. ground sesame mixed with salt

□ **식초** [식초] sik-cho n. vinegar

□ **식용유** [시공뉴] si-gyong-nyu n. cooking oil

□ **올리브유** [올리브유] ol-ri-beu-yu n. olive oil

□ **참기름** [참기름] cham-gi-reum n. sesame oil

   □ **들기름** [들기름] deul-gi-reum n. perilla oil

□ **버터** [버터] beo-teo n. butter

□ **마요네즈** [마요네즈] ma-yo-ne-jeu n. mayonnaise, mayo

   □ **케첩** [케첩] ke-cheop n. ketchup

   □ **꿀** [꿀] ggul n. honey

   □ **잼** [잼] jaem n. jam

□ **겨자** [겨자] gyeo-ja n. mustard

   □ **고추냉이** [고추냉이] go-chu-naeng-i n. wasabi

□ **요리법** [요리뻡] yo-ri-bbeop n. recipe

   = **조리법** [조리뻡] jo-ri-bbeop

   = **레시피** [레시피] re-si-pi

□ **다듬다** [다듬따] da-deum-dda v. prepare (for cooking)

   채소 다듬는 것을 도와주세요.
   chae-so da-deum-neun geo-seul do-wa-ju-se-yo
   Please help me to prepare the vegetables.

□ **자르다** [자르다] ja-reu-da v. cut

   □ **썰다** [썰:다] sseol-da v. chop

   □ **다지다** [다지다] da-ji-da v. mince

   □ **벗기다** [벋끼다] beot-ggi-da v. peel

□ **섞다** [석따] seok-dda v. mix

= **버무리다** [버무리다] beo-mu-ri-da

= **무치다** [무치다] mu-chi-da •

tip. '무치다' is the verb used for '나물 [na-mul] (herbs, vegetables)'. '나물 요리' are vegetabales dishes with seasonings.

□ **무침** [무침] mu-chim n. some vegetables seasoned with some condiments

□ **볶다** [복따] bok-dda v. stir-fry

□ **볶음** [보끔] bo-ggeum n. stir-frying

□ **튀기다** [튀기다] twi-gi-da v. deep fry

□ **튀김** [튀김] twi-gim n. deep-frying

□ **굽다** [굽:따] gup-dda v. roast, grill

□ **구이** [구이] gu-i n. roast, grill, grilled dishes

□ **삶다** [삼:따] sam-dda v. boil

□ **찌다** [찌다] jji-da v. steam

□ **찜** [찜] jjim n. steamed dish

□ **도마** [도마] do-ma n. cutting board

□ **칼** [칼] kal n. knife

□ **식칼** [식칼] sik-kal n. kitchen knife

= **부엌칼** [부억칼] bu-eok-kal

□ **과일칼** [과:일칼] gwa-il-kal n. fruit knife

= **과도** [과:도] gwa-do

□ **국자** [국짜] guk-jja n. ladle

□ **밥주걱** [밥쭈걱] bap-jju-geok n. rice scoop

□ **뒤집개** [뒤집깨] dwi-jip-ggae n. spatula

□ **냄비** [냄비] naem-bi n. pot, saucepan

□ **솥** [솓] sot n. Sot, Korean traditional caldron made of cast iron

□ **밥솥** [밥쏟] bap-ssot n. rice cooker

□ **프라이팬** [프라이팬] peu-ra-i-paen n. frying pan

□ **식기** [식끼] sik-ggi n. tableware

□ **그릇** [그륻] geu-reut n. bowl

= **사발** [사발] sa-bal

□ **밥그릇** [밥끄륻] bap-ggeu-reut n. rice bowl

□ **국그릇** [국끄륻] guk-ggeu-reut n. soup bowl

□ **접시** [접씨] jeop-ssi n. plate

□ **쟁반** [쟁반] jaeng-ban n. tray

12. 음식 투정

Useful Conversation

김미나   남기지 말고 다 먹어.
nam-gi-ji mal-go da meo-geo
Finish your meal.

이준서   콩 싫어. 맛이 없어.
kong si-reo. ma-si eop-sseo
I don't like peas. They're disgusting.

김미나   그렇게 음식을 가리면 안 돼.
geu-reo-ke eum-si-geul ga-ri-myeon an dwae
Don't be so picky about your food.

이준서   알았어. 그럼 케첩 뿌려도 돼?
a-ra-sseo. geu-reom ke-cheop bbu-ryeo-do dwae?
Okay. Then can I put some ketchup on them?

Hobbies 취미 chwi-mi

□ **취미** [취:미] chwi-mi

n. hobby

□ **운동** [운:동] un-dong

= **스포츠** [스포츠]

seu-po-cheu

n. sport

□ **달리다** [달리다] dal-ri-da

= **뛰다** [뛰다] ddwi-da

v. run, dash

□ **수영** [수영] su-yeong

n. swimming

□ **테니스** [테니스]

te-ni-seu

n. tennis

□ **배드민턴** [배드민턴]

bae-deu-min-teon

n. badminton

□ **축구** [축꾸] chuk-ggu

n. football, soccer

□ **야구** [야:구] ya-gu

n. baseball

□ **농구** [농구] nong-gu

n. basketball

□ **배구** [배구] bae-gu

n. volleyball

□ **요가** [요가] yo-ga

n. yoga

□ **골프** [골프] gol-peu

n. golf

□ **음악** [으막] eu-mak

n. music

□ **노래** [노래] no-rae

n. song

□ **가수** [가수] ga-su

n. singer

□ **악기** [악끼] ak-ggi

n. musical instrument

□ **연주** [연:주] yeon-ju

n. performance

□ **피아노** [피아노] pi-a-no

n. piano

□ **바이올린** [바이올린]

ba-i-ol-rin

n. violin

□ **기타** [기타] gi-ta

n. guitar

□ **북** [북] buk

= **드럼** [드럼] deu-reom

n. drum

□ **음악회** [으마쾨/으마퀘]

eu-ma-koe/eu-ma-kwe

= **콘서트** [콘서트]

kon-seo-teu

n. concert

□ **오페라** [오페라]

o-pe-ra

n. opera

□ **뮤지컬** [뮤지컬]

myu-ji-keol

n. musical

□ **연극** [연:극] yeon-geuk
n. play

□ **영화** [영화] yeong-hwa
n. movie, film

□ **극장** [극짱] geuk-jjang
n. theater

□ **책** [책] chaek
n. book

□ **독서** [독써] dok-sseo
n. reading

□ **읽다** [익따] yik-dda
v. read

□ **쓰다** [쓰다] sseu-da
v. write

□ **도서관** [도서관]
do-seo-gwan
n. library

□ **서점** [서점] seo-jeom
n. bookstore

□ **문학** [문학] mun-hak
n. literature

□ **만화책** [만:화책]
man-hwa-chaek
n. comic book

□ **동화책** [동:화책]
dong-hwa-chaek
n. fairy tale book

□ **잡지** [잡찌] jap-jji
n. magazine

□ **사진** [사진] sa-jin

n. photograph,
photo, picture

□ **카메라** [카메라]

ka-me-ra

n. camera

□ **그림** [그:림] geu-rim

n. picture

□ **그리다** [그:리다]

geu-ri-da

v. draw

□ **물감** [물깜] mul-ggam

n. color

□ **종이** [종이] jong-i

n. paper

□ **체스** [체스] che-seu

n. chess

□ **장기** [장:기] jang-gi

n. Korean chess

□ **등산** [등산] deung-san

n. climbing

□ **낚시** [낙씨] nak-ssi

n. fishing

□ **야영** [야:영] ya-yeong

= **캠핑** [캠핑] kaem-ping

n. camping

□ **뜨개질** [뜨개질]

ddeu-gae-jil

n. knitting

□ **취미** [취:미] chwi-mi n. hobby

취미가 뭐예요?
chwi-mi-ga mwo-ye-yo?
What are your hobbies?

□ **운동** [운:동] un-dong n. sport
= **스포츠** [스포츠] seu-po-cheu

□ **경기** [경:기] gyeong-gi n. game
= **게임** [게임] ge-im
□ **시합** [시합] si-hap n. match

□ **달리다** [달리다] dal-ri-da v. run, dash
= **뛰다** [뛰다] ddwi-da
□ **조깅** [조깅] jo-ging n. jogging

□ **산책** [산:책] san-chaek n. walk
= **산보** [산:뽀] san-bbo

□ **체육관** [체육꽌] che-yuk-ggwan n. gym
□ **헬스클럽** [헬스클럽] hel-seu-keul-reop n. fitness center

□ **수영** [수영] su-yeong n. swimming
□ **수영장** [수영장] su-yeong-jang n. swimming pool, pool

□ **공** [공:] gong n. ball
□ **셔틀콕** [셔틀콕] syeo-teul-kok n. shuttlecock

□ **라켓** [라켇] ra-ket n. racket

□ **테니스** [테니스] te-ni-seu n. tennis

□ **배드민턴** [배드민턴] bae-deu-min-teon n. badminton

□ **축구** [축꾸] chuk-ggu n. football, soccer

  □ **미식축구** [미식축꾸] mi-sik-chuk-ggu n. American football

□ **야구** [야ː구] ya-gu n. baseball

□ **농구** [농구] nong-gu n. basketball

□ **배구** [배구] bae-gu n. volleyball

□ **탁구** [탁꾸] tak-ggu n. table tennis, ping-pong

□ **당구** [당구] dang-gu n. billiards

□ **요가** [요가] yo-ga n. yoga

□ **골프** [골프] gol-peu n. golf

　요즘 골프에 빠져 있어요.
　yo-jeum gol-peu-e bba-jeo i-sseo-yo
　I'm passionate about golf these days.

□ **사이클링** [사이클링] sa-i-keul-ring n. cycling

□ **권투** [권ː투] gwon-tu n. boxing

　= **복싱** [복씽] bok-ssing

□ **스키** [스키] seu-ki n. skiing

  □ **스노보드** [스노보드] seu-no-bo-deu n. snowboarding

  □ **스키장** [스키장] seu-ki-jang n. ski resort

□ **스케이트** [스케이트] seu-ke-i-teu n. skating

  □ **인라인스케이트** [인라인스케이트] in-ra-in-seu-ke-i-teu n. inline skating

  □ **스케이트보드** [스케이트보드] seu-ke-i-teu-bo-deu n. skateboarding

  □ **스케이트장** [스케이트장] seu-ke-i-teu-jang n. ice rink

□ **음악** [으막] eu-mak n. music

  □ **듣다** [듣따] deut-dda v. listen to, hear

  음악 듣는 것을 좋아해요.
  eu-mak deun-neun geu-seul jo-a-hae-yo
  I like listening to music.

□ **노래** [노래] no-rae n. song

  □ **가수** [가수] ga-su n. singer

□ **가사** [가사] ga-sa n. lyrics

  □ **가락** [가락] ga-rak n. melody

  = **멜로디** [멜로디] mel-ro-di

  = **선율** [서뉼] seo-nyul

  □ **작사** [작싸] jak-ssa n. writing lyrics

  □ **작곡** [작꼭] jak-ggok n. composition

□ **음반** [음반] eum-ban n. record disc, LP

  = **디스크** [디스크] di-seu-keu

□ **악기** [악끼] ak-ggi n. musical instrument

  □ **연주** [연주] yeon-ju n. performance

  악기를 다룰 줄 알아요?
  ak-ggi-reul da-rul jul a-ra-yo?
  Do you play any musical instruments?

□ **피아노** [피아노] pi-a-no n. piano

□ **바이올린** [바이올린] ba-i-ol-rin n. violin

□ **비올라** [비올라] bi-ol-ra n. viola

□ **첼로** [첼로] chel-ro n. cello

□ **하프** [하프] ha-peu n. harp

□ **기타** [기타] gi-ta n. guitar

□ **플루트** [플루트] peul-ru-teu n. flute

□ **트럼펫** [트럼펟] teu-reom-pet n. trumpet

□ **색소폰** [색소폰] saek-so-pon n. saxophone

□ **북** [북] buk n. drum

= **드럼** [드럼] deu-reom

□ **음악회** [으마괴/으마퀘] eu-ma-koe/eu-ma-kwe n. concert

= **콘서트** [콘서트] kon-seo-teu

□ **관현악단** [관혀낙딴] gwan-hyeo-nak-ddan n. orchestra

= **교향악단** [교향악딴] gyo-hyang-ak-ddan

= **오케스트라** [오케스트라] o-ke-seu-teu-ra

□ **지휘자** [지휘자] ji-hwi-ja n. conductor

□ **오페라** [오페라] o-pe-ra n. opera

□ **뮤지컬** [뮤지컬] myu-ji-keol n. musical

□ **연극** [연:극] yeon-geuk n. play

□ **영화** [영화] yeong-hwa n. movie, film

□ **보다** [보다] bo-da v. see, watch

□ **개봉하다** [개봉하다] gae-bong-ha-da v. release

오늘 밤에 영화 보러 가요.
o-neul ba-me yeong-hwa bo-reo ga-yo
Let's go to see a movie tonight.

□ **극장** [극짱] geuk-jjang n. theater

　□ **영화관** [영화관] yeong-hwa-gwan n. movie theater, cinema

□ **블록버스터** [블록뻐스터] beul-rok-bbeo-seu-teo blockbuster

□ **영화감독** [영화감독] yeong-hwa-gam-dok n. movie director

□ **배우** [배우] bae-u n. actor, actress

　□ **여배우** [여배우] yeo-bae-u n. actress

□ **주인공** [주인공] ju-in-gong n. main character

□ **관객** [관객] gwan-gaek n. audience

□ **책** [책] chaek n. book

　□ **독서** [독써] dok-sseo n. reading

　□ **읽다** [익따] ik-dda v. read

　한 달에 몇 권 읽으세요?
　han da-re myeot ggwon il-geu-se-yo?
　How many books do you read a month?

□ **도서관** [도서관] do-seo-gwan n. library

□ **서점** [서점] seo-jeom n. bookstore

□ **쓰다** [쓰다] sseu-da v. write

　= **저술하다** [저:술하다] jeo-sul-ha-da

□ **문학** [문학] mun-hak n. literature

　□ **소설** [소:설] so-seol n. novel

　□ **시** [시] si n. poem

　□ **수필** [수필] su-pil n. essay

　= **에세이** [에세이] e-se-i

□ **만화책** [만ː화책] man-hwa-chaek n. comic book

□ **동화책** [동ː화책] dong-hwa-chaek n. fairy tale book

□ **위인전** [위인전] wi-in-jeon n. biography

□ **잡지** [잡찌] jap-jji n. magazine

□ **작가** [작까] jak-gga n. writer

　□ **저자** [저ː자] jeo-ja n. author

□ **소설가** [소ː설가] so-seol-ga n. novelist

□ **시인** [시인] si-in n. poet

□ **수필가** [수필가] su-pil-ga n. essayist

□ **사진** [사진] sa-jin n. photograph, photo, picture

□ **촬영** [촤령] chwa-ryeong n. photography

　□ **카메라** [카메라] ka-me-ra n. camera

　사진 촬영 금지
　sa-jin chwa-ryeong geum-ji
　No Photography Allowed

□ **그림** [그ː림] geu-rim n. picture

　□ **유화** [유화] yu-hwa n. oil painting

　□ **수채화** [수채화] su-chae-hwa n. watercolor

　□ **삽화** [사퐈] sa-pwa n. illustration

　= **일러스트레이션** [일러스트레이션] il-reo-seu-teu-re-i-syeon

□ **그리다** [그ː리다] geu-ri-da v. draw

　□ **스케치** [스케치] seu-ke-chi n. sketch

□ **소묘** [소:묘] so-myo n. drawing

□ **색칠하다** [색칠하다] saek-chil-ha-da v. paint

= **채색하다** [채:새카다] chae-sae-ka-da

□ **화가** [화:가] hwa-ga n. painter

□ **물감** [물깜] mul-ggam n. color

□ **붓** [붇] but n. brush

□ **종이** [종이] jong-i n. paper

　□ **도화지** [도화지] do-hwa-ji n. drawing paper

　□ **스케치북** [스케치북] seu-ke-chi-buk n. sketchbook

　□ **캔버스** [캔버스] kaen-beo-seu n. canvas

□ **보드게임** [보드게임] bo-deu-ge-im n. board game

□ **주사위** [주사위] ju-sa-wi n. dice

□ **체스** [체스] che-seu n. chess

□ **장기** [장:기] jang-gi n. Korean chess

□ **바둑** [바둑] ba-duk n. go

□ **등산** [등산] deung-san n. climbing

　□ **암벽등반** [암벽등반] am-byeok-deung-ban rock-climbing

　예전부터 등산을 좋아했어요.
　ye-jeon-bu-teo deung-sa-neul jo-a-hae-sseo-yo
　I've been interested in climbing.

□ **낚시** [낙씨] nak-ssi n. fishing

□ **소풍** [소풍] so-pung n. picnic

170

□ **야영** [야:영] ya-yeong **n.** camping

  = **캠핑** [캠핑] kaem-ping

□ **공예** [공예] gong-ye **n.** craft

□ **원예** [워녜] wo-nye **n.** gardening

□ **꽃꽂이** [꼳꼬지] ggot-ggo-ji **n.** flower arrangement

□ **수집** [수집] su-jip **n.** collection

□ **뜨개질** [뜨개질] ddeu-gae-jil **n.** knitting

13. 기타

Useful Conversation

김미나   넌 시간 있을 때 뭐 해?
     neon si-gan i-sseul ddae mwo hae?
     What do you do when you have free time?

송하영   난 기타를 쳐.
     nan gi-ta-reul cheo
     I play the guitar.

김미나   멋진데! 한 곡 연주해 줄 수 있니?
     meot-jjin-de! han gok yeon-ju-hae jul ssu in-ni?
     Great! Could you play me a melody?

송하영   사실은, 이제 막 배우기 시작했는데 한번 시도해 볼게.
     sa-si-reun, i-je mak bae-u-gi si-jak-haet-neun-de han-beon
     si-do-hae bol-ge
     **Actually, I've just started learning but I'll give it
     a try.**

Telephone & the Internet 전화 & 인터넷 jeon-hwa & in-teo-net

☐ **전화** [전:화] jeon-hwa
n. telephone, phone

☐ **휴대폰** [휴대폰] hyu-dae-pon
= **핸드폰** [핸드폰] haen-deu-pon
= **휴대전화** [휴대전화] hyu-dae-jeon-hwa
n. cellular phone, cell phone, mobile phone

☐ **전화하다** [전:화하다]
jeon-hwa-ha-da
= **걸다** [걸:다] geol-da
v. call

☐ **받다** [받따] bat-dda
v. answer/take
(the phone),
receive (a message)

☐ **끊다** [끈타] ggeun-ta
v. hang up

☐ **전화번호** [전:화번호]
jeon-hwa-beon-ho
n. phone number

☐ **로밍 서비스** [로밍 서비스]
ro-ming seo-bi-seu
roaming service

☐ **문자메시지** [문짜메시지]
mun-jja-me-si-ji
SMS, text message

☐ **전송** [전:송] jeon-song
n. transmission

☐ **벨 소리** [벨 소리]
bel so-ri
ring-tone

☐ **진동모드** [진:동모드]
jin-dong-mo-deu
vibrate mode

☐ **애플리케이션** [애플리케이션]

ae-peul-ri-ke-i-syeon

n. application, app

☐ **다운로드** [다운로드]

da-un-ro-deu

n. download

☐ **업로드** [업로드]

eop-ro-deu

n. upload

☐ **배터리** [배터리]

bae-teo-ri

n. battery

☐ **충전** [충전] chung-jeon

n. charge

☐ **켜다** [켜다] kyeo-da

v. turn on

☐ **끄다** [끄다] ggeu-da

v. turn off

☐ **와이파이** [와이파이] wa-i-pa-i

n. Wi-Fi

☐ **인터넷** [인터넷] in-teo-net

n. Internet

☐ **온라인 게임** [올라인 게임]

ol-ra-in ge-im

online game

☐ **인터넷 쇼핑** [인터넷 쇼핑]

in-teo-net syo-ping

online shopping

173

□ **즐겨찾기** [즐겨찯끼]
jeul-gyeo-chat-ggi
n. favorite

□ **접속** [접쏙]
jeop-ssok
n. connect

□ **이메일** [이메일] i-me-il
= **전자우편** [전자우편]
jeon-ja-u-pyeon
n. e-mail

□ **웹 사이트** [웹 사이트] wep sa-i-teu
website

□ **홈페이지** [홈페이지] hom-pe-i-ji
n. homepage

□ **검색** [검:색] geom-saek
n. search

□ **컴퓨터** [컴퓨터] keom-pyu-teo
n. computer

□ **노트북** [노트북] no-teu-buk
n. laptop computer

□ **태블릿** [태블릳] tae-beul-rit
n. tablet computer

□ **모니터** [모니터] mo-ni-teo
n. monitor

□ **키보드** [키보드]
ki-bo-deu
n. keyboard

□ **치다** [치다] chi-da
v. tap

□ **마우스** [마우스]
ma-u-seu
n. mouse

□ **클릭** [클릭] keul-rik
n. making a click

□ **프린터** [프린터]
peu-rin-teo
n. printer

□ **웹캠** [웹캠] wep-kaem
n. webcam

□ **파일** [파일] pa-il
n. file

□ **폴더** [폴더] pol-deo
n. folder

□ **저장** [저:장] jeo-jang
n. save

□ **삭제** [삭쩨] sak-jje
n. deletion

□ **보안** [보:안] bo-an
n. security

□ **블로그** [블로그]
beul-ro-geu
n. blog

175

☐ **전화** [전:화] jeon-hwa n. telephone, phone

☐ **휴대폰** [휴대폰] hyu-dae-pon n. cellular phone, cell phone, mobile phone

　= **핸드폰** [핸드폰] haen-deu-pon

　= **휴대전화** [휴대전화] hyu-dae-jeon-hwa

　　영화 시작 전에 휴대폰을 꺼 두세요.
　　yeong-hwa si-jak jeo-ne hyu-dae-po-neul ggeo du-se-yo
　　Turn your cell phone off before the movie starts.

☐ **스마트폰** [스마트폰] seu-ma-teu-pon n. smartphone

☐ **전화하다** [전:화하다] jeon-hwa-ha-da v. call

　= **걸다** [걸:다] geol-da

　= **발신하다** [발씬하다] bal-ssin-ha-da

☐ **받다** [받따] bat-dda v. answer/take (the phone), receive (a message)

　= **수신하다** [수신하다] su-sin-ha-da

　☐ **수신** [수신] su-sin n. receiving

　☐ **수신음** [수신음] su-sin-eum n. received sound

☐ **통화** [통화] tong-hwa n. phone call, telephone conversation

☐ **통화 중** [통화 중] tong-hwa jung on the phone, busy line

☐ **끊다** [끈타] ggeun-ta v. hang up

☐ **바꾸다** [바꾸다] ba-ggu-da v. transfer, change

☐ **공중전화** [공중전화] gong-jung-jeon-hwa n. public phone, pay phone

　☐ **긴급 전화** [긴급 전화] gin-geup jeon-hwa emergency call

□ **전화번호** [전:화번호] jeon-hwa-beon-ho n. phone number

□ **로밍 서비스** [로밍 서비스] ro-ming seo-bi-seu roaming service

□ **자동응답기** [자동응:답끼] ja-dong-eung-dap-ggi answering machine

□ **메신저** [메신저] me-sin-jeo n. messenger

□ **메시지** [메시지] me-si-ji n. message

　□ **문자메시지** [문짜메시지] mun-jja-me-si-ji SMS, text message

　□ **음성메시지** [음성메시지] eum-seong-me-si-ji voice mail,

voice message

메시지를 남기시겠어요?
me-si-ji-reul nam-gi-si-ge-sseo-yo?
Can I take a message?

□ **보내다** [보내다] bo-nae-da v. send (a message)

　□ **전송** [전:송] jeon-song n. transmission

□ **벨 소리** [벨 소리] bel so-ri ring-tone

□ **진동모드** [진:동모드] jin-dong-mo-deu vibrate mode

　= **매너모드** [매너모드] mae-neo-mo-deu

□ **애플리케이션** [애플리케이션] ae-peul-ri-ke-i-syeon n. application, app

　= **어플** [어플] eo-peul ————→ **tip.** '어플' and '앱' are short for '애플리케이션'.

　= **앱** [앱] aep

□ **다운로드** [다운로드] da-un-ro-deu n. download

□ **업로드** [업로드] eop-ro-deu n. upload

□ **업데이트** [업떼이트] eop-dde-i-teu n. update

□ **배터리** [배터리] bae-teo-ri n. battery

배터리가 얼마 없어요.
bae-teo-ri-ga eol-ma eop-sseo-yo
My battery is low.

□ **충전** [충전] chung-jeon n. charge

□ **충전기** [충전기] chung-jeon-gi n. charger

□ **방전** [방:전] bang-jeon n. electric discharge

□ **전원** [저:눤] jeo-nwon n. power supply

□ **켜다** [켜다] kyeo-da v. turn on

□ **끄다** [끄다] ggeu-da v. turn off

□ **영상통화** [영상통화] yeong-sang-tong-hwa n. video call

□ **와이파이** [와이파이] wa-i-pa-i n. Wi-Fi(wireless fidelity)

= **근거리 무선망** [근:거리 무선망] geun-geo-ri mu-seon-mang

□ **인터넷** [인터넫] in-teo-net n. Internet

□ **온라인** [올라인] ol-ra-in n. online

□ **오프라인** [오프라인] o-peu-ra-in n. offline

□ **온라인 게임** [올라인 게임] ol-ra-in ge-im online game

□ **인터넷 뱅킹** [인터넫 뱅킹] in-teo-net baeng-king Internet banking

□ **인터넷 쇼핑** [인터넫 쇼핑] in-teo-net syo-ping online shopping

□ **즐겨찾기** [즐겨찯끼] jeul-gyeo-chat-ggi n. favorite

□ **접속** [접쏙] jeop-ssok n. connect

□ **무선데이터** [무선데이터] mu-seon-de-i-teo wireless data

□ **이메일** [이메일] i-me-il n. **e-mail**

　= **전자우편** [전자우편] jeon-ja-u-pyeon

　□ **이메일주소** [이메일주:소] i-me-il-ju-so **e-mail address**

　　이메일주소가 뭐예요?
　　i-me-il-ju-so-ga mwo-ye-yo?
　　Could I get your e-mail address?

□ **받은 메일함** [바든 메일함] ba-deun me-il-ham **inbox (by e-mail)**

　□ **보낸 메일함** [보낸 메일함] bo-naen me-il-ham **sent mail**

□ **답장** [답짱] dap-jjang n. **response for mail**

□ **전달** [전달] jeon-dal n. **forwarding**

□ **첨부 파일** [첨부 파일] cheom-bu pa-il **attached file, attachment**

　　첨부 파일이 열리지 않아요.
　　cheom-bu pa-i-ri yeol-ri-ji a-na-yo
　　I can't open the attachment.

□ **스팸 메일** [스팸 메일] seu-paem me-il **spam mail**

□ **로그인** [로그인] ro-geu-in n. **log-on, log-in, sign in**

　□ **로그아웃** [로그아웃] ro-geu-a-ut n. **log-off, log-out, sign out**

□ **회원가입** [회:원가입/훼:원가입] hoe-won ga-ip **sign in**

　□ **탈퇴** [탈퇴/탈퉤] tal-toe/tal-twe **drop out**

□ **계정** [계:정/게:정] gye-jeong/ge-jeong n. **account**

□ **웹 사이트** [웹 사이트] wep sa-i-teu **website**

□ **홈페이지** [홈페이지] hom-pe-i-ji n. **homepage**

□ **브라우저** [브라우저] beu-ra-u-jeo n. **browser**

□ **검색** [검:색] geom-saek n. search

  □ **검색창** [검:색창] geom-saek-chang n. search bar

  □ **주소창** [주:소창] ju-so-chang address bar

  □ **웹 서핑** [웹 서핑] wep seo-ping browsing through a website

□ **아이디** [아이디] a-i-di n. ID

  □ **비밀번호** [비:밀번호] bi-mil-beon-ho n. password, PIN(personal identification number)

□ **컴퓨터** [컴퓨터] keom-pyu-teo n. computer

□ **데스크톱** [데스크톱] de-seu-keu-top n. desktop computer

  = **데스크톱 컴퓨터** [데스크톱 컴퓨터] de-seu-keu-top keom-pyu-teo

  □ **노트북** [노트북] no-teu-buk n. laptop computer

  = **노트북 컴퓨터** [노트북 컴퓨터] no-teu-buk keom-pyu-teo

  □ **태블릿** [태블릳] tae-beul-rit n. tablet computer

  = **태블릿 컴퓨터** [태블릳 컴퓨터] tae-beul-rit keom-pyu-teo

□ **모니터** [모니터] mo-ni-teo n. monitor

  □ **액정** [액쩡] aek-jjeong n. display

  □ **화면** [화:면] hwa-myeon n. screen

  □ **바탕화면** [바탕화:면] ba-tang-hwa-myeon wallpaper

□ **키보드** [키보드] ki-bo-deu n. keyboard

  □ **단축키** [단축키] dan-chuk-ki n. shortcut

  □ **타이핑** [타이핑] ta-i-ping n. typing

  □ **치다** [치다] chi-da v. type

□ **마우스** [마우스] ma-u-seu n. mouse

  □ **무선 마우스** [무선 마우스] mu-seon ma-u-seu wireless mouse

□ **마우스 패드** [마우스 패드] ma-u-seu pae-deu **mouse pad**

□ **클릭** [클릭] keul-rik n. **making a click**

  열기 버튼을 클릭해 봐요.
  yeol-gi beo-teu-neul keul-ri-kae bwa-yo
  Click the open button.

□ **헤드셋** [헤드셋] he-deu-set n. **headset**

□ **하드디스크** [하드디스크] ha-deu-di-seu-keu **hard disk, hard drive**

□ **디스크드라이브** [디스크드라이브] di-seu-keu-deu-ra-i-beu **disk drive**

□ **램** [램] raem n. **RAM(random-access memory)**

  = **랜덤액세스메모리** [랜덤액쎄스메모리] raen-deom-aek-sse-seu-me-mo-ri

□ **롬** [롬] rom n. **ROM(read-only memory)**

  = **고정기억장치** [고정기억짱치] go-jeong-gi-eok-jjang-chi

□ **프로그램** [프로그램] peu-ro-geu-raem n. **program**

  □ **오에스** [오에스] o-e-seu n. **OS(operating system)**

  = **운영체제** [우:녕체제] u-nyeong-che-je

□ **설치** [설치] seol-chi n. **installation**

□ **하드웨어** [하드웨어] ha-deu-we-eo n. **hardware**

  □ **소프트웨어** [소프트웨어] so-peu-teu-we-oe n. **software**

□ **프린터** [프린터] peu-rin-teo n. **printer**

□ **복사기** [복싸기] bok-ssa-gi n. **copy machine, copier**

□ **스캐너** [스캐너] seu-kae-neo n. **scanner**

□ **웹캠** [웹캠] wep-kaem n. **webcam**

□ **파일** [파일] pa-il n. file

□ **폴더** [폴더] pol-deo n. folder

□ **저장** [저:장] jeo-jang n. save

　□ **저장하다** [저:장하다] jeo-jang-ha-da v. save

　어느 폴더에 저장했어요?
　eo-neu pol-deo-e jeo-jang-hae-sseo-yo?
　Which folder did you save it in?

□ **수정** [수정] su-jeong n. modification

□ **복사** [복싸] bok-ssa n. copy

　= **카피** [카피] ka-pi

□ **붙여넣기** [부처너:키] bu-cheo-neo-ki paste

□ **삭제** [삭쩨] sak-jje n. deletion

　□ **삭제하다** [삭쩨하다] sak-jje-ha-da v. delete

　= **지우다** [지우다] ji-u-da

　= **제거하다** [제거하다] je-geo-ha-da

　실수로 파일을 지웠어요.
　sil-ssu-ro pa-i-reul ji-wo-sseo-yo
　I accidentally deleted the file.

□ **공유** [공:유] gong-yu n. sharing

□ **보안** [보:안] bo-an n. security

□ **차단** [차:단] cha-dan n. block

□ **바이러스** [바이러스] ba-i-reo-seu n. virus

　□ **백신** [백신] baek-sin n. antivirus

□ **에스엔에스** [에스엔에스] e-seu-en-e-seu n. SNS

(Social Networking Service)

= **소셜 네트워크 서비스** [소셜 네트워크 서비스]

so-syeol ne-teu-wo-keu seo-bi-seu

□ **블로그** [블로그] beul-ro-geu n. blog

□ **해커** [해커] hae-keo n. hacker

□ **피시방** [피시방] pi-si-bang n. Internet café

#14. 이메일

Useful Conversation

김 상무   내 이메일 확인했나요?
nae i-mae-il hwa-gin haen-na-yo?
Did you read my e-mail?

이 대리   아니요, 아직이요.
a-ni-yo, a-ji-gi-yo
No, not yet.

김 상무   그거 보면 답장 좀 해 주세요.
geu-geo bo-meon dap-jjang jom hae ju-se-yo
Please reply to me after reading it.

이 대리   네, 물론이지요. 곧 답 드릴게요.
ne, mul-ro-ni-ji-yo. got dap deu-ril-ge-yo
Yes, of course. I'll reply soon.

Exercise

Read and Match.

1. 가구 •		• bag
2. 가방 •		• book
3. 과일 •		• clothes
4. 사진 •		• food
5. 신발 •		• fruit
6. 옷 •		• furniture
7. 운동 •		• hobby
8. 음식 •		• house, home
9. 음악 •		• music
10. 집 •		• photograph, photo, picture
11. 책 •		• shoes
12. 취미 •		• sport

1. 가구 – furniture 2. 가방 – bag 3. 과일 – fruit 4. 사진 – photograph, photo, picture
5. 신발 – shoes 6. 옷 – clothes 7. 운동 – sport 8. 음식 – food
9. 음악 – music 10. 집 – house, home 11. 책 – book 12. 취미 – hobby

5장

Social Life

School 학교 hak-ggyo

□ **학교** [학꾜] hak-ggyo
  n. school

□ **유치원** [유치원] yu-chi-won
  n. kindergarten

□ **초등학교** [초등학꾜] cho-deung-hak-ggyo
  n. elementary school,
  primary school

□ **중학교** [중학꾜] jung-hak-ggyo
  n. middle school,
  junior high school

□ **고등학교** [고등학꾜] go-deung-hak-ggyo
  n. high school, senior high school

□ **대학교** [대:학꾜] dae-hak-ggyo
  n. college, university

□ **입학** [이팍] i-pak
  n. enrollment, admission

□ **졸업** [조럽] jo-reop
  n. graduation

□ **출석** [출썩] chul-sseok

　n. attendance

□ **결석** [결썩] gyeol-sseok

　n. absence

□ **지각** [지각] ji-gak

　n. lateness, tardiness

□ **가르치다** [가르치다] ga-reu-chi-da

　v. teach

□ **배우다** [배우다] bae-u-da v. **learn**

□ **공부** [공부] gong-bu n. **study**

□ **교사** [교:사] gyo-sa

　= **선생** [선생] seon-saeng

　n. teacher

□ **학생** [학쌩] hak-ssaeng

　n. student

□ **수업** [수업] su-eop

　= **강의** [강:의/강:이] gang-ui/gang-i

　n. class, lecture, course, lesson

187

□ **질문** [질문] jil-mun n. question

□ **묻다** [묻:따] mut-dda
= **물어보다** [무러보다] mu-reo-bo-da
v. ask

□ **대답** [대:답] dae-dap
= **답** [답] dap
n. answer

□ **공책** [공책] gong-chaek
= **노트** [노트] no-teu
n. notebook

□ **연필** [연필] yeon-pil
n. pencil

□ **지우개** [지우개] ji-u-gae
n. eraser

□ **필기** [필기] pil-gi
n. taking notes

□ **숙제** [숙쩨] suk-jje n. homework

□ **과제** [과제] gwa-je n. assignment

□ **제출** [제출] je-chul
n. submission

□ **시험** [시험] si-heom

n. examination, exam, test

□ **성적** [성적] seong-jeok

n. grade, achievement

□ **쉽다** [쉽:따] swip-dda

a. easy

□ **어렵다** [어렵따] eo-ryeop-dda

a. difficult

□ **합격** [합껵] hap-ggeok

n. passing the exam

□ **평가** [평:까] pyeong-gga

n. appreciation

□ **학위** [하귀] ha-gwi

n. degree

□ **장학금** [장:학끔] jang-hak-ggeum

n. scholarship

□ **여름방학** [여름방학]

yeo-reum-bang-hak

summer break

□ **겨울방학** [겨울방학]

gyeo-ul-bang-hak

winter break

189

□ **학교** [학꾜] hak-ggyo n. school

□ **유치원** [유치원] yu-chi-won n. kindergarten
　□ **어린이집** [어리니집] eo-ri-ni-jip n. daycare center

□ **초등학교** [초등학꾜] cho-deung-hak-ggyo n. elementary school, primary school

□ **중학교** [중학꾜] jung-hak-ggyo n. middle school, junior high school

□ **고등학교** [고등학꾜] go-deung-hak-ggyo n. high school, senior high school
　= **고교** [고교] go-gyo

□ **대학교** [대:학꾜] dae-hak-ggyo n. college, university
　□ **대학** [대:학] dae-hak n. college
　= **단과대학** [단꽈대:학] dan-ggwa-dae-hak
　□ **종합대학** [종합대:학] jong-hap-dae-hak university

□ **대학원** [대:하권] dae-ha-gwon n. graduate school, postgraduate school

□ **연구소** [연:구소] yeon-gu-so n. institute

□ **학회** [하쾨/하퀘] ha-koe/ha-kwe n. society

□ **학원** [하권] ha-gwon n. academy

□ **전공** [전공] jeon-gong n. major
　□ **부전공** [부:전공] bu-jeon-gong n. minor

□ **입학** [이팍] i-pak n. enrollment, admission
　□ **입학식** [이팍씩] i-pak-ssik n. entrance ceremony

□ **입학 허가** [이팍 허가] i-pak heo-ga admission

□ **입학시험** [이팍씨험] i-pak-ssi-heom n. entrance exam

= **입시** [입씨] ip-ssi

□ **수능** [수능] su-neung n. college scholastic ability test

= **대학 수학 능력 시험** [대:학 수학 능녁 시험]

dae-hak su-hak neung-nyeok si-heom

□ **졸업** [조럽] jo-reop n. graduation

□ **졸업식** [조럽씩] jo-reop-ssik n. graduation ceremony

□ **출석** [출썩] chul-sseok n. attendance

한 선생님이 출석 확인했어요?

han seon-saeng-ni-mi chul-sseok hwa-gin-hae-sseo-yo?

Did Mr. Han check the attendance?

□ **결석** [결썩] gyeol-sseok n. absence

□ **지각** [지각] ji-gak n. lateness, tardiness

□ **조퇴** [조:퇴/조:퉤] jo-toe/jo-twe n. leaving early

□ **등록** [등녹] deung-nok n. registration, enrollment

□ **신청** [신청] sin-cheong n. application

□ **수강 신청하다** [수강 신청하다] su-gang sin-cheong-ha-da

sign up for classes

□ **가르치다** [가르치다] ga-reu-chi-da v. teach

□ **가르침** [가르침] ga-reu-chim n. teaching, lesson

tip. '가르치다' means teach something to someone. A similar word, '가리키다[ga-ri-ki-da]' means to point to something / somebody with a finger, pen, etc.

□ **배우다** [배우다] bae-u-da v. learn

  □ **학습** [학씁] hak-sseup n. study, learning

□ **수업** [수업] su-eop n. class, lecture, course, lesson

  = **강의** [강:의/강:이] gang-ui/gang-i

□ **공부** [공부] gong-bu n. study

□ **자습** [자습] ja-seup n. study by oneself

□ **교사** [교:사] gyo-sa n. teacher

  = **선생** [선생] seon-saeng

tip. In Korea, students usually call the teacher, '선생님', not the teacher's name. '님' is added to '선생' to show respect. This is different from Western culture.

□ **교수** [교:수] gyo-su n. professor

  □ **부교수** [부:교수] bu-gyo-su n. associate professor

  □ **조교수** [조:교수] jo-gyo-su n. assistant professor

□ **강사** [강:사] gang-sa n. instructor, lecturer

  □ **시간강사** [시간강:사] si-gan-gang-sa part-time lecturer

□ **가정교사** [가정교사] ga-jeong-gyo-sa tutor, private teacher

□ **학생** [학쌩] hak-ssaeng n. student

  □ **제자** [제:자] je-ja n. pupil

□ **학우** [하구] ha-gu n. schoolmate

  □ **급우** [그부] geu-bu n. classmate

□ **신입생** [시닙쌩] si-nip-ssaeng n. freshman

□ **재학생** [재:학쌩] jae-hak-ssaeng n. enrolled student

□ **교실** [교:실] gyo-sil n. classroom

□ **학년** [항년] hang-nyeon n. grade, school year

□ **반** [반] ban n. class

나는 2학년 3반이에요.
na-neun i-hang-nyeon sam-ba-ni-e-yo
I'm in grade 2, class 3.

□ **학기** [학끼] hak-ggi n. semester, term

이번 학기에 몇 과목 들어요?
i-beon hak-ggi-e meot gwa-mok deu-reo-yo?
How many classes are you taking this semester?

tip. The Korean school system has two semesters. The first semester is from March to August and the second is from September to February of the next year.

□ **교육** [교:육] gyo-yuk n. education

□ **교육과정** [교:육과정] gyo-yuk-gwa-jeong curriculum

= **교과과정** [교:과과정/교:꽈과정] gyo-gwa-gwa-jeong/gyo-ggwa-gwa-jeong

= **학과과정** [학꽈과정] hak-ggwa-gwa-jeong

□ **방과 후 교실** [방과 후 교실] bang-gwa hu gyo-sil extra-curricular

□ **방과 후 돌보미** [방과 후 돌보미] bang-gwa hu dol-bo-mi
after school's caregiver

□ **과외** [과외/과웨] gwa-oe/gwa-we n. extra classes, private tutoring

= **과외수업** [과외수업/과웨수업] gwa-oe-su-eop/gwa-we-su-eop

□ **질문** [질문] jil-mun n. question

□ **묻다** [묻:따] mut-dda v. ask

= **물어보다** [무러보다] mu-reo-bo-da

□ **대답** [대:답] dae-dap n. answer

= **답** [답] dap

☐ **과목** [과목] gwa-mok n. subject

  ☐ **학과** [학꽈] hak-ggwa n. department

좋아하는 과목이 뭐예요?
jo-a-ha-neun gwa-mo-gi mwo-ye-yo?
What's your favorite subject?

☐ **국어** [구거] gu-geo n. official language, mother tongue

  ☐ **한국어** [한:구거] han-gu-geo n. Korean (language)

  tip. '국어' means the language of one's country.
     In Korea, '국어' means the Korean language.

☐ **영어** [영어] yeong-eo n. English

☐ **문학** [문학] mun-hak n. literature

☐ **수학** [수:학] su-hak n. math, mathematics

  ☐ **숫자** [수:짜/숟:짜] su-jja/sut-jja n. numbers

  = **수** [수:] su

  ☐ **연산** [연:산] yeon-san n. arithmetic

  = **산수** [산:수] san-su

  ☐ **계산** [계:산/게:산] gye-san/ge-san n. calculation, figures, sum

  = **셈** [셈:] sem

☐ **과학** [과학] gwa-hak n. science

☐ **화학** [화:학] hwa-hak n. chemistry

☐ **물리학** [물리학] mul-ri-hak n. physics

☐ **생물학** [생물학] saeng-mul-hak n. biology

☐ **천문학** [천문학] cheon-mun-hak n. astronomy

□ **사회학** [사회학/사훼학] sa-hoe-hak/sa-hwe-hak n. social studies

□ **역사** [역싸] yeok-ssa n. history

　□ **국사** [국싸] guk-ssa n. national history

tip. '국사' means national history, so in Korea it refers to Korean history.
You can also say '한국사 [한:국싸 han-guk-ssa]'.

□ **지리학** [지리학] ji-ri-hak n. geography

□ **지질학** [지질학] ji-jil-hak n. geology

□ **정치학** [정치학] jeong-chi-hak n. politics

□ **경제학** [경제학] gyeong-je-hak n. economics

□ **회계학** [회:계학/훼:게학] hoe-gye-hak/hwe-ge-hak n. accounting

□ **인문학** [인문학] in-mun-hak n. humanities

□ **심리학** [심니학] sim-ni-hak n. psychology

□ **철학** [철학] cheol-hak n. philosophy

□ **윤리** [율리] yul-ri n. ethics

□ **음악** [으막] eu-mak n. music

□ **미술** [미:술] mi-sul n. art

□ **체육** [체육] che-yuk n. physical education, PE

□ **칠판** [칠판] chil-pan n. blackboard

　□ **분필** [분필] bun-pil n. chalk

　□ **칠판지우개** [칠판지우개] chil-pan-ji-u-gae n. chalk eraser

□ **화이트보드** [화이트보드] hwa-i-teu-bo-deu n. whiteboard

　□ **펠트펜** [펠트펜] pel-teu-pen n. marker, a pen with a broad felt tip

　= **보드 마커** [보드 마커] bo-deu ma-keo

□ **책가방** [책까방] chaek-gga-bang n. school bag

□ **교과서** [교:과서/교:꽈서] gyo-gwa-seo/gyo-ggwa-seo n. textbook

□ **공책** [공책] gong-chaek n. notebook
= **노트** [노트] no-teu

□ **연필** [연필] yeon-pil n. pencil
□ **색연필** [생년필] saeng-nyeon-pil n. colored pencil

□ **볼펜** [볼펜] bol-pen n. ball-point pen

□ **만년필** [만:년필] man-nyeon-pil n. fountain pen

□ **형광펜** [형광펜] hyeong-gwang-pen n. highlighter pen, highlighter

□ **사인펜** [사인펜] sa-in-pen n. marker, felt-tip pen

□ **지우개** [지우개] ji-u-gae n. eraser
□ **수정액** [수정액] su-jeong-aek correction fluid
□ **수정 테이프** [수정 테이프] su-jeong te-i-peu correction tape

□ **필기** [필기] pil-gi n. taking notes

그는 필기를 정말 잘해요.
geu-neun pil-gi-reul jeong-mal jal-hae-yo
He takes notes very neatly.

□ **받아쓰기** [바다쓰기] ba-da-sseu-gi n. dictation

□ **숙제** [숙쩨] suk-jje n. homework
□ **과제** [과제] gwa-je n. assignment

□ **보고서** [보:고서] bo-go-seo n. report
= **리포트** [리포트] ri-po-teu

□ **제출** [제출] je-chul n. submission

□ **시험** [시험] si-heom n. examination, exam, test

  □ **쪽지 시험** [쪽찌 시험] jjok-jji si-heom quiz

  □ **중간고사** [중간고사] jung-gan-go-sa n. midterm exam

  □ **기말고사** [기말고사] gi-mal-go-sa n. final exam

    기말고사가 2주 후에 있어요.
    gi-mal-go-sa-ga i-ju hu-e i-sseo-yo
    Final exams are in 2 weeks.

□ **합격** [합격] hap-ggeok n. passing the exam

  □ **불합격** [불합격] bul-hap-ggeok n. failure

□ **커닝** [커닝] keo-ning n. cheating

  = **부정행위** [부정행위] bu-jeong-haeng-wi

□ **쉽다** [쉽:따] swip-dda a. easy

□ **어렵다** [어렵따] eo-ryeop-dda a. difficult

□ **평가** [평:까] pyeong-gga n. appreciation

□ **결과** [결과] gyeol-gwa n. result

□ **점수** [점쑤/점수] jeom-ssu/jeom-su n. score

□ **평균** [평균] pyeong-gyun n. average

□ **학점** [학쩜] hak-jjeom n. credit

□ **성적** [성적] seong-jeok n. grade, achievement

  □ **성적표** [성적표] seong-jeok-pyo n. report card, report

    tip. If you say [성:쩍 seong-jjeok], it means something sexual.

□ **자격증** [자격쯩] ja-gyeok-jjeung n. certificate, license

□ **학위** [하귀] ha-gwi n. degree

  □ **준학사** [준:학싸] jun-hak-ssa a person with an associate's degree

  □ **학사** [학싸] hak-ssa n. a person with a bachelor's degree

  □ **석사** [석싸] seok-ssa n. a person with a master's degree

  □ **박사** [박싸] bak-ssa n. a person with a Ph.D. or doctorate

□ **장학금** [장:학끔] jang-hak-ggeum n. scholarship

□ **쉬는 시간** [쉬는 시간] swi-neun si-gan break

  쉬는 시간은 10분이에요.
  swi-neun si-ga-neun sip-bbu-ni-e-yo
  We have a 10-minute break.

□ **방학** [방학] bang-hak n. vacation

  □ **여름방학** [여름방학] yeo-reum-bang-hak summer break

  □ **겨울방학** [겨울방학] gyeo-ul-bang-hak winter break

  □ **봄방학** [봄방학] bom-bang-hak spring break

□ **소풍** [소풍] so-pung n. picnic

  다음 주에 학교 소풍이 있어요.
  da-eum ju-e hak-ggyo so-pung-i i-sseo-yo
  There will be a school picnic next week.

□ **운동장** [운:동장] un-dong-jang n. playground

  □ **운동회** [운:동회/운:동훼] un-dong-hoe/un-dong-hwe n. field day, sports day

□ **강당** [강:당] gang-dang n. auditorium

□ **도서관** [도서관] do-seo-gwan n. library

□ **과학실** [과학씰] gwa-hak-ssil science lab

□ **음악실** [으막씰] eu-mak-ssil n. music classroom

□ **교복** [교:복] gyo-bok n. school uniform

□ **급식** [급씩] geup-ssik n. meal service

□ **도시락** [도시락] do-si-rak n. lunch box

#15. 시험 결과

Useful Conversation

최지훈　시험을 잘 못 봤어.
　　　　si-heo-meul jal mot bwa-sseo
　　　　I didn't do very well on the exam.

이준서　나도 그래. 시험 결과가 만족스럽지 않아.
　　　　na-do geu-rae. si-heom gyeol-gwa-ga man-jok-sseu-reop-jji a-na
　　　　Neither did I. I wasn't very happy with my grade.

최지훈　기말고사는 더 공부할 거야.
　　　　gi-mal-go-sa-neun deo gong-bu-hal ggeo-ya
　　　　I'll study more for the final exam.

이준서　나도. 우리 같이 공부하자!
　　　　na-do. u-ri ga-chi gong-bu-ha-ja!
　　　　Me too. Let's study together!

Work & Jobs 일 & 직업 il & ji-geop

☐ 일 [일:] il n. work

☐ 일하다 [일:하다] il-ha-da

  v. work, do one's job, labor

☐ 회사원 [회:사원/훼:사원]

  hoe-sa-won/hwe-sa-won

  n. worker

☐ 임금 [임:금] im-geum n. wage

☐ 급여 [그벼] geu-byeo

  n. allowance, wage

☐ 출근 [출근] chul-geun

  n. going to work

☐ 회사 [회:사/훼:사] hoe-sa/hwe-sa

  n. company

☐ 사무실 [사:무실] sa-mu-sil

  n. office

☐ 회의 [회:의/훼:이] hoe-ui/hwe-i

  n. meeting, conference

☐ 상여금 [상여금] sang-yeo-geum

  = 보너스 [보너스] bo-neo-seu

  n. bonus

☐ 퇴근 [퇴:근/퉤:근] toe-geun/twe-geun

  n. getting off work

□ **퇴직** [퇴:직/퉤:직] toe-jik/twe-jik

　 n. retirement

□ **사직** [사직] sa-jik n. resignation

□ **해고** [해:고] hae-go

　 n. dismissal

□ **휴가** [휴가] hyu-ga

　 n. vacation, holiday, leave

□ **출산 휴가** [출싼 휴가]

　 chul-ssan hyu-ga

　 parental leave, paternity leave,
　 maternity leave

□ **구직** [구직] gu-jik n. job-hunting

□ **구인** [구인] gu-in n. recruitment

□ **이력서** [이:력써] i-ryeok-sseo

　 n. resume

□ **자기소개서** [자기소개서]

　 ja-gi-so-gae-seo

　 n. a letter of self-introduction

□ **면접시험** [면:접씨험] myeon-jeop-ssi-heom

　 n. interview

□ **직업** [지겁] ji-geop

n. job, occupation, profession

□ **의사** [의사] ui-sa

n. doctor

□ **수의사** [수의사/수이사]

su-ui-sa/su-i-sa

n. veterinarian, vet

□ **간호사** [간호사]

gan-ho-sa

n. nurse

□ **약사** [약싸] yak-ssa

n. pharmacist

□ **교사** [교:사] gyo-sa

n. teacher

□ **건축가** [건:축까]

geon-chuk-gga

n. architect

□ **프로그래머** [프로그래머]

peu-ro-geu-rae-meo

n. programmer

□ **기자** [기자] gi-ja

n. reporter

□ **판사** [판사] pan-sa

n. judge

□ **변호사** [변:호사] byeon-ho-sa n. lawyer

□ **검사** [검:사] geom-sa

n. prosecutor, district attorney

□ **비서** [비:서] bi-seo

n. secretary

□ **정치가** [정치가]

jeong-chi-ga

n. politician

□ **경찰** [경:찰]

gyeong-chal

n. police officer

□ **소방관** [소방관]

so-bang-gwan

n. firefighter

□ **엔지니어** [엔지니어]

en-ji-ni-eo

n. engineer

□ **정비공** [정:비공]

jeong-bi-gong

n. mechanic

□ **요리사** [요리사]

yo-ri-sa

n. cook

□ **제빵사** [제:빵사]

je-bbang-sa

n. baker

□ **식당 종업원** [식땅 종어뷘]

sik-ddang jong-eo-bwon

waiter, waitress

□ **미용사** [미:용사]

mi-yong-sa

n. hairdresser,

beautician

□ **농부** [농부] nong-bu

n. farmer

□ **어부** [어부] eo-bu

n. fisherman

□ **일** [일:] il n. work

　□ **업무** [엄무] eom-mu n. work, task, business

　□ **근무** [근:무] geun-mu n. work

　□ **일중독** [일:중독] il-jung-dok n. workaholic

　무슨 일 하세요?
　mu-seun il ha-se-yo?
　What do you work for?

□ **일하다** [일:하다] il-ha-da v. work, do one's job, labor

□ **회사** [회:사/훼:사] hoe-sa/hwe-sa n. company

　□ **사무실** [사:무실] sa-mu-sil n. office

□ **회사원** [회:사원/훼:사원] hoe-sa-won/hwe-sa-won n. worker

　□ **신입 사원** [시닙 사원] si-nip sa-won new employee

□ **야근** [야:근] ya-geun n. overtime

　□ **잔업** [자넙] ja-neop n. extra work

□ **출장** [출짱] chul-jjang n. business trip

□ **회의** [회:의/훼:이] hoe-ui/hwe-i n. meeting, conference

　□ **회의실** [회:의실/훼:이실] hoe-ui-sil/hwe-i-sil n. meeting room, conference room

　□ **주제** [주제] ju-je n. topic, subject

　□ **안건** [안:껀] an-ggeon n. agenda

□ **발표** [발표] bal-pyo n. presentation

　오늘 발표 준비 다 됐어요?
　o-neul bal-pyo jun-bi da dwae-sseo-yo?
　Are you ready for today's presentation?

□ **서류** [서류] seo-ryu n. document

= **문서** [문서] mun-seo

□ **부서** [부서] bu-seo n. department

□ **총무부** [총:무부] chong-mu-bu n. general affairs department

□ **경리부** [경니부] gyeong-ni-bu n. finance department

□ **인사부** [인사부] in-sa-bu HR(human resources) department, personnel department

□ **영업부** [영업뿌] yeong-eop-bbu n. sales department

□ **홍보부** [홍보부] hong-bo-bu PR(public relations) department

□ **구매부** [구매부] gu-mae-bu n. purchasing department

안녕하세요. AB사 영업부의 김호찬입니다.
an-nyeong-ha-se-yo. e-i-bi-sa yeong-eop-bbu-e gim-ho-chan-im-ni-da
Hello. AB Company, the sales department, Ho-chan Kim speaking.

□ **상사** [상:사] sang-sa n. boss

□ **부하** [부하] bu-ha n. subordinate

□ **동료** [동뇨] dong-nyo n. coworker

□ **지위** [지위] ji-wi n. position

□ **회장** [회:장/훼:장] hoe-jang/hwe-jang n. chairperson, chairman

□ **부회장** [부:회장/부:훼장] bu-hoe-jang/bu-hwe-jang n. vice-chairperson, vice-chairman

□ **사장** [사장] sa-jang n. president

□ **부사장** [부:사장] bu-sa-jang n. executive vice-president

□ **전무** [전무] jeon-mu n. managing director

□ **이사** [이:사] i-sa n. director

☐ **국장** [국짱] guk-jjang n. general manager

  ☐ **부장** [부:장] bu-jang n. manager

  ☐ **차장** [차장] cha-jang n. chief

  ☐ **과장** [과장] gwa-jang n. section chief, section manager

  ☐ **대리** [대:리] dae-ri n. administrative manager

  ☐ **주임** [주임] ju-im n. assistant section manager

  ☐ **사원** [사원] sa-won n. staff

☐ **승진** [승진] seung-jin n. promotion

☐ **임금** [임:금] im-geum n. wage

  ☐ **최저임금** [최저임:금] choe-jeo-im-geum minimum wage

☐ **봉급** [봉:급] bong-geup n. salary

  ☐ **월급** [월급] wol-geup n. monthly salary

  ☐ **연봉** [연봉] yeon-bong n. annual salary

☐ **급여** [그벼] geu-byeo n. allowance, wage

  ☐ **실수령액** [실쑤령액] sil-ssu-ryeong-aek net wages

  ☐ **기본급** [기본급] gi-bon-geup n. basic wage

☐ **상여금** [상여금] sang-yeo-geum n. bonus

  = **보너스** [보너스] bo-neo-seu

☐ **수당** [수당] su-dang n. allowance

  ☐ **출장 수당** [출짱 수당] chul-jjang su-dang travel allowance

  ☐ **야근 수당** [야근 수당] ya-geun su-dang overtime allowance

  급여 및 수당은 조정 가능해요.
  geu-byeo mit su-dang-eun jo-jeong ga-neung-hae-yo
  Salary and benefits are negotiable.

□ **세금** [세:금] se-geum n. tax

□ **고용 보험** [고용 보험] go-yong bo-heom employment insurance

□ **건강 보험** [건강 보험] geon-gang bo-heom health insurance

□ **공제** [공:제] gong-je n. deduction

□ **인상** [인상] in-sang n. pay raise

□ **삭감** [삭깜] sak-ggam n. pay cut

□ **동결** [동:결] dong-gyeol n. wage freeze

□ **출근** [출근] chul-geun n. going to work

□ **퇴근** [퇴:근/퉤:근] toe-geun/twe-geun n. getting off work

□ **출퇴근** [출퇴근/출퉤근] chul-toe-geun/chul-twe-geun

n. going to and getting off work

8시까지 출근해야 해요.
yeo-deol-si-gga-ji chul-geun-hae-ya hae-yo
I have to get to work by 8 o'clock.

□ **퇴직** [퇴:직/퉤:직] toe-jik/twe-jik n. retirement

= **은퇴** [은퇴/은퉤] eun-toe/eun-twe

□ **사직** [사직] sa-jik n. resignation

□ **명예퇴직** [명예퇴직/명예퉤직] myeong-ye-toe-jik/myeong-ye-twe-jik

n. voluntary resignation

= **명퇴** [명퇴/명퉤] myeong-toe/myeong-twe

= **희망퇴직** [히망퇴직/히망퉤직] hi-mang-toe-jik/hi-mang-twe-jik

□ **퇴직금** [퇴:직끔/퉤:직끔] toe-jik-ggeum/twe-jik-ggeum

n. retirement allowance

□ **파업** [파:업] pa-eop n. strike

□ **해고** [해:고] hae-go n. **dismissal**

□ **휴가** [휴가] hyu-ga n. **vacation, holiday, leave**

　□ **유급 휴가** [유:급 휴가] yu-geup hyu-ga **paid leave**

　□ **무급 휴가** [무급 휴가] mu-geup hyu-ga **unpaid leave**

　□ **출산 휴가** [출싼 휴가] chul-ssan hyu-ga **parental leave, paternity leave, maternity leave**

　□ **병가** [병:가] byeong-ga n. **sick leave**

　나은 씨는 휴가 중이에요.
　na-eun ssi-neun hyu-ga jung-i-e-yo
　Na-eun is away on vacation.

□ **직업** [지겁] ji-geop n. **job, occupation, profession**

□ **의사** [의사] ui-sa n. **doctor**

□ **치과의사** [치꽈의사/치꽈이사] chi-ggwa-ui-sa/chi-ggwa-i-sa **dentist**

□ **수의사** [수의사/수이사] su-ui-sa/su-i-sa n. **veterinarian, vet**

□ **간호사** [간호사] gan-ho-sa n. **nurse**

□ **약사** [약싸] yak-ssa n. **pharmacist**

□ **교사** [교:사] gyo-sa n. **teacher**

□ **건축가** [건:축까] geon-chuk-gga n. **architect**

□ **프로그래머** [프로그래머] peu-ro-geu-rae-meo n. **programmer**

□ **기자** [기자] gi-ja n. **reporter**

□ **편집자** [편집짜] pyeon-jip-jja n. **editor**
　= **편집인** [편지빈] pyeon-ji-bin

□ **디자이너** [디자이너] di-ja-i-neo n. designer

□ **사진작가** [사진작까] sa-jin-jak-gga n. photographer

□ **판사** [판사] pan-sa n. judge

    □ **변호사** [변:호사] byeon-ho-sa n. lawyer

    □ **검사** [검:사] geom-sa n. prosecutor, district attorney

□ **회계사** [회:계사/훼:게사] hoe-gye-sa/hwe-ge-sa n. accountant

□ **비서** [비:서] bi-seo n. secretary

□ **정치가** [정치가] jeong-chi-ga n. politician

    = **정치인** [정치인] jeong-chi-in

□ **경찰** [경:찰] gyeong-chal n. police officer

    = **경찰관** [경:찰관] gyeong-chal-gwan

□ **소방관** [소방관] so-bang-gwan n. firefighter

□ **우편집배원** [우편집빼원] u-pyeon-jip-bbae-won n. mail carrier

    = **우편배달부** [우편배달부] u-pyeon-bae-dal-bu

□ **엔지니어** [엔지니어] en-ji-ni-eo n. engineer

□ **정비공** [정:비공] jeong-bi-gong n. mechanic

    = **정비사** [정:비사] jeong-bi-sa

□ **배관공** [배:관공] bae-gwan-gong n. plumber

□ **요리사** [요리사] yo-ri-sa n. cook

□ **주방장** [주방장] ju-bang-jang n. chef

□ **제빵사** [제:빵사] je-bbang-sa n. baker

□ **조종사** [조종사] jo-jong-sa n. **pilot**

= **파일럿** [파일럳] pa-il-reot

□ **승무원** [승무원] seung-mu-won n. **crew, flight attendant, cabin crew**

  □ **스튜어드** [스튜어드] seu-tyu-eo-deu n. **steward**

  □ **스튜어디스** [스튜어디스] seu-tyu-eo-di-seu n. **stewardess**

□ **상인** [상인] sang-in n. **merchant, trader, seller**

  □ **점원** [점:원] jeom-won n. **salesclerk, salesperson**

  = **판매원** [판매원] pan-mae-won

  □ **식당 종업원** [식땅 종어붠] sik-ddang jong-eo-bwon **waiter, waitress**

□ **미용사** [미:용사] mi-yong-sa n. **hairdresser, beautician**

□ **플로리스트** [플로리스트] peul-ro-ri-seu-teu **florist**

□ **농부** [농부] nong-bu n. **farmer**

□ **어부** [어부] eo-bu n. **fisherman**

□ **구직** [구직] gu-jik n. **job-hunting**

  □ **구인** [구인] gu-in n. **recruitment**

  □ **지원** [지원] ji-won n. **application**

  □ **이력서** [이:력써] i-ryeok-sseo n. **resume**

  □ **자기소개서** [자기소개서] ja-gi-so-gae-seo

n. **a letter of self-introduction**

  = **자소서** [자소서] ja-so-seo

  □ **프로필** [프로필] peu-ro-pil n. **profile**

이력서는 이메일로 보내 주세요.
i-ryeok-sseo-neun i-me-il-ro bo-nae ju-se-yo
Send your resume by e-mail.

□ **경력** [경녁] gyeong-nyeok n. **career, work experience**

□ **학력** [항녁] hang-nyeok n. **academic career**

□ **필기시험** [필기시험] pil-gi-si-heom n. **written test**

□ **면접시험** [면:접씨험] myeon-jeop-ssi-heom n. **interview**

= **면접** [면:접] myeon-jeop

언제 면접을 보나요?
eon-je myeon-jeo-beul bo-na-yo?
When will you have an interview?

Useful Conversation

#16. 보너스

김미나   추석 보너스를 받았어.
chu-seok bo-neo-seu-reul ba-da-sseo
I got a Chuseok bonus.

이준서   잘됐다! 부럽네.
jal-dwaet-dda! bu-reop-ne
That's good! I envy you.

김미나   너는 못 받았어?
neo-neun mot ba-da-sseo?
Didn't you get one?

이준서   응. 우리 사장님은 올해 보너스를 없앴거든.
eung. u-ri sa-jang-ni-meun ol-hae bo-neo-seu-reul
eop-ssaet-ggeo-deun
No. My boss eliminated bonuses this year.

Restaurants & Cafés 음식점 & 카페 eum-sik-jjeom & ka-pe

□ **음식점** [음:식쩜] eum-sik-jjeom
= **식당** [식땅] sik-ddang
n. restaurant

□ **카페** [카페] ka-pe
= **커피숍** [커피숍] keo-pi-syop
n. café, coffee shop

□ **요리** [요리] yo-ri
n. dish, cooking

□ **메뉴판** [메뉴판]
me-nyu-pan
n. menu

□ **예약** [예:약] ye-yak
n. reservation, booking

□ **추천** [추천] chu-cheon
n. recommendation

□ **주문** [주:문] ju-mun
n. order

□ **테이크아웃** [테이크아웃] te-i-keu-a-ut
n. takeout, takeaway

212

☐ **애피타이저** [애피타이저]
ae-pi-ta-i-jeo
n. appetizer

☐ **주요리** [주요리] ju-yo-ri
n. main dish

☐ **반찬** [반찬] ban-chan
n. side dish

☐ **후식** [후:식] hu-sik
= **디저트** [디저트]
di-jeo-teu
n. dessert

☐ **밥** [밥] bap n. rice

☐ **비빔밥** [비빔빱]
bi-bim-bbap
n. bibimbap

☐ **국** [국] guk n. soup

☐ **미역국** [미역꾹]
mi-yeok-gguk
n. seaweed soup

☐ **찌개** [찌개] jji-gae
n. stew, casserole

☐ **나물** [나물] na-mul
n. vegetables mixed
with seasonings

☐ **마른반찬** [마른반찬]
ma-reun-ban-chan
n. dried meat or fish

☐ **불고기** [불고기]
bul-go-gi
n. bulgogi,
barbecued beef

☐ **스테이크** [스테이크]
seu-te-i-keu
n. steak

☐ **갈비** [갈비] gal-bi
n. ribs

☐ **감자튀김** [감자튀김]
gam-ja-twi-gim

n. fried potatoes

☐ **잡채** [잡채] jap-chae

n. jap-chae

☐ **떡볶이** [떡뽀끼]
ddeok-bbo-ggi

n. tteok-bokki,
stir-fried rice cake

☐ **아이스크림** [아이스크림]
a-i-seu-keu-rim

n. ice cream

☐ **치즈** [치즈] chi-jeu

n. cheese

☐ **초콜릿** [초콜릳]
cho-kol-rit

n. chocolate

☐ **사탕** [사탕] sa-tang

n. candy

☐ **빵** [빵] bbang

n. bread

☐ **케이크** [케이크] ke-i-keu

n. cake

☐ **과자** [과자] gwa-ja

n. cookie, biscuit

☐ **음료** [음:뇨] eum-nyo
= **음료수** [음:뇨수]
eum-nyo-su

n. beverage, drink

☐ **커피** [커피] keo-pi

n. coffee

214

□ **차** [차] cha
n. tea

□ **주스** [주스] ju-seu
n. juice

□ **탄산수** [탄:산수]
tan-san-su
n. carbonated
water

□ **숟가락** [숟까락]
sut-gga-rak
n. spoon

□ **젓가락** [저까락/젇까락]
jeo-gga-rak/
jeot-gga-rak
n. chopsticks

□ **포크** [포크] po-keu
n. fork

□ **맛있다** [마딛따/마싣따]
ma-dit-dda/ma-sit-dda
a. delicious, tasty

□ **짜다** [짜다] jja-da
a. salty

□ **달다** [달다] dal-da
a. sweet

□ **맵다** [맵따] maep-dda
a. hot, spicy

□ **시다** [시다] si-da
a. sour

□ **쓰다** [쓰다] sseu-da
a. bitter

□ **음식점** [음:식쩜] eum-sik-jjeom n. restaurant

　= **식당** [식땅] sik-ddang

　= **레스토랑** [레스토랑] re-seu-to-rang

　이 근처에 맛있는 음식점 있어요?
　i geun-cheo-e ma-din-neun eum-sik-jjeom i-seo-yo?
　Is there a good restaurant around here?

□ **카페** [카페] ka-pe n. café, coffee shop

　= **커피숍** [커피숍] keo-pi-syop

　= **찻집** [차찝/찯찝] cha-jjip/chat-jjip

　= **다방** [다방] da-bang ●————————→ **tip.** '다방' is an old-fashioned term.

□ **요리** [요리] yo-ri n. dish, cooking

□ **메뉴판** [메뉴판] me-nyu-pan n. menu

　= **메뉴** [메뉴] me-nyu

　= **차림표** [차림표] cha-rim-pyo

　메뉴판 좀 볼 수 있을까요?
　me-nyu-pan jom bol su i-sseul-gga-yo?
　Can I see the menu, please?

□ **오늘의 메뉴** [오느릐 메뉴/오느레 메뉴] o-neu-rui me-nyu/o-neu-re me-nyu

special of the day

　□ **특선 메뉴** [특썬 메뉴] teuk-sseon me-nyu specialty

　이곳의 특선 메뉴는 무엇인가요?
　i-go-se teuk-sseon me-nyu-neun mu-eo-sin-ga-yo?
　What is the specialty of the house?

□ **예약** [예:약] ye-yak n. reservation, booking

□ **추천** [추천] chu-cheon n. recommendation

□ **주문** [주:문] ju-mun n. order

주문을 하시겠어요?
ju-mu-neul ha-si-ge-sseo-yo?
Shall I take your order?

□ **포장** [포장] po-jang n. packing

　□ **테이크아웃** [테이크아웉] te-i-keu-a-ut n. takeout, takeaway

□ **식자재** [식짜재] sik-jja-jae n. ingredient

　= **음식 재료** [음:식 재료] eum-sik jae-ryo

□ **애피타이저** [애피타이저] ae-pi-ta-i-jeo n. appetizer

　= **전채** [전채] jeon-chae

　= **오르되브르** [오르되브르] o-reu-doe-beu-reu

□ **주요리** [주요리] ju-yo-ri n. main dish

　= **주메뉴** [주메뉴] ju-me-nyu

□ **반찬** [반찬] ban-chan n. side dish

　= **사이드 메뉴** [사이드 메뉴] sa-i-deu me-nyu

□ **후식** [후:식] hu-sik n. dessert

　= **디저트** [디저트] di-jeo-teu

□ **밥** [밥] bap n. rice

tip. Traditional Korean food consists of rice and some side dishes such as seasoned
　vegetables, grilled foods, pancakes, salted seafood and so on.
　Soup and kimchi are often served and are not counted as side dishes.

□ **비빔밥** [비빔빱] bi-bim-bbap n. bibimbap

tip. 'Bibimbap' is a Korean dish consisting of rice topped with sauteed vegetables,
　chilli paste, beef or other meat, and sometimes the addition of a raw or fried egg.

□ **김밥** [김:밥/김:빱] gim-bap/gim-bbap n. gimbap(cooked rice and other ingredients rolled in a sheet of dried seaweed)

□ **김치** [김치] gim-chi n. kimchi(Korean traditional side dish made from salted and fermented vegetables with a variety of seasonings)

□ **국** [국] guk n. soup

　□ **미역국** [미역꾹] mi-yeok-gguk n. seaweed soup

　　tip. '미역국' is traditionally consumed by Korean women after giving birth. And it is also eaten for breakfast on birthday, as a celebration of one's mother.

　□ **소고기 뭇국** [소고기 무:꾹/소고기 묻:꾹] so-go-gi mu-gguk/ so-go-gi mut-gguk beef radish soup

□ **탕** [탕] tang n./suf. soup

　□ **삼계탕** [삼계탕/삼게탕] sam-gye-tang/sam-ge-tang

　n. chicken soup with ginseng •———→ **tip.** '삼계탕' is a warm soup for hot summer days.

　□ **설렁탕** [설렁탕] seol-reong-tang

　n. stock soup of bone and stew meat

　　tip. '탕' is a suffix, it means the soup boiled longer than '국'; for example, '설렁탕 seol-reong-tang', '갈비탕 gal-bi-tang'.

□ **찌개** [찌개] jji-gae n. stew, casserole

　□ **된장찌개** [된:장찌개/뒌:장찌개] doen-jang-jji-gae/dwen-jang-jji-gae

　n. soy bean paste stew

　□ **김치찌개** [김치찌개] gim-chi-jji-gae n. kimchi stew

□ **찜** [찜] jjim n. steamed dish

□ **구이** [구이] gu-i n. roast, grill, grilled dishes

□ **마른반찬** [마른반찬] ma-reun-ban-chan n. dried meat or fish ↗

tip. '마른반찬' is cooked with dried anchovies, dried squids, dried lavers and so on.

□ **나물** [나물] na-mul n. vegetables mixed with seasonings

□ **조림** [조림] jo-rim n. food boiled in soy sauce or other seasonings

□ **젓갈** [젇깔] jeot-ggal n. salted seafood

□ **전** [전:] jeon n. Korean style pancake

= **부침개** [부침개] bu-chim-gae

= **지짐이** [지지미] ji-ji-mi

□ **불고기** [불고기] bul-go-gi n. bulgogi, barbecued beef

□ **갈비** [갈비] gal-bi n. ribs

□ **수프** [수프] su-peu n. soup(Western dish)

□ **샐러드** [샐러드] sael-reo-deu n. salad

□ **소시지** [소시지] so-si-ji n. sausage

□ **감자튀김** [감자튀김] gam-ja-twi-gim n. fried potatoes

□ **잡채** [잡채] jap-chae n. jap-chae(a sweet and savory dish of stire-fried glass noodle and vegetables)

□ **떡볶이** [떡뽀끼] ddeok-bbo-ggi n. tteok-bokki, stir-fried rice cake

□ **조개** [조개] jo-gae n. clam

□ **홍합** [홍합] hong-hap n. mussel

□ **굴** [굴] gul n. oyster

= **석화** [서콰] seo-kwa

□ **꼬막** [꼬막] ggo-mak n. cockle

□ **바지락** [바지락] ba-ji-rak n. Manila clam

□ **모시조개** [모시조개] mo-si-jo-gae n. short-necked clam

□ **전복** [전복] jeon-bok n. abalone

□ **바닷가재** [바다까재/바닫까재] ba-da-gga-jae/ba-dat-gga-jae n. lobster
= **랍스터** [랍쓰터] rap-sseu-teo

□ **버섯** [버섣] beo-seot n. mushroom

  □ **표고** [표고] pyo-go n. shiitake

  □ **송이버섯** [송이버섣] song-i-beo-seot n. pine mushroom

  □ **양송이** [양송이] yang-song-i n. champignon

  □ **느타리** [느타리] neu-ta-ri n. agaric

  □ **팽이버섯** [팽이버섣] paeng-i-beo-seot n. enoki mushroom

    tip. '표고, 양송이, 느타리' are also called '표고버섯, 양송이버섯, 느타리버섯'.

□ **요구르트** [요구르트] yo-gu-reu-teu n. yogurt

□ **아이스크림** [아이스크림] a-i-seu-keu-rim n. ice cream

□ **치즈** [치즈] chi-jeu n. cheese

□ **초콜릿** [초콜릳] cho-kol-rit n. chocolate

□ **사탕** [사탕] sa-tang n. candy

□ **빵** [빵] bbang n. bread

  □ **마늘빵** [마늘빵] ma-neul-bbang n. garlic bread

  □ **바게트** [바게트] ba-ge-teu n. baguette

  □ **크루아상** [크루아상] keu-ru-a-sang n. croissant

  □ **소보로빵** [소보로빵] so-bo-ro-bbang n. streusel bread
  = **곰보빵** [곰:보빵] gom-bo-bbang

  □ **크림빵** [크림빵] keu-rim-bbang n. cream bun

  □ **팥빵** [팓빵] pat-bbang n. red bean bun

□ **고로케** [고로케] go-ro-ke n. croquette

= **크로켓** [크로켇] keu-ro-ket

□ **카스텔라** [카스텔라] ka-seu-tel-ra n. castella

□ **토스트** [토스트] to-seu-teu n. toast

□ **샌드위치** [샌드위치] saen-deu-wi-chi n. sandwich

□ **케이크** [케이크] ke-i-keu n. cake

　□ **스펀지케이크** [스펀지케이크] seu-peon-ji-ke-i-keu n. sponge cake

　□ **팬케이크** [팬케이크] paen-ke-i-keu n. pancake

　= **핫케이크** [핟케이크] hat-ke-i-keu

□ **과자** [과자] gwa-ja n. cookie, biscuit

　□ **쿠키** [쿠키] ku-ki n. cookie

　□ **비스킷** [비스킫] bi-seu-kit n. biscuit

□ **음료** [음:뇨] eum-nyo n. beverage, drink

　= **음료수** [음:뇨수] eum-nyo-su

□ **커피** [커피] keo-pi n. coffee

tip. There are also Americano(아메리카노 [a-me-ri-ka-no]) and cappuccino(카푸치노 [ka-pu-chi-no]) as Korean favorite coffee.

　□ **아이스커피** [아이스커피] a-i-seu-keo-pi n. iced coffee

　= **냉커피** [냉커피] naeng-keo-pi

　□ **에스프레소** [에스프레소] e-seu-peu-re-so n. espresso

　□ **카페라테** [카페라테] ka-pe-ra-te n. caffe latte

　□ **카페모카** [카페모카] ka-pe-mo-ka n. mocha

　□ **캐러멜마키아토** [캐러멜마키아토] kae-reo-mel-ma-ki-a-to

　n. caramel macchiato

　커피 한잔하면서 얘기해요.
　keo-pi han-jan-ha-myeon-seo yae-gi-hae-yo
　Let's talk over a cup of coffee.

221

□ **차** [차] cha n. tea

  □ **홍차** [홍차] hong-cha n. (black) tea

  □ **녹차** [녹차] nok-cha n. green tea

  □ **허브차** [허브차] heo-beu-cha n. herb tea

  □ **인삼차** [인삼차] in-sam-cha n. ginseng tea

  □ **생강차** [생강차] saeng-gang-cha n. ginger tea

  □ **대추차** [대:추차] dae-chu-cha n. jujube tea

  커피보다 차를 좋아해요.
  keo-pi-bo-da cha-reul jo-a-hae-yo
  I prefer tea to coffee.

□ **주스** [주스] ju-seu n. juice

  □ **오렌지주스** [오렌지주스] o-ren-ji-ju-seu n. orange juice

□ **레모네이드** [레모네이드] re-mo-ne-i-deu n. lemonade

□ **탄산수** [탄:산수] tan-san-su n. carbonated water

  = **소다수** [소다수] so-da-su

□ **탄산음료** [탄:사늠뇨] tan-sa-neum-nyo n. soda

  □ **콜라** [콜라] kol-ra n. Coke

  □ **사이다** [사이다] sa-i-da n. Sprite, 7UP

□ **술** [술] sul n. alcohol

  □ **샴페인** [샴페인] syam-pe-in n. champagne

  □ **맥주** [맥쭈] maek-jju n. beer

  저 술집에 가서 맥주 한잔합시다!
  jeo sul-jji-be ga-seo maek-jju han-jan-hap-ssi-da!
  Let's get a beer in that bar!

□ **양주** [양주] yang-ju n. liquor, spirits

　□ **위스키** [위스키] wi-seu-ki n. whisky

□ **포도주** [포도주] po-do-ju n. wine

　= **와인** [와인] wa-in

□ **소주** [소주] so-ju n. Korean distilled spirits

□ **막걸리** [막껄리] mak-ggeol-ri n. white rice wine

　□ **동동주** [동동주] dong-dong-ju n. sweet rice wine

　　tip. '막걸리' and '동동주' are kinds of Korean traditional alcohols made from rice.

□ **얼음** [어름] eo-reum n. ice

□ **컵** [컵] keop n. cup

　□ **유리컵** [유리컵] yu-ri-keop n. glass

　= **유리잔** [유리잔] yu-ri-jan

　□ **찻잔** [차짠/찯짠] cha-jjan/chat-jjan n. teacup

□ **빨대** [빨때] bbal-ddae n. straw

□ **계산서** [계:산서/게:산서] gye-san-seo/ge-san-seo n. bill

□ **팁** [팁] tip n. tip

　= **봉사료** [봉:사료] bong-sa-ryo

　　tip. Customers don't have to tip for service in restaurants in Korea.

□ **냅킨** [냅킨] naep-kin n. napkin

□ **수저** [수저] su-jeo n. spoon and chopsticks

　□ **숟가락** [숟까락] sut-gga-rak n. spoon

　= **숟갈** [숟깔] sut-ggal

□ **찻숟가락** [차쑫까락/찯쑫까락] cha-ssut-gga-rak/chat-ssut-gga-rak

n. teaspoon

= **티스푼** [티스푼] ti-seu-pun

□ **젓가락** [저까락/젇까락] jeo-gga-rak/jeot-gga-rak n. chopsticks

= **젓갈** [저깔/젇깔] jeo-ggal/jeot-ggal

□ **나이프** [나이프] na-i-peu n. knife (for Western dishes)

□ **포크** [포크] po-keu n. fork

□ **맛** [맏] mat n. taste

　□ **맛보다** [맏뽀다] mat-bbo-da v. taste

　□ **맛있다** [마딛따/마싣따] ma-dit-dda/ma-sit-dda a. delicious, tasty

　□ **맛없다** [마덥따] ma-deop-dda a. tasteless

□ **짜다** [짜다] jja-da a. salty

　□ **짭짤하다** [짭짤하다] jjap-jjal-ha-da a. a bit salty

□ **달다** [달다] dal-da a. sweet

　□ **달콤하다** [달콤하다] dal-kom-ha-da a. sugary, honeyed

　좀 단 것 같아요.
　jom dan geot ga-ta-yo
　It's a little too sweet for me.

□ **시다** [시다] si-da a. sour

　□ **새콤하다** [새콤하다] sae-kom-ha-da a. a bit sour

□ **쓰다** [쓰다] sseu-da a. bitter

　□ **씁쓸하다** [씁쓸하다] sseup-sseul-ha-da a. a bit bitter

□ **맵다** [맵따] maep-dda a. hot, spicy

　□ **매콤하다** [매콤하다] mae-kom-ha-da a. a bit hot, a bit spicy

너무 맵지 않게 해 주세요.
neo-mu maep-jji an-ke hae ju-se-yo
Don't make it not too spicy, please.

□ **담백하다** [담:배카다] dam-bae-ka-da a. plain

□ **싱겁다** [싱겁따] sing-geop-dda a. plain, not salty

맛이 담백해요. / 맛이 싱거워요.
ma-si dam-bae-kae-yo / ma-si sing-geo-wo-yo
It's plain.

□ **느끼하다** [느끼하다] neu-ggi-ha-da

a. greasy

17. 음식 주문

Useful Conversation

김미나   오늘의 메뉴는 뭐예요?
o-neu-re me-nyu-neun mwo-ye-yo?
What's today's special?

종업원   불고기덮밥입니다.
bul-go-gi-deop-bba-bim-ni-da
Bulgogi with rice.

이준서   파전과 막걸리 한 병도 주세요.
pa-jeon-gwa mak-ggeol-ri han byeong-do ju-se-yo
I'll have that with a green onion pancake and
a bottle of rice wine, please.

종업원   알겠습니다. 곧 가져올게요.
al-get-sseum-ni-da. got ga-jeo-ol-ge-yo
Great. Coming right up.

Stores & Shops 상점 sang-jeom

□ **상점** [상점] sang-jeom

= **가게** [가:게] ga-ge

n. store, shop

□ **시장** [시:장] si-jang

n. market

□ **벼룩시장** [벼룩씨장]

byeo-ruk-ssi-jang

n. flea market

□ **슈퍼마켓** [슈퍼마켇]

syu-peo-ma-ket

= **슈퍼** [슈퍼] syu-peo

n. supermarket

□ **백화점** [배콰점]

bae-kwa-jeom

n. department store

□ **편의점** [펴늬점/펴니점]

pyeo-nui-jeom/

pyeo-ni-jeom

n. convenience store

□ **구입** [구입] gu-ip n. buy, purchase

□ **사다** [사다] sa-da v. buy

□ **판매** [판매] pan-mae n. sale

□ **팔다** [팔다] pal-da v. sell

□ **장보기** [장보기] jang-bo-gi

= **쇼핑** [쇼핑] syo-ping

n. shopping

□ **상품** [상품] sang-pum

= **물건** [물건] mul-geon

n. product, goods

□ **계산대** [계:산대/게:산대]
gye-san-dae/ge-san-dae
n. counter

□ **영수증** [영수증] yeong-su-jeung
n. receipt

□ **지불하다** [지불하다] ji-bul-ha-da
= **내다** [내:다] nae-da
v. pay

□ **신용카드** [시:뇽카드]
si-nyong-ka-deu
credit card

□ **바꾸다** [바꾸다] ba-ggu-da
v. change, transfer

□ **환불** [환불] hwan-bul
n. refund

□ **교환하다** [교환하다] gyo-hwan-ha-da
v. exchange

□ **반품** [반:품] ban-pum
n. return

□ **비싸다** [비싸다] bi-ssa-da
a. expensive, high-priced

□ **싸다** [싸다] ssa-da
= **저렴하다** [저:렴하다]
jeo-ryeom-ha-da
a. cheap, low-priced

227

□ **빵집** [빵찝] bbang-jjip

  n. bakery

□ **채소 가게** [채:소 가:게] chae-so ga-ge

  vegetable store

□ **과일 가게** [과:일 가:게] gwa-il ga-ge

  fruit store

□ **정육점** [정육쩜] jeong-yuk-jjeom

  n. butcher shop, meat market

□ **생선 가게** [생선 가:게]

  saeng-seon ga-ge

  fish shop, seafood store

□ **서점** [서점] seo-jeom

= **책방** [책빵] chaek-bbang

  n. bookstore

□ **문방구** [문방구] mun-bang-gu

= **문구점** [문구점] mun-gu-jeom

  n. stationery store

□ **안경원** [안:경원] an-gyeong-won

= **안경점** [안:경점] an-gyeong-jeom

  n. optician

□ **옷 가게** [옫 가:게] ot ga-ge

clothing store

□ **신발 가게** [신발 가:게] sin-bal ga-ge

shoe store

□ **화장품 가게** [화장품 가:게]

hwa-jang-pum ga-ge

cosmetics store

□ **세탁소** [세:탁쏘] se-tak-sso

n. laundry

□ **미용실** [미:용실] mi-yong-sil

n. beauty parlor, beauty salon

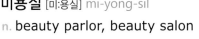

□ **이발소** [이:발쏘] i-bal-sso

n. barbershop

□ **꽃집** [꼳찝] ggot-jjip

n. flower shop

□ **공인중개소** [공인중개소]

gong-in-jung-gae-so

real estate agent

□ **여행사** [여행사] yeo-haeng-sa

n. travel agency

□ **상점** [상점] sang-jeom n. store, shop

  = **가게** [가:게] ga-ge

  □ **구멍가게** [구멍가게] gu-meong-ga-ge n. small store

□ **시장** [시:장] si-jang n. market

  □ **재래시장** [재:래시장] jae-rae-si-jang n. traditional market, bazaar

  □ **벼룩시장** [벼룩씨장] byeo-ruk-ssi-jang n. flea market

□ **쇼핑센터** [쇼핑센터] syo-ping-sen-teo n. shopping mall

  = **쇼핑몰** [쇼핑몰] syo-ping-mol

□ **슈퍼마켓** [슈퍼마켇] syu-peo-ma-ket n. supermarket

  = **슈퍼** [슈퍼] syu-peo

□ **편의점** [펴늬점/펴니점] pyeo-nui-jeom/pyeo-ni-jeom n. convenience store

□ **백화점** [배콰점] bae-kwa-jeom n. department store

□ **장보기** [장보기] jang-bo-gi n. shopping

  = **쇼핑** [쇼핑] syo-ping

  □ **쇼핑하다** [쇼핑하다] syo-ping-ha-da v. go shopping

□ **장바구니** [장빠구니] jang-bba-gu-ni n. shopping bag

  = **시장바구니** [시:장빠구니] si-jang-bba-gu-ni

  □ **카트** [카트] ka-teu n. cart, trolley

    장바구니를 가져오면 100원 보상해 드려요.
    jang-bba-gu-ni-reul ga-jeo-o-myeon bae-gwon bo-sang-hae deu-ryeo-yo
    Bring your own shopping bags and get 100 won rewards.

□ **구입** [구입] gu-ip n. buy, purchase

  = **구매** [구매] gu-mae

tip. Thesedays, for environmental protection, many markets make the customers use own shopping bags.

□ **사다** [사다] sa-da v. buy

□ **판매** [판매] pan-mae n. sale

  □ **팔다** [팔다] pal-da v. sell

□ **판촉** [판촉] pan-chok n. sales promotion

  □ **판촉물** [판총물] pan-chong-mul n. sales promotion gift

□ **상품** [상품] sang-pum n. product, goods

  = **물건** [물건] mul-geon

  □ **재고** [재:고] jae-go n. stock

  = **재고품** [재:고품] jae-go-pum

□ **유통기한** [유통기한] yu-tong-gi-han date of expiration

□ **품질** [품:질] pum-jil n. quality

□ **품절** [품:절] pum-jeol n. out of stock, sold-out

  죄송하지만, 지금은 품절이에요.
  joe-song-ha-ji-man, ji-geu-meun pum-jeo-ri-e-yo
  I'm sorry, it's out of stock right now.

□ **냉동품** [냉:동품] naeng-dong-pum n. frozen products

□ **농산물** [농산물] nong-san-mul n. farm products

□ **수산물** [수산물] su-san-mul n. seafood

□ **유제품** [유제품] yu-je-pum n. dairy products

□ **인스턴트식품** [인스턴트식품] in-seu-teon-teu-sik-pum n. instant food

  = **즉석식품** [즉썩씩품] jeuk-sseok-ssik-pum

□ **공산품** [공산품] gong-san-pum n. industrial products

□ **전자 제품** [전:자 제품] jeon-ja je-pum electric appliances

□ **상인** [상인] sang-in n. merchant, trader, seller

   = **장사꾼** [장사꾼] jang-sa-ggun ⟶ **tip.** '장사꾼' is the informal word for seller.

□ **점원** [점:원] jeom-won n. salesclerk, salesperson

   = **판매원** [판매원] pan-mae-won

□ **계산** [계:산/게:산] gye-san/ge-san n. payment, calculation

   □ **계산대** [계:산대/게:산대] gye-san-dae/ge-san-dae n. counter

   □ **계산원** [계:사뭔/게:사뭔] gye-sa-nwon/ge-sa-nwon n. cashier

□ **영수증** [영수증] yeong-su-jeung n. receipt

   □ **계산서** [계:산서/게:산서] gye-san-seo/ge-san-seo n. bill

   = **청구서** [청구서] cheong-gu-seo

   여기 영수증이요.
   yeo-gi yeong-su-jeung-i-yo
   Here is your receipt.

□ **지불** [지불] ji-bul n. payment

   □ **내다** [내:다] nae-da v. pay

   어떻게 지불하실 건가요?
   eo-ddeo-ke ji-bul-ha-sil geon-ga-yo?
   How would you like to pay?

□ **신용카드** [시:뇽카드] si-nyong-ka-deu credit card

   = **크레디트카드** [크레디트카드] keu-re-di-teu-ka-deu

□ **체크카드** [체크카드] che-keu-ka-deu debit card

□ **현금** [현:금] hyeon-geum n. cash

   = **현찰** [현:찰] hyeon-chal

□ **교환** [교환] gyo-hwan n. exchange

  □ **바꾸다** [바꾸다] ba-ggu-da v. change, transfer

□ **환불** [환불] hwan-bul n. refund

  이것을 환불해 주시겠어요?
  i-geo-seul hwan-bul-hae ju-si-ge-sseo-yo?
  I'd like to get a refund for this.

□ **반품** [반ː품] ban-pum n. return

□ **진열** [지ː녈] ji-nyeol n. showcase

□ **고객** [고객] go-gaek n. customer, shopper

  □ **단골손님** [단골손님] dan-gol-son-nim n. regular customer

  = **단골** [단골] dan-gol

□ **비싸다** [비싸다] bi-ssa-da a. expensive, high-priced

□ **싸다** [싸다] ssa-da a. cheap, low-priced

  = **저렴하다** [저ː렴하다] jeo-ryeom-ha-da

  □ **싸구려** [싸구려] ssa-gu-ryeo n. cheapie

□ **절약하다** [저랴카다] jeo-rya-ka-da v. save

  = **아끼다** [아끼다] a-ggi-da

□ **할인** [하린] ha-rin n. discount, sale

  = **세일** [세일] se-il

  = **에누리** [에누리] e-nu-ri

□ **특가** [특까] teuk-gga n. special price

  □ **염가** [염까] yeom-gga n. bargain price

□ **덤** [덤ː] deom n. extra, addition, something thrown in

□ **빵집** [빵찝] bbang-jjip n. bakery

□ **분식집** [분식찝] bun-sik-jjip n. small restaurant, snack bar

□ **채소 가게** [채:소 가:게] chae-so ga-ge vegetable store

□ **과일 가게** [과:일 가:게] gwa-il ga-ge fruit store

□ **정육점** [정육쩜] jeong-yuk-jjeom n. butcher shop, meat market

□ **생선 가게** [생선 가:게] saeng-seon ga-ge fish shop, seafood store

□ **아이스크림 가게** [아이스크림 가:게] a-i-seu-keu-rim ga-ge
  n. ice-cream parlor

□ **피자 가게** [피자 가:게] pi-ja ga-ge pizza parlor

□ **패스트푸드점** [패스트푸드점] pae-seu-teu-pu-deu-jeom
  n. fast food restaurant

□ **카페** [카페] ka-pe n. café, coffee shop
  = **커피숍** [커피숍] keo-pi-syop

□ **보석상** [보:석쌍] bo-seok-ssang n. jewelry store
  = **금은방** [그믄빵] geo-meun-bbang

□ **서점** [서점] seo-jeom n. bookstore
  = **책방** [책빵] chaek-bbang
    □ **헌책방** [헌:책빵] heon-chaek-bbang n. second-hand bookshop

□ **문방구** [문방구] mun-bang-gu n. stationery store
  = **문구점** [문구점] mun-gu-jeom

□ **완구점** [완:구점] wan-gu-jeom n. toy store
  = **장난감 가게** [장난깜 가:게] jang-nan-ggam ga-ge

□ **안경원** [안:경원] an-gyeong-won n. optician

　= **안경점** [안:경점] an-gyeong-jeom

□ **옷 가게** [옫 가:게] ot ga-ge clothing store

　□ **사이즈** [사이즈] sa-i-jeu n. size

　□ **옷걸이** [옫꺼리] ot-ggeo-ri n. hanger

　□ **마네킹** [마네킹] ma-ne-king n. mannequin

　□ **거울** [거울] geo-ul n. mirror

　□ **탈의실** [타:뤼실/타:리실] ta-rui-sil/ta-ri-sil n. fitting room

　= **피팅 룸** [피팅 룸] pi-ting rum

　　탈의실에서 입어 볼 수 있어요.
　　ta-ri-si-re-seo i-beo bol su i-sseo-yo
　　You can try it on in the fitting room.

□ **신발 가게** [신발 가:게] sin-bal ga-ge shoe store

□ **스포츠용품 가게** [스포츠용:품 가:게] seu-po-cheu-yong-pum ga-ge
　sporting-goods store

□ **향수 가게** [향수 가:게] hyang-su ga-ge perfumery

　□ **향수** [향수] hyang-su n. perfume

□ **화장품 가게** [화장품 가:게] hwa-jang-pum ga-ge cosmetics store

　□ **스킨** [스킨] seu-kin n. (skin) toner

　□ **로션** [로션] ro-syeon n. lotion

　□ **크림** [크림] keu-rim n. cream

　□ **아이 크림** [아이 크림] a-i keu-rim eye cream

　□ **수분 크림** [수분 크림] su-bun keu-rim moisturizing cream

　□ **미백 크림** [미:백 크림] mi-baek keu-rim whitening cream

□ **재생 크림** [재생 크림] jae-saeng keu-rim regenerating cream

□ **선크림** [선크림] seon-keu-rim n. sunscreen

□ **파운데이션** [파운데이션] pa-un-de-i-syeon n. foundation

□ **콤팩트파우더** [콤팩트파우더] kom-paek-teu-pa-u-deo
n. compact powder

□ **립스틱** [립쓰틱] rip-sseu-tik n. lipstick

□ **립글로스** [립끌로스] rip-ggeul-ro-seu n. lip gloss

□ **아이섀도** [아이섀도] a-i-syae-do n. eye shadow

□ **아이라이너** [아이라이너] a-i-ra-i-neo n. eye liner

□ **마스카라** [마스카라] ma-seu-ka-ra n. mascara

□ **블러셔** [블러셔] beul-reo-syeo n. blush, blusher

□ **매니큐어** [매니큐어] mae-ni-kyu-eo n. nail polish

□ **세탁소** [세:탁쏘] se-tak-sso n. laundry

이 양복을 세탁소에 좀 맡겨 줄래요?
i yang-bo-geul se-tak-sso-e jom mat-gyeo jul-rae-yo?
Can you take this suit to the laundry?

□ **드라이클리닝** [드라이클리닝] deu-ra-i-keul-ri-ning n. dry cleaning

□ **얼룩** [얼룩] eol-ruk n. stain

□ **제거** [제거] je-geo n. removal

□ **다리미질** [다리미질] da-ri-mi-jil n. ironing

= **다림질** [다림질] da-rim-jil ●————————→ **tip.** '다림질' is short for '다리미질'.

□ **수선** [수선] su-seon n. repair, mending

이 코트는 수선이 필요해요.
i ko-teu-neun su-seo-ni pi-ryo-hae-yo
This coat needs mending.

□ **미용실** [미:용실] mi-yong-sil **n.** beauty parlor, beauty salon

= **미장원** [미:장원] mi-jang-won

□ **이발소** [이:발쏘] i-bal-sso **n.** barbershop

= **이발관** [이:발관] i-bal-gwan

□ **약국** [약꾹] yak-gguk **n.** pharmacy

□ **꽃집** [꼳찝] ggot-jjip **n.** flower shop

□ **공인중개소** [공인중개소] gong-in-jung-gae-so real estate agent

□ **여행사** [여행사] yeo-haeng-sa

n. travel agency

18. 원피스

Useful Conversation

판매원   무엇을 도와드릴까요?
mu-eo-seul do-wa-deu-ril-gga-yo?
May I help you?

김미나   이 원피스를 입어 봐도 될까요?
i won-pi-seu-reul i-beo bwa-do doel-gga-yo?
Can I try on this dress?

판매원   물론이죠. 사이즈가 어떻게 되세요?
mul-ro-ni-jyo. sa-i-jeu-ga eo-ddeo-ke doe-se-yo?
Of course. What size do you wear?

김미나   10호예요.
si-po-ye-yo
I'm a size 10.

Hospitals & Banks 병원 & 은행 byeong-won & eun-haeng

□ **병원** [병:원] byeong-won

n. hospital, clinic

□ **종합병원** [종합병:원] jong-hap-byeong-won

hospital

□ **환자** [환:자] hwan-ja

n. patient

□ **의사** [의사] ui-sa

n. doctor

□ **간호사** [간호사]

gan-ho-sa

n. nurse

□ **진찰** [진:찰] jin-chal

n. consult

□ **증세** [증세] jeung-se

= **증상** [증상] jeung-sang

n. symptom

□ **고통** [고통] go-tong

n. pain, agony

□ **두통** [두통] du-tong

n. headache

□ **치통** [치통] chi-tong

n. toothache

□ **화상** [화:상] hwa-sang

n. burn, scald

□ **다치다** [다치다]

da-chi-da

v. be hurt

□ **부상** [부:상] bu-sang

= **상처** [상처] sang-cheo

n. injury, wound, cut

□ **멍** [멍] meong

n. bruise, black-and-blue mark

□ **감기** [감:기] gam-gi

n. cold

□ **기침** [기침] gi-chim

n. cough

□ **열나다** [열라다]

yeol-ra-da

v. run a fever

□ **소화불량** [소화불량]

so-hwa-bul-ryang

indigestion, dyspepsia

□ **구토** [구토] gu-to

n. vomiting

□ **현기증** [현:기쯩]

hyeon-gi-jjeung

n. dizziness

□ **입원** [이붠] i-bwon

n. hospitalization

□ **퇴원** [퇴:원/퉤:원] toe-won/twe-won

n. discharge from a hospital

239

□ 약국 [약꾹] yak-gguk

n. pharmacy

□ 약 [약] yak

n. medicine

□ 진통제 [진:통제] jin-tong-je

n. painkiller, analgesic

□ 해열제 [해:열쩨]

hae-yeol-jje

n. antifebrile

□ 소화제 [소화제]

so-hwa-je

n. digestive medicine

□ 수면제 [수면제]

su-myeon-je

n. sleeping pill

□ 연고 [연:고] yeon-go

n. ointment

□ 붕대 [붕대] bung-dae

n. bandage

□ 반창고 [반창고]

ban-chang-go

n. Band-Aid,
sticking plaster

□ 은행 [은행] eun-haeng

n. bank

□ 돈 [돈:] don n. money

□ 현금 [현:금] hyeon-geum n. cash

□ 지폐 [지폐/지폐] ji-pye/ji-pe

n. bill, note

□ 동전 [동전] dong-jeon

n. coin

240

□ **저축** [저:축] jeo-chuk
= **저금** [저:금] jeo-geum
= **예금** [예:금] ye-geum
n. deposit, saving

□ **통장** [통장] tong-jang
n. bankbook,
passbook

□ **입금** [입끔]
ip-ggeum
n. deposit

□ **출금** [출금] chul-geum
n. withdrawal

□ **이체** [이체] i-che
n. credit transfer

□ **송금** [송·금] song-geum
n. transfer

□ **이자** [이:자] i-ja
n. interest

□ **대출** [대:출] dae-chul
n. loan

□ **환전** [환:전] hwan-jeon
n. exchange

□ **신용카드** [시:뇽카드]
si-nyong-ka-deu
credit card

□ **에이티엠** [에이티엠]
e-i-ti-em
n. ATM

□ **인터넷 뱅킹** [인터넫 뱅킹]
in-teo-net baeng-king
Internet banking

□ **비밀번호** [비:밀번호]
bi-mil-beon-ho
n. password, PIN

241

☐ **병원** [병ː원] byeong-won n. hospital, clinic

   ☐ **종합병원** [종합병ː원] jong-hap-byeong-won hospital

   ☐ **진료소** [질ː료소] jil-ryo-so n. clinic

   ☐ **보건소** [보ː건소] bo-geon-so n. public health center

☐ **의사** [의사] ui-sa n. doctor

☐ **간호사** [간호사] gan-ho-sa n. nurse

☐ **환자** [환ː자] hwan-ja n. patient

☐ **진찰** [진ː찰] jin-chal n. consult

☐ **증세** [증세] jeung-se n. symptom

   = **증상** [증상] jeung-sang

   증세가 어때요?
   jeung-se-ga eo-ddae-yo?
   What are your symptoms?

☐ **고통** [고통] go-tong n. pain, agony

   ☐ **통증** [통ː쯩] tong-jjeung n. pain, agony

☐ **아프다** [아프다] a-peu-da a. painful

   = **고통스럽다** [고통스럽따] go-tong-seu-reop-dda

   = **괴롭다** [괴롭따/궤롭따] goe-rop-dda/gwe-rop-dda

☐ **따갑다** [따갑따] dda-gap-dda a. sore

☐ **쑤시다** [쑤시다] ssu-si-da v. ache

☐ **욱신거리다** [욱씬거리다] uk-ssin-geo-ri-da v. throb, sore

   ☐ **욱신욱신** [욱씨눅씬] uk-ssi-nuk-ssin ad. throbbingly

   ☐ **뻐근하다** [뻐근하다] bbeo-geun ha da a. stiff

□ **두통** [두통] du-tong n. headache

두통이 심해요.
du-tong-i sim-hae-yo
I have a terrible headache.

□ **치통** [치통] chi-tong n. toothache

□ **화상** [화:상] hwa-sang n. burn, scald

□ **의식불명** [의:식불명] ui-sik-bul-myeong unconsciousness

□ **다치다** [다치다] da-chi-da v. be hurt

□ **부상** [부:상] bu-sang n. injury, wound, cut

= **상처** [상처] sang-cheo

□ **타박상** [타:박쌍] ta-bak-ssang n. contusion

□ **찰과상** [찰과상] chal-gwa-sang n. abrasion

□ **멍** [멍] meong n. bruise, black-and-blue mark

□ **피멍** [피멍] pi-meong n. bruise

□ **흉터** [흉터] hyung-teo n. scar

= **흉** [흉] hyung

□ **할퀴다** [할퀴다] hal-kwi-da v. scratch, claw

□ **삐다** [삐:다] bbi-da v. sprain, wrench

= **접질리다** [접찔리다] jeop-jjil-ri-da

□ **붓다** [붇:따] but-dda v. swell, become swollen

□ **목발** [목빨] mok-bbal n. crutch

□ **깁스** [깁쓰] gip-sseu n. plaster cast

= **석고붕대** [석꼬붕대] seok-ggo-bung-dae

□ **감기** [감:기] gam-gi n. cold

  □ **감기에 걸리다** [감:기에 걸리다] gam-gi-e geol-ri-da catch a cold

  감기에 걸린 것 같아요.
  gam-gi-e geol-rin geot ga-ta-yo
  I seem to have caught a cold.

□ **독감** [독깜] dok-ggam n. influenza, the flu

  = **인플루엔자** [인플루엔자] in-peul-ru-en-ja

  = **유행성감기** [유행썽감:기] yu-haeng-sseong-gam-gi

□ **기침** [기침] gi-chim n. cough

  □ **재채기** [재채기] jae-chae-gi n. sneezing

  □ **콜록콜록** [콜록콜록] kol-rok-kol-rok ad. cough cough

□ **열** [열] yeol n. fever

  □ **열나다** [열라다] yeol-ra-da v. run a fever

  □ **고열** [고열] go-yeol n. high fever

  □ **미열** [미열] mi-yeol n. slight fever

  열이 나요.
  yeo-ri na-yo
  I have a fever.

□ **몸살** [몸살] mom-sal n. ache all over one's body from a cold

  □ **오한** [오한] o-han n. chill

□ **소화불량** [소화불량] so-hwa-bul-ryang indigestion, dyspepsia

  □ **속 쓰림** [속 쓰림] sok sseu-rim sour stomach

  □ **위염** [위염] wi-yeom n. gastritis

□ **맹장염** [맹장념] maeng-jang-nyeom n. appendicitis

□ **메스껍다** [메스껍따] me-seu-ggeop-dda a. nauseous

□ **체** [체] che n. upset stomach

= **배탈** [배탈] bae-tal

□ **체하다** [체하다] che-ha-da v. have an upset stomach

□ **구토** [구토] gu-to n. vomiting

□ **입덧** [입떧] ip-ddeot n. morning sickness

□ **설사** [설싸] seol-ssa n. diarrhea

□ **변비** [변비] byeon-bi n. constipation

설사를 해요.
seol-ssa-ruel hae-yo
I have diarrhea.

□ **혈압** [혀랍] hyeo-rap n. blood pressure

□ **고혈압** [고혀랍] go-hyeo-rap n. high blood pressure, hypertension

□ **저혈압** [저:혀랍] jeo-hyeo-rap n. low blood pressure, hypotension

나는 고혈압이 있어요.
na-neun go-hyeo-ra-bi i-sseo-yo
I have high blood pressure.

□ **현기증** [현:기쯩] hyeon-gi-jjeung n. dizziness

= **어지럼증** [어지럼쯩] eo-ji-reom-jjeung

□ **어지럽다** [어지럽따] eo-ji-reop-dda a. dizzy

□ **빈혈** [빈혈] bin-hyeol n. anemia

□ **두드러기** [두드러기] du-deu-reo-gi n. hives

□ **뽀루지** [뽀루지] bbyo-ru-ji n. pimple, eruption, rash

□ **알레르기** [알레르기] al-re-reu-gi n. allergy → **tip.** Some people also say '알러지 [al-reo-ji]'.

□ **가렵다** [가렵따] ga-ryeop-dda a. itchy

□ **부르트다** [부르트다] bu-reu-teu-da v. blister

□ **유전병** [유전뼝] yu-jeon-bbyeong n. hereditary disease

□ **치과** [치꽈] chi-ggwa n. dental clinic

   □ **앞니** [암니] am-ni n. front tooth

   □ **송곳니** [송:곤니] song-gon-ni n. canine tooth

   □ **어금니** [어금니] eo-geum-ni n. back tooth

   □ **사랑니** [사랑니] sa-rang-ni n. wisdom tooth

   □ **충치** [충치] chung-chi n. cavity, decayed tooth

   □ **잇몸** [인몸] in-mom n. gum

□ **스케일링** [스케일링] seu-ke-il-ring n. scaling

   □ **치아 교정** [치아 교:정] chi-a gyo-jeong orthodontics

   □ **치아 교정기** [치아 교:정기] chi-a gyo-jeong-gi brace

□ **입원** [이뷘] i-bwon n. hospitalization

   □ **입원하다** [이뷘하다] i-bwon-ha-da v. go into a hospital,
be hospitalized

□ **퇴원** [퇴:원/퉤:원] toe-won/twe-won n. discharge from a hospital

   □ **퇴원하다** [퇴:원하다/퉤:원하다] toe-won-ha-da/twe-won-ha-da
v. leave the hospital

   입원해야 하나요?
   i-beon-hae-ya ha-na-yo?
   Should I be hospitalized?

□ **수술** [수술] su-sul n. surgery, operation

□ **마취** [마취] ma-chwi n. anesthesia

  □ **전신마취** [전신마취] jeon-sin-ma-chwi general anesthesia

  □ **국소마취** [국쏘마취] guk-sso-ma-chwi local anesthesia

  = **국부마취** [국뿌마취] guk-bbu-ma-chwi

□ **의료보험** [의료보:험] ui-ryo-bo-heom medical insurance

□ **진단서** [진:단서] jin-dan-seo n. medical certificate

□ **처방서** [처:방서] cheo-bang-seo n. prescription

  = **처방전** [처:방전] cheo-bang-jeon

  처방서를 써 드릴게요.
  cheo-bang-seo-reul sseo deu-ril-ge-yo
  I'm going to write you a prescription.

□ **약국** [약꾹] yak-gguk n. pharmacy

□ **약** [약] yak n. medicine

  □ **진통제** [진:통제] jin-tong-je n. painkiller, analgesic

  □ **해열제** [해:열쩨] hae-yeol-jje n. antifebrile

  □ **소화제** [소화제] so-hwa-je n. digestive medicine

  □ **수면제** [수면제] su-myeon-je n. sleeping pill

  요즘 복용하는 약이 있나요?
  yo-jeum bo-gyong-ha-neun ya-gi in-na-yo?
  Are you taking any medicine these days?

□ **부작용** [부:자굥] bu-ja-gyong n. side effect

  이 약에 부작용은 없나요?
  i ya-ge bu-ja-gyong-eun eom-na-yo?
  Does this medicine have any side effects?

□ **연고** [연:고] yeon-go n. ointment

□ **붕대** [붕대] bung-dae n. bandage

　□ **반창고** [반창고] ban-chang-go n. Band-Aid, sticking plaster

□ **은행** [은행] eun-haeng n. bank

□ **돈** [돈:] don n. money

　□ **화폐** [화:폐/화:페] hwa-pye/hwa-pe n. money, currency

　□ **통화** [통화] tong-hwa n. currency

□ **현금** [현:금] hyeon-geum n. cash

　□ **지폐** [지폐/지페] ji-pye/ji-pe n. bill, note

　□ **동전** [동전] dong-jeon n. coin

　= **주화** [주:화] ju-hwa

□ **수표** [수표] su-pyo n. check, cheque

□ **증권** [증꿘] jeung-ggwon n. stock

□ **계좌** [계:좌/게:좌] gye-jwa/ge-jwa n. account

　저축 계좌를 개설하고 싶어요.
　jeo-chuk gye-jwa-reul gae-seol-ha-go si-peo-yo
　I'd like to open a bank account.

□ **통장** [통장] tong-jang n. bankbook, passbook

□ **저축** [저:축] jeo-chuk n. deposit, saving

　= **저금** [저:금] jeo-geum

　= **예금** [예:금] ye-geum

　□ **보통예금** [보:통예:금] bo-tong-ye-geum regualr savings account

　□ **정기예금** [정:기예:금] jeong-gi-ye-geum fixed deposit account

□ **적금** [적끔] jeok-ggeum n. installment savings account

□ **입금** [입끔] ip-ggeum n. deposit

　　□ **입금하다** [입끔하다] ip-ggeum-ha-da v. deposit

□ **출금** [출금] chul-geum n. withdrawal

　= **인출** [인출] in-chul

　　□ **출금하다** [출금하다] chul-geum-ha-da v. withdraw

　= **인출하다** [인출하다] in-chul-ha-da

　= **돈을 찾다** [도늘 찯따] do-neul chat-dda

　　얼마를 인출하실 거예요?
　　eol-ma-reul in-chul-ha-sil geo-ye-yo?
　　How much do you want to withdraw?

□ **잔고** [잔고] jan-go n. balance

　　이 청구서를 지불하기에는 당신의 계좌 잔고가 부족합니다.
　　i cheong-gu-seo-reul ji-bul-ha-gi-e-neun dang-si-ne gye-jwa jan-go-ga
　　bu-jo-kam-ni-da
　　Your balance is insufficient to pay this bill.

□ **조회** [조:회/조:훼] jo-hoe/jo-hwe n. inquiry

□ **이체** [이체] i-che n. credit transfer

　　□ **자동이체** [자동이체] ja-dong-i-che automatic withdrawal

　　□ **송금** [송:금] song-geum n. transfer

□ **이자** [이:자] i-ja n. interest

　　□ **금리** [금니] geum-ni n. rate of interest

□ **대출** [대:출] dae-chul n. loan

　　□ **빚** [빋] bit n. debt

□ **금융** [금늉/그뮹] geum-nyung/geu-myung n. finance

□ **외화** [외ː화/웨ː화] oe-hwa/we-hwa n. foreign currency

□ **환율** [화ː뉼] hwa-nyul n. exchange rate

오늘 환율이 어떻게 돼요?
o-neul hwa-nyu-ri eo-ddeo-ke dwae-yo?
What's the current exchange rate?

□ **환전** [환ː전] hwan-jeon n. exchange

□ **환전하다** [환ː전하다] hwan-jeon-ha-da v. exchange, change into

□ **환전소** [환ː전소] hwan-jeon-so n. currency exchange booth

□ **원화** [원화] won-hwa n. won(Korean currency unit)

□ **원** [원] won b.n. won(Korean currency unit)

□ **달러** [달러] dal-reo n./b.n. dollar

달러를 원화로 환전하고 싶어요.
dal-reo-reul won-hwa-ro hwan-jeon-ha-go si-peo-yo
I'd like to exchange US dollars for Korean won.

□ **모기지** [모기지] mo-gi-ji n. mortgage

□ **모기지대출** [모기지대출] mo-gi-ji-dae-chul mortgage loan

□ **신용카드** [시ː뇽카드] si-nyong-ka-deu credit card

□ **체크카드** [체크카드] che-keu-ka-deu debit card

□ **발급** [발급] bal-geup n. issue

□ **수수료** [수수료] su-su-ryo n. fee

은행 이체 수수료가 있어요?
eun-haeng i-che su-su-ryo-ga i-sseo-yo?
Is there a bank fee for transferring money?

□ **에이티엠** [에이티엠] e-i-ti-em n. ATM(automated teller machine)

= **현금인출기** [현:금인출기] hyeon-geum-in-chul-gi

□ **인터넷 뱅킹** [인터넷 뱅킹] in-teo-net baeng-king Internet banking

인터넷 뱅킹을 신청하고 싶어요.
in-teo-net baeng-king-eul sin-cheong-ha-go si-peo-yo
I want to start Internet banking.

□ **비밀번호** [비:밀번호] bi-mil-beon-ho n. password,

PIN(personal identification number)

= **패스워드** [패스워드] pae-seu-wo-deu

비밀번호를 입력하세요.
bi-mil-beon-ho-reul im-nyeo-ka-se-yo
Please enter your PIN.

Useful Conversation

\# 19. 두통

김미나 누구 진통제 가지고 있는 사람?
nu-gu jin-tong-je ga-ji-go in-neun sa-ram?
Does anyone have a painkiller?

이준서 왜? 무슨 문제 있니?
wae? mu-seun mun-je in-ni?
Why? What's the problem?

김미나 두통이 엄청 심해.
du-tong-i eom-cheong sim-hae
I have a severe headache.

이준서 약통에 좀 있을 거야.
yak-tong-e jom i-sseul geo-ya
I might have something in the medicine cabinet.

Exercise

Read and Match.

1. 병원	•	• bank
2. 상점, 가게	•	• café, coffee shop
3. 요리	•	• coffee
4. 은행	•	• company
5. 음식점, 식당, 레스토랑	•	• dish, cooking
		• hospital, clinic
6. 장보기, 쇼핑	•	• job, occupation, profession
7. 직업	•	
8. 카페, 커피숍	•	• restaurant
9. 커피	•	• school
10. 학교	•	• shopping
11. 학생	•	• store, shop
12. 회사	•	• student

1. 병원 – hospital, clinic   2. 상점, 가게 – store, shop   3. 요리 – dish, cooking
4. 은행 – bank   5. 음식점, 식당, 레스토랑 – restaurant   6. 장보기, 쇼핑 – shopping
7. 직업 – job, occupation, profession   8. 카페, 커피숍 – café, coffee shop
9. 커피 – coffee   10. 학교 – school   11. 학생 – student   12. 회사 – company

6장

Traveling

Transportation 교통 gyo-tong

□ **교통** [교통] gyo-tong
n. transportation

□ **표** [표] pyo n. ticket

□ **차표** [차표] cha-pyo
= **승차권** [승차꿘] seung-cha-ggwon
n. (bus/train) ticket

□ **매표소** [매:표소] mae-pyo-so
n. ticket office

□ **개찰구** [개:찰구] gae-chal-gu
n. wicket

□ **노선** [노:선] no-seon n. line

□ **지하철노선도** [지하철노:선도]
ji-ha-cheol-no-seon-do
subway line map

□ **목적지** [목쩍찌] mok-jjeok-jji
= **행선지** [행선지] haeng-seon-ji
n. destination

□ **정류장** [정뉴장] jeong-nyu-jang
= **정류소** [정뉴소] jeong-nyu-so
n. stop

□ **환승** [환:승] hwan-seung
n. transfer

☐ **지하철** [지하철] ji-ha-cheol
　 n. subway, metro

☐ **버스** [버스] beo-seu
　 n. bus

☐ **택시** [택씨] taek-ssi
　 n. taxi, cab

☐ **기차** [기차] gi-cha
　 = **열차** [열차] yeol-cha
　 n. train

☐ **기차역** [기차역] gi-cha-yeok
　 n. train station

☐ **플랫폼** [플랟폼] peul-raet-pom
　 n. platform

☐ **선로** [설로] seol-ro
　 n. railroad

☐ **객실** [객씰] gaek-ssil
　 n. cabin

□ **비행기** [비행기] bi-haeng-gi
n. plane, airplane

□ **공항** [공항] gong-hang
n. airport

□ **일반석** [일반석] il-ban-seok
n. economy class

□ **비즈니스 클래스** [비즈니스 클래스]
bi-jeu-ni-seu keul-rae-seu
business class

□ **항공권** [항:공꿘] hang-gong-ggwon
n. airline ticket

□ **탑승권** [탑쓩꿘] tap-sseung-ggwon
n. boarding pass, boarding card

□ **퍼스트 클래스** [퍼스트 클래스]
peo-seu-teu keul-rae-seu
first class

□ **여권** [여꿘] yeo-ggwon
= **패스포트** [패스포트] pae-seu-po-teu
n. passport

□ **비자** [비자] bi-ja
n. visa

□ **터미널** [터미널] teo-mi-neol
n. terminal

□ **탑승구** [탑쓩구] tap-sseung-gu
n. departure gate

□ **출발** [출발] chul-bal

n. departure

□ **도착** [도ː착] do-chak

n. arrival

□ **이륙** [이ː륙] i-ryuk

n. take-off

□ **착륙** [창뉵] chang-nyuk

n. landing

□ **수하물** [수하물]

su-ha-mul

n. baggage, luggage

□ **비상구** [비ː상구]

bi-sang-gu

n. emergency exit

□ **면세점** [면ː세점]

myeon-se-jeom

n. duty free shop

□ **자전거** [자전거]

ja-jeon-geo

n. bicycle, bike

□ **오토바이** [오토바이]

o-to-ba-i

n. motorcycle

□ **배** [배] bae n. ship

□ **보트** [보트] bo-teu

n. boat

257

□ **교통** [교통] gyo-tong n. transportation

□ **대중교통** [대:중교통] dae-jung-gyo-tong n. public transportation

□ **표** [표] pyo n. ticket

    □ **차표** [차표] cha-pyo n. (bus/train) ticket

    = **승차권** [승차꿘] seung-cha-ggwon

    □ **기차표** [기차표] gi-cha-pyo n. (railroad) ticket

□ **매표소** [매:표소] mae-pyo-so n. ticket office

□ **요금** [요:금] yo-geum n. fare, charge, fee

□ **개찰구** [개:찰구] gae-chal-gu n. wicket

□ **시간표** [시간표] si-gan-pyo n. timetable

□ **노선** [노:선] no-seon n. line

    □ **지하철노선도** [지하철노:선도] ji-ha-cheol-no-seon-do subway line map

□ **목적지** [목쩍찌] mok-jjeok-jji n. destination

    = **행선지** [행선지] haeng-seon-ji

□ **차선** [차선] cha-seon n. lane

    □ **버스전용차선** [버스저뇽차선] beo-seu-jeo-nyong-cha-seon bus lane

    = **버스전용차로** [버스저뇽차로] beo-seu-jeo-nyong-cha-ro

□ **정류장** [정뉴장] jeong-nyu-jang n. stop

    = **정류소** [정뉴소] jeong-nyu-so

□ **종점** [종쩜] jong-jjeom n. last stop

□ **환승** [환:승] hwan-seung n. transfer

    □ **환승하다** [환:승하다] hwan-seung-ha-da v. transfer

□ **환승역** [환:승녁] hwan-seung-nyeok n. transfer station

어디에서 환승해야 해요?
eo-di-e-seo hwan-seung-hae-ya hae-yo?
Where should I transfer?

□ **지하철** [지하철] ji-ha-cheol n. subway, metro

　□ **지하철역** [지하철력] ji-ha-cheol-ryeok n. subway station

근처에 지하철역이 있어요?
geun-cheo-e ji-ha-cheol-ryeo-gi i-sseo-yo?
Is there a subway station around here?

□ **버스** [버스] beo-seu n. bus

　□ **시내버스** [시:내버스] si-nae-beo-seu n. city bus

　□ **고속버스** [고속뻐스] go-sok-bbeo-seu n. express bus

이 버스가 공항으로 가나요?
i beo-seu-ga gong-hang-eu-ro ga-na-yo?
Does this bus go to the airport?

□ **택시** [택씨] taek-ssi n. taxi, cab

□ **전차** [전:차] jeon-cha n. streetcar, trolley car, tram

□ **기차** [기차] gi-cha n. train

　= **열차** [열차] yeol-cha

　□ **기차역** [기차역] gi-cha-yeok n. train station

□ **급행열차** [그팽녈차] geu-paeng-nyeol-cha n. express train

　= **급행** [그팽] geu-paeng

□ **완행열차** [완:행녈차] wan-haeng-nyeol-cha n. local train

　= **완행** [완:행] wan-haeng

□ **플랫폼** [플랟폼] peul-raet-pom n. **platform**

　= **승강장** [승강장] seung-gang-jang

□ **선로** [설로] seol-ro n. **railroad**

□ **객실** [객씰] gaek-ssil n. **cabin**

□ **침대칸** [침:대칸] chim-dae-kan n. **sleeping compartment, sleeper**

□ **짐칸** [짐칸] jim-kan n. **cargo**

　= **화물칸** [화:물칸] hwa-mul-kan

□ **식당 칸** [식땅 칸] sik-ddang kan **dining car**

□ **비행기** [비행기] bi-haeng-gi n. **plane, airplane**

　□ **항공** [항:공] hang-gong n. **aviation**

　□ **항공편** [항:공편] hang-gong-pyeon n. **flight**

　□ **항공사** [항:공사] hang-gong-sa n. **airlines**

□ **공항** [공항] gong-hang n. **airport**

　내가 공항으로 마중 나갈게요.
　nae-ga gong-hang-eu-ro ma-jung na-gal-ge-yo
　I'll pick you up at the airport.

□ **터미널** [터미널] teo-mi-neol n. **terminal**

□ **탑승구** [탑쓩구] tap-sseung-gu n. **departure gate**

□ **항공권** [항:공꿘] hang-gong-ggwon n. **airline ticket**

　돌아갈 항공권을 갖고 있어요?
　do-ra-gal hang-gong-ggwo-neul gat-ggó i-sseo-yo?
　Do you have a return ticket?

□ **탑승** [탑쓩] tap sscung n. **boarding**

260

□ **체크인** [체크인] che-keu-in n. **check-in**

= **탑승수속** [탑씅수속] tap-sseung-su-sok

늦어도 출발 한 시간 전에는 체크인해 주세요.
neu-jeo-do chul-bal han si-gan jeo-ne-neun che-keu-in-hae ju-se-yo
Please check in at least 1 hour before departure time.

□ **탑승권** [탑씅꿘] tap-sseung-ggwon n. **boarding pass, boarding card**

탑승권을 보여 주실래요?
tap-sseung-ggwo-neul bo-yeo ju-sil-rae-yo?
May I see your boarding pass, please?

□ **여권** [여꿘] yeo-ggwon n. **passport**

= **패스포트** [패스포트] pae-seu-po-teu

여권을 신청하려는데요.
yeo-ggwo-neul sin-cheong-ha-reo-neun-de-yo
I'd like to apply for a passport.

□ **비자** [비자] bi-ja n. **visa**

= **사증** [사쯩] sa-jjeung

□ **신청** [신청] sin-cheong n. **application**

□ **발급** [발급] bal-geup n. **issue**

□ **갱신** [갱:신] gaeng-sin n. **renewal**

□ **출발** [출발] chul-bal n. **departure**

□ **떠나다** [떠나다] ddeo-na-da v. **leave, depart**

언제 떠날 예정인가요?
eon-je ddeo-nal ye-jeong-in-ga-yo?
When would you like to leave?

□ **이륙** [이ː륙] i-ryuk n. take-off

  □ **이륙하다** [이ː류카다] i-ryu-ka-da v. take off

  잠시 후에 이륙해요.
  jam-si hu-e i-ryu-kae-yo
  We are taking off shortly.

□ **착륙** [창뉵] chang-nyuk n. landing

  □ **착륙하다** [창뉴카다] chang-nyu-ka-da v. land

□ **도착** [도ː착] do-chak n. arrival

  □ **도착하다** [도ː차카다] do-cha-ka-da v. arrive

  탑승수속을 위해 출발 두 시간 전까지 공항에 도착해야 해요.
  tap-sseung-su-so-geul wi-hae chul-bal du si-gan jeon-gga-ji gong-hang-e
  do-cha-kae-ya hae-yo
  You should arrive at the airport at least 2 hours before your flight
  time to check in.

□ **편도** [편도] pyeon-do a. one-way

  □ **왕복** [왕ː복] wang-bok n. round trip

  부산행 편도로 한 장 주세요.
  bu-san-haeng pyeon-do-ro han jang ju-se-yo
  A one-way ticket to Busan, please.

□ **직항** [지캉] ji-kang n. direct flight

  □ **경유** [경유] gyeong-yu n. via

  □ **기항지** [기항지] gi-hang-ji n. port of call, a way station

□ **좌석** [좌ː석] jwa-seok n. seat

  □ **창가석** [창까석] chang-gga-seok n. window seat

  □ **통로석** [통노석] tong-no-seok n. aisle seat

창가석으로 주세요.

chang-gga-seo-geu-ro ju-se-yo

I'd like a window seat, please.

☐ **일반석** [일반석] il-ban-seok n. economy class

= **보통석** [보:통석] bo-tong-seok

☐ **비즈니스 클래스** [비즈니스 클래스] bi-jeu-ni-seu keul-rae-seu

business class

= **이등석** [이:등석] i-deung-seok n.

☐ **퍼스트 클래스** [퍼스트 클래스] peo-seu-teu keul-rae-seu first class

= **일등석** [일뜽석] il-ddeung-seok n.

☐ **여행 가방** [여행 가방] yeo-haeng ga-bang suitcase, trunk

= **트렁크** [트렁크] teu-reong-keu n.

☐ **수하물** [수하물] su-ha-mul n. baggage, luggage

= **수화물** [수화물] su-hwa-mul

☐ **수하물확인증** [수하물화긴쯩] su-ha-mul-hwa-gin-jjeung

baggage check, luggage ticket

☐ **초과수하물** [초과수하물] cho-gwa-su-ha-mul excess baggage

☐ **출입국** [추립꾹] chu-rip-gguk

n. entry into and departure from the country

☐ **출입국심사** [추립꾹심사] chu-rip-gguk-sim-sa immigration

☐ **출입국신고서** [추립꾹신고서] chu-rip-gguk-sin-go-seo

departure and landing card

☐ **출입국카드** [추립꾹카드] chu-rip-gguk-ka-deu

embarkation and disembarkation card

□ **조사** [조사] jo-sa n. check

= **확인** [화긴] hwa-gin

□ **보안 검색** [보:안 검ː색] bo-an geom-saek security check

□ **보안 검색대** [보:안 검ː색때] bo-an geom-saek-ddae airport security

□ **세관** [세ː관] se-gwan n. customs

□ **세관 검사** [세ː관 검ː사] se-gwan geom-sa customs inspection

□ **세관 신고서** [세ː관 신고서] se-gwan sin-go-seo declaration card

□ **기내** [기내] gi-nae n. on the plane

□ **기내식** [기내식] gi-nae-sik n. in-flight meal

□ **안전띠** [안전띠] an-jeon-ddi n. seatbelt, seat belt

= **안전벨트** [안전벨트] an-jeon-bel-teu

안전벨트를 매도록 해요.
an-jeon-bel-teu-reul mae-do-rok hae-yo
Fasten your seat belt.

□ **구명조끼** [구명조끼] gu-myeong-jo-ggi n. life vest, life jacket

□ **비상구** [비ː상구] bi-sang-gu n. emergency exit

□ **면세점** [면ː세점] myeon-se-jeom n. duty free shop

□ **면세품** [면ː세품] myeon-se-pum n. duty free goods

□ **자전거** [자전거] ja-jeon-geo n. bicycle, bike

□ **자전거도로** [자전거도로] ja-jeon-geo-do-ro bicycle path

□ **오토바이** [오토바이] o-to-ba-i n. motorcycle

□ **헬멧** [헬멛] hel-met n. helmet

□ **배** [배] bae n. ship

　= **선박** [선박] seon-bak

□ **보트** [보트] bo-teu n. boat

　□ **요트** [요트] yo-teu n. yacht

□ **항구** [항ː구] hang-gu n. port, harbor

□ **멀미** [멀미] meol-mi n. sickness

20. 항공권 예약

Useful Conversation

이준서　서울행 비행기표를 예약하려고요.
　　　seo-ul-haeng bi-haeng-gi-pyo-reul ye-ya-ka-ryeo-go-yo
　　　I'd like to book a ticket for Seoul, Korea.

직원　언제 떠날 예정이세요?
　　　eon-je ddeo-nal ye-jeong-i-se-yo?
　　　When do you plan on departing?

이준서　12월 20일에서 23일 사이에 떠나고 싶은데요.
　　　si-bi-wol i-si-bil-e-seo i-sip-sa-mil sa-i-e ddeo-na-go si-peun-de-yo
　　　I'd like to leave between December 20th and the 23rd.

직원　편도예요, 왕복이에요?
　　　pyeon-do-ye-yo, wang-bo-gi-e-yo?
　　　One-way, or round trip?

이준서　왕복으로 주세요.
　　　wang-bo-geu-ro ju-se-yo
　　　Round trip, please.

Driving 운전 un-jeon

□ **운전** [운:전] un-jeon n. driving

□ **운전하다** [운:전하다] un-jeon-ha-da
  v. drive

□ **자동차** [자동차] ja-dong-cha
  n. car

□ **에스유브이** [에스유브이]
  e-seu-yu-beu-i
  n. SUV(sport utility vehicle)

□ **오픈카** [오픈카] o-peun-ka
  n. convertible (car)

□ **밴** [밴] baen
  n. van

□ **트럭** [트럭] teu-reok
  = **화물자동차** [화:물자동차]
  hwa-mul-ja-dong-cha
  n. truck

□ **핸들** [핸들] haen-deul
  n. steering wheel, handlebar

□ **밟다** [밥:따] bap-dda
  v. step on

266

□ **정지하다** [정지하다] jeong-ji-ha-da
= **멈추다** [멈추다] meom-chu-da
v. stop

□ **헤드라이트** [헤드라이트]
he-deu-ra-i-teu
= **전조등** [전조등] jeon-jo-deung
n. headlight

□ **경적** [경:적] gyeong-jeok
= **클랙슨** [클랙쓴] keul-raek-sseun
n. horn, klaxon

□ **백미러** [백미러] baek-mi-reo
n. rearview mirror

□ **바퀴** [바퀴] ba-kwi n. wheel

□ **타이어** [타이어] ta-i-eo n. tire

□ **위반** [위반] wi-ban
n. violation

□ **속도위반** [속또위반]
sok-ddo-wi-ban
n. speeding

□ **음주 운전** [음:주 운:전]
eum-ju un-jeon
drunk driving

267

□ **벌금** [벌금] beol-geum

= **범칙금** [범:칙끔] beom-chik-ggeum

n. fine, penalty

□ **교통표지판** [교통표지판]

gyo-tong-pyo-ji-pan

traffic sign

□ **신호등** [신:호등] sin-ho-deung

n. traffic lights

□ **건널목** [건:널목] geon-neol-mok

n. (railway) crossing

□ **횡단보도** [횡단보도/휑단보도)

hoeng-dan-bo-do/hweng-dan-bo-do

n. pedestrian crossing

□ **속도** [속또] sok-ddo

n. speed

□ **빠르다** [빠르다] bba-reu-da a. fast

□ **빨리** [빨리] bbal-ri ad. fast, quickly

□ **느리다** [느리다] neu-ri-da a. slow

□ **천천히** [천:천히] cheon-cheon-hi

ad. slowly

□ **주유** [주:유] ju-yu

n. refueling

□ **주유소** [주:유소] ju-yu-so

n. gas station

□ **세차** [세:차] se-cha

n. washing a car

□ **세차장** [세:차장] se-cha-jang

n. car wash

□ **주차** [주:차] ju-cha

n. parking

□ **주차장** [주:차장] ju-cha-jang

n. parking lot, car park

□ **도로** [도:로] do-ro

n. road, street

□ **보도** [보:도] bo-do

= **인도** [인도] in-do

n. sidewalk

□ **운전** [운:전] un-jeon n. driving

□ **운전하다** [운:전하다] un-jeon-ha-da v. drive

운전할 수 있어요?
un-jeon-hal ssu i-sseo-yo?
Can you drive a car?

□ **운전면허** [운:전면허] un-jeon-myeon-heo n. driver's license

□ **운전면허 시험** [운:전면허 시험] un-jeon-myeon-heo si-heom
driving test

□ **국제운전면허증** [국제운:전면허쯩] guk-jje-un-jeon-myeon-heo-jjeung
international driving license, international driving permit

□ **자동차** [자동차] ja-dong-cha n. car

□ **대형자동차** [대:형자동차] dae-hyeong-ja-dong-cha full-size car
= **대형차** [대:형차] dae-hyeong-cha n.

□ **소형자동차** [소:형자동차] so-hyeong-ja-dong-cha compact car
= **소형차** [소:형차] so-hyeong-cha n.

□ **에스유브이** [에스유브이] e-seu-yu-beu-i n. SUV(sport utility vehicle)

□ **오픈카** [오픈카] o-peun-ka n. convertible (car)

□ **밴** [밴] baen n. van

□ **트럭** [트럭] teu-reok n. truck
= **화물자동차** [화:물자동차] hwa-mul-ja-dong-cha

□ **렌터카** [렌터카] ren-teo-ka n. rental car

□ **핸들** [핸들] haen-deul n. steering wheel, handlebar

□ **파워핸들** [파워핸들] pa-wo-haen-deul power steering

□ **변속기어** [변ː속기어] byeon-sok-gi-eo gearshift

  □ **자동변속기** [자동변ː속끼] ja-dong-byeon-sok-ggi
  automatic transmission

  □ **수동변속기** [수동변ː속끼] su-dong-byeon-sok-ggi
  manual transmission

□ **안전띠** [안전띠] an-jeon-ddi n. seatbelt, seat belt

  = **안전벨트** [안전벨트] an-jeon-bel-teu

□ **밟다** [밥ː따] bap-dda v. step on

□ **액셀러레이터** [액셀러레이터] aek-sel-reo-re-i-teo n. accelerator

  = **액셀** [액셀] aek-sel

  = **가속페달** [가속페달] ga-sok-pe-dal

□ **클러치** [클러치] keul-reo-chi n. clutch

  = **클러치페달** [클러치페달] keul-reo-chi-pe-dal

□ **브레이크** [브레이크] beu-re-i-keu n. brake

  □ **사이드브레이크** [사이드브레이크] sa-i-deu-beu-re-i-keu side brake,
  emergency brake

□ **정지** [정지] jeong-ji n. stop

  □ **정지하다** [정지하다] jeong-ji-ha-da v. stop

  = **멈추다** [멈추다] meom-chu-da

□ **범퍼** [범퍼] beom-peo n. bumper, fender

□ **보닛** [보닏] bo-nit n. hood, bonnet

□ **와이퍼** [와이퍼] wa-i-peo n. wiper

□ **트렁크** [트렁크] teu-reong-keu n. suitcase, trunk

□ **헤드라이트** [헤드라이트] he-deu-ra-i-teu n. headlight
   = **전조등** [전조등] jeon-jo-deung

□ **깜빡이** [깜빠기] ggam-bba-gi n. turn signal
   = **방향지시등** [방향지시등] bang-hyang-ji-si-deung
      □ **비상등** [비:상등] bi-sang-deung n. emergency light

□ **경적** [경:적] gyeong-jeok n. **horn, klaxon**
   = **클랙슨** [클랙쓴] keul-raek-sseun

□ **백미러** [백미러] baek-mi-reo n. **rearview mirror**
      □ **사이드미러** [사이드미러] sa-i-deu-mi-reo side-view mirror

□ **후방카메라** [후:방카메라] hu-bang-ka-me-ra **rear-facing camera**

□ **번호판** [번호판] beon-ho-pan n. license plate

□ **바퀴** [바퀴] ba-kwi n. wheel
      □ **타이어** [타이어] ta-i-eo n. tire
      □ **스노타이어** [스노타이어] seu-no-ta-i-eo n. snow tire
      □ **스페어타이어** [스페어타이어] seu-pe-eo-ta-i-eo n. spare tire

   타이어 점검해 주세요.
   ta-i-eo jeom-geom-hae ju-se-yo
   Would you check my tires?

□ **펑크** [펑크] peong-keu n. flat tire

□ **도로교통법** [도:로교통법] do-ro-gyo-tong-beop the Road Traffic Law

□ **위반** [위반] wi-ban n. violation
      □ **주차위반** [주:차위반] ju-cha wi-ban parking violation

☐ **신호위반** [신:호위반] sin-ho-wi-ban signal violation

☐ **속도위반** [속또위반] sok-ddo-wi-ban n. speeding

tip. '속도위반' can also mean that a couple has a baby before getting married.

☐ **음주 운전** [음:주 운:전] eum-ju un-jeon drunk driving

☐ **음주측정기** [음:주측쩡기] eum-ju-cheuk-jjeong-gi breathalyzer, drunkometer

음주측정기를 부세요.
eum-ju-cheuk-jjeong-gi-reul bu-se-yo
Please blow into this breathalyzer.

☐ **벌금** [벌금] beol-geum n. fine, penalty

= **범칙금** [범:칙끔] beom-chik-ggeum

벌금이 얼마예요?
beol-geu-mi eol-ma-ye-yo?
How much is the fine?

☐ **표지판** [표지판] pyo-ji-pan n. sign

☐ **교통표지판** [교통표지판] gyo-tong-pyo-ji-pan traffic sign

☐ **도로표지판** [도로표지판] do-ro-pyo-ji-pan road sign

☐ **일방통행** [일방통행] il-bang-tong-haeng n. one way

☐ **신호등** [신:호등] sin-ho-deung n. traffic lights

☐ **빨간불** [빨간불] bbal-gan-bul n. red light

= **적신호** [적씬호] jeok-ssin-ho

☐ **파란불** [파란불] pa-ran-bul n. green light

= **청신호** [청신호] cheong-sin-ho

= **초록불** [초록뿔] cho-rok-bbul

= **녹색등** [녹쌕뜽] nok-ssaek-ddeung

☐ **노란불** [노란불] no-ran-bul n. yellow light, orange light

tip. '신호등' has red, green and yellow(orage) lights. '파란불' means 'blue light', but for traffic, green lights are usually called '파란불'.

□ **횡단보도** [횡단보도/휑단보도] hoeng-dan-bo-do/hweng-dan-bo-do

　n. pedestrian crossing

　□ **무단횡단** [무단횡단/무단휑단] mu-dan-hoeng-dan/mu-dan-hweng-dan

　jaywalk

　　무단횡단을 하면 안 됩니다.
　　mu-dan-hoeng-da-neul ha-myeon an doem-ni-da
　　You shouldn't jaywalk.

□ **건널목** [건ː널목] geon-neol-mok n. (railway) crossing

□ **육교** [육꾜] yuk-ggyo n. pedestrian overpass

□ **지하도** [지하도] ji-ha-do n. underpass

□ **운전자** [운ː전자] un-jeon-ja n. driver

□ **보행자** [보ː행자] bo-haeng-ja n. pedestrian, walker

　= **행인** [행인] haeng-in

□ **속도** [속또] sok-ddo n. speed

　= **스피드** [스피드] seu-pi-deu

　□ **제한속도** [제한속또] je-han-sok-ddo speed limit

　□ **과속** [과ː속] gwa-sok n. over the speed limit

□ **빠르다** [빠르다] bba-reu-da a. fast

　□ **빨리** [빨리] bbal-ri ad. fast, quickly

□ **급하다** [그파다] geo-pa-da a. urgent

　□ **급히** [그피] geu-pi ad. in a hurry

□ **느리다** [느리다] neu-ri-da a. slow

　□ **천천히** [천ː천히] cheon-cheon-hi ad. slowly

□ **주유** [주ː유] ju-yu n. refueling

  □ **주유소** [주ː유소] ju-yu-so n. gas station

  □ **셀프 주유소** [셀프 주ː유소] sel-peu ju-yu-so self serve station

  이 근처에 주유소가 있어요?
  i geun-cheo-e ju-yu-so-ga i-sseo-yo?
  Is there a gas station around here?

□ **휘발유** [휘발류] hwi-bal-ryu n. gasoline, gas

  = **가솔린** [가솔린] ga-sol-rin

□ **경유** [경유] gyeong-yu n. diesel

  = **디젤유** [디젤류] di-jel-ryu

□ **천연가스** [처년가스] cheo-nyeon-ga-seu n. natural gas

□ **리터** [리터] li-teo b.n. liter

□ **양** [양] yang n. quantity

□ **연비** [연비] yeon-bi n. fuel efficiency

□ **세차** [세ː차] se-cha n. washing a car

  □ **세차장** [세ː차장] se-cha-jang n. car wash

□ **주차** [주ː차] ju-cha n. parking

  □ **정차** [정차] jeong-cha n. stop

  □ **주차장** [주ː차장] ju-cha-jang n. parking lot, car park

  □ **무료 주차장** [무료 주ː차장] mu-ryo ju-cha-jang free parking

  □ **유료 주차장** [유ː료 주ː차장] yu-ryo ju-cha-jang paid parking

  주차장이 어디에 있어요?
  ju-cha-jang-i eo-di-e i-sseo-yo?
  Where is the parking lot?

□ **주차금지** [주:차금:지] ju-cha-geum-ji **no parking**

　□ **불법주차** [불법주:차/불뻡주:차] bul-beop-ju-cha/bul-bbeop-ju-cha

　illegal parking

　= **무단주차** [무단주:차] mu-dan-ju-cha

　□ **주차단속** [주:차단속] ju-cha-dan-sok **crackdown on illegal parking**

□ **러시아워** [러시아워] reo-si-a-wo n. **rush hour**

　□ **교통체증** [교통체증] gyo-tong-che-jeung **traffic jam**

　= **교통정체** [교통정체] gyo-tong-jeong-che

□ **찻길** [차낄/찯낄] cha-ggil/chat-ggil n. **roadway**

　= **차도** [차도] cha-do

□ **차선** [차선] cha-seon n. **lane**

　□ **중앙선** [중앙선] jung-ang-seon n. **the center line**

　□ **유턴** [유턴] yu-teon n. **U-turn**

　□ **좌회전** [좌:회전/좌:훼전] jwa-hoe-jeon/jwa-hwe-jeon n. **left-turn**

　□ **우회전** [우:회전/우:훼전] u-hoe-jeon/u-hwe-jeon n. **right-turn**

　이 차선은 좌회전 전용입니다.
　i cha-seo-neun jwa-hoe-jeon jeo-nyong-im-ni-da
　This lane is left-turns only.

□ **도로** [도:로] do-ro n. **road, street**

　□ **고속도로** [고속도:로] go-sok-do-ro n. **highway, expressway**

　□ **유료도로** [유:료도:로] yu-ryo-do-ro **toll road**

　□ **통행료** [통행뇨] tong-haeng-nyo n. **toll fee**

□ **교차로** [교차로] gyo-cha-ro n. **intersection, junction**

　□ **사거리** [사:거리] sa-geo-ri n. **crossroads**

□ **로터리** [로터리] ro-teo-ri **n.** roundabout

□ **갓길** [가:낄/갇:낄] ga-ggil/gat-ggil **n.** shoulder (of the road)

□ **터널** [터널] teo-neol **n.** tunnel

□ **보도** [보:도] bo-do **n.** sidewalk

= **인도** [인도] in-do

= **보행로** [보:행노] bo-haeng-no

21. 교통 위반

Useful Conversation

경찰　　안녕하세요. 운전면허를 보여 주세요.
　　　　an-nyoung-ha-se-yo. un-jeon myeon-heo-reul bo-yeo ju-se-yo
　　　　Hello. May I see your driver's license?

준서　　왜요? 제가 너무 빨리 갔나요?
　　　　wae-yo? je-ga neo-mu bbal-ri gan-na-yo?
　　　　Why? Was I going too fast?

경찰　　아니요, 안전벨트를 안 매셨습니다.
　　　　a-ni-yo, an-jeon-bel-teu-reul an mae-syeot-sseum-ni-da
　　　　No, you didn't burkle your seatbelt.

준서　　죄송합니다. 급히 출발하느라. 딱지를 끊어야 하나요?
　　　　joe-song-ham-ni-da. geu-pi chul-bal-ha-neu-ra.
　　　　ddak-ji-reul ggeu-neo-ya ha-na-yo?
　　　　Sorry, I was in a hurry. Is a a ticket necessary?

경찰　　네, 3만 원의 범칙금이 있습니다.
　　　　ne, sam-man wo-ne beom-chik-ggeu-mi it-sseum-ni-da
　　　　Yes, that's a 30,000 won fine.

Staying Overnight 숙박 suk-bbak

□ **머무르다** [머무르다] meo-mu-reu-da
= **묵다** [묵따] muk-dda
= **체류하다** [체류하다] che-ryu-ha-da
v. stay

□ **숙소** [숙쏘] suk-sso
= **숙박 시설** [숙빡 시:설]
suk-bbak si-seol
n. accommodation

□ **호텔** [호텔] ho-tel
n. hotel

□ **로비** [로비] ro-bi
n. lobby

□ **체크인** [체크인] che-keu-in
n. check-in

□ **체크아웃** [체크아웃] che-keu-a-ut
n. check-out

□ **객실** [객씰] gaek-ssil
n. room

□ **싱글룸** [싱글룸] sing-geul-rum
single room

□ **더블룸** [더블룸] deo-beul-rum
double room

□ **스위트룸** [스위트룸] seu-wi-teu-rum
n. suite

278

□ **룸서비스** [룸서비스] rum-seo-bi-seu

n. room service

□ **불평** [불평] bul-pyeong

n. complaint

□ **냉방** [냉:방] naeng-bang

n. air conditioning

□ **난방** [난:방] nan-bang

n. heating

□ **화장실** [화장실] hwa-jang-sil

n. toilet, restroom

□ **세탁실** [세:탁씰] se-tak-ssil

n. laundry room

□ **깨끗하다** [깨끄타다]

ggae-ggeu-ta-da

a. clean

□ **더럽다** [더:럽따] deo-reop-dda

a. dirty

279

□ **편안하다** [펴난하다] pyeo-nan-ha-da
= **안락하다** [알라카다] al-ra-ka-da
a. comfortable

□ **불편하다** [불편하다]
bul-pyeon-ha-da
a. uncomfortable,
inconvenient

□ **예약** [예:약] ye-yak
n. reservation, booking

□ **예약하다** [예:야카다] ye-ya-ka-da
v. reserve, book,
make a reservation

□ **취소** [취:소] chwi-so
n. cancellation

□ **취소하다** [취:소하다]
chwi-so-ha-da
v. cancel

□ **침구** [침:구] chim-gu n. bedding

□ **시트** [시트] si-teu n. sheet

□ **이불** [이불] i-bul n. duvet

□ **담요** [담:뇨] dam-nyo n. blanket

□ **베개** [베개] be-gae
n. pillow

□ **수건** [수:건] su-geon
n. towel

□ **샴푸** [샴푸] syam-pu n. shampoo

□ **린스** [린스] rin-seu n. rinse

□ **보디 샴푸** [보디 샴푸] bo-di syam-pu
body wash

□ **비누** [비누] bi-nu
n. soap

□ **칫솔** [치쏠/칟쏠] chi-ssol/chit-ssol
n. toothbrush

□ **치약** [치약] chi-yak n. toothpaste

□ **빗** [빋] bit
= **머리빗** [머리빋] meo-ri-bit
n. comb

□ **면도기** [면:도기] myeon-do-gi
n. razor, shaver

□ **드라이어** [드라이어] deu-ra-i-eo
= **헤어드라이어** [헤어드라이어]
he-eo-deu-ra-i-eo
n. blower, hair drier, hair dryer

□ **화장지** [화장지] hwa-jang-ji
= **휴지** [휴지] hyu-ji
n. toilet paper

□ **티슈** [티슈] ti-syu
n. tissue

281

☐ **숙박** [숙빡] suk-bbak n. stay

☐ **머무르다** [머무르다] meo-mu-reu-da v. stay

= **묵다** [묵따] muk-dda

= **체류하다** [체류하다] che-ryu-ha-da

친구네에서 머무를 거예요.
chin-gu-ne-e-seo meo-mu-reul geo-ye-yo
I'm going to stay at my friend's house.

☐ **숙소** [숙쏘] suk-sso n. accommodation

= **숙박 시설** [숙빡 시:설] suk-bbak si-seol

☐ **호텔** [호텔] ho-tel n. hotel

☐ **호스텔** [호스텔] ho-seu-tel n. hostel

☐ **유스호스텔** [유스호스텔] yu-seu-ho-seu-tel youth hostel

☐ **모텔** [모텔] mo-tel n. motel

☐ **여관** [여관] yeo-gwan n. inn

☐ **민박** [민박] min-bak n. B&B(Bed and Breakfast)

☐ **프런트** [프런트] peu-reon-teu n. reception, front desk

☐ **로비** [로비] ro-bi n. lobby

☐ **체크인** [체크인] che-keu-in n. check-in

체크인은 몇 시부터입니까?
che-keu-i-neun meot si-bu-teo-im-ni-gga?
What time is check-in?

☐ **체크아웃** [체크아웉] che-keu-a-ut n. check-out

□ **객실** [객씰] gaek-ssil n. room

  □ **싱글룸** [싱글룸] sing-geul-rum single room

  □ **더블룸** [더블룸] deo-beul-rum double room

  □ **스위트룸** [스위트룸] seu-wi-teu-rum n. suite

□ **룸서비스** [룸서비스] rum-seo-bi-seu n. room service

□ **만족** [만족] man-jok n. satisfaction

  □ **만족하다** [만조카다] man-jo-ka-da a. satisfied v. satisfy

□ **불평** [불평] bul-pyeong n. complaint

  □ **불평하다** [불평하다] bul-pyeong-ha-da v. complain

  = **투덜거리다** [투덜거리다] tu-deol-geo-ri-da

□ **시설** [시:설] si-seol n. facility

  □ **설비** [설비] seol-bi n. equipment

□ **냉난방** [냉:난방] naeng-nan-bang n. air conditioning and heating

  □ **냉방** [냉:방] naeng-bang n. air conditioning

  □ **난방** [난:방] nan-bang n. heating

□ **통풍** [통풍] tong-pung n. ventilation

  = **환기** [환:기] hwan-gi

□ **호텔종사자** [호텔종사자] ho-tel-jong-sa-ja hotel staff

  □ **도어맨** [도어맨] do-eo-man n. doorman

  □ **호텔포터** [호텔포터] ho-tel-po-teo bellhop, bellboy

□ **화장실** [화장실] hwa-jang-sil n. toilet, restroom

□ **세탁실** [세:탁씰] se-tak-ssil n. laundry room

□ **음식점** [음ː식쩜] eum-sik-jjeom n. restaurant

  = **식당** [식땅] sik-ddang

  = **레스토랑** [레스토랑] re-seu-to-rang

□ **뷔페** [뷔페] bwi-pe n. buffet

□ **무선인터넷** [무선인터넫] mu-seon in-teo-net wireless Internet

  □ **근거리 무선망** [근ː거리 무선망] geun-geo-ri mu-seon-mang Wi-Fi

> **tip.** '와이파이 [wa-i-pa-i]' is used more than '근거리 무선망' in Korea.

□ **깨끗하다** [깨끄타다] ggae-ggeu-ta-da a. clean

  = **청결하다** [청결하다] cheong-gyeol-ha-da

□ **더럽다** [더ː럽따] deo-reop-dda a. dirty

  = **지저분하다** [지저분하다] ji-jeo-bun-ha-da

  = **불결하다** [불결하다] bul-gyeol-ha-da

□ **편안하다** [펴난하다] pyeo-nan-ha-da a. comfortable

  = **안락하다** [알라카다] al-ra-ka-da

□ **불편하다** [불편하다] bul-pyeon-ha-da a. uncomfortable, inconvenient

□ **전망** [전ː망] jeon-mang n. view

  바다 전망 방으로 주세요.
  ba-da jeon-mang bang-eu-ro ju-se-yo
  I'd like a room with a view of the ocean.

□ **비치파라솔** [비치파라솔] bi-chi-pa-ra-sol n. beach umbrella

  = **파라솔** [파라솔] pa-ra-sol

□ **수영장** [수영장] su-yeong-jang n. swimming pool, pool

  = **풀장** [풀짱] pul-jang

□ **요금** [요ː금] yo-geum n. charge, fare, fee

□ **할인요금** [하린요:금] ha-rin-yo-geum discount

□ **추가 요금** [추가 요:금] chu-ga yo-geum extra charge

이 항목은 무슨 요금입니까?
i hang-mo-geun mu-seun yo-geu-mim-ni-gga?
What is this charge?

□ **가격** [가격] ga-gyeok n. price

= **값** [갑] gap

□ **비용** [비:용] bi-yong n. cost

= **경비** [경비] gyeong-bi

□ **보증금** [보증금] bo-jeung-geum n. deposit — **tip.** Most hotels require a deposit when you check in.

□ **지불** [지불] ji-bul n. payment

= **결제** [결쩨] gyeol-jje

　□ **선불** [선불] seon-bul n. prepayment

　□ **후불** [후:불] hu-bul n. paying later

□ **추가** [추가] chu-ga n. addition

□ **세금** [세:금] se-geum n. tax

　□ **면세** [면:세] myeon-se n. tax-free

□ **박** [박] bak b.n. (a trip for) night

3박 4일 묵으려고요.
sam-bak sa-il mu-geu-ryeo-go-yo
I'm going to stay for four days and three nights.

□ **예약** [예:약] ye-yak n. reservation, booking

　□ **예약하다** [예:야카다] ye-ya-ka-da v. reserve, book, make a reservation

□ **취소** [취:소] chwi-so n. cancellation

  □ **취소하다** [취:소하다] chwi-so-ha-da v. cancel

□ **빈방** [빈:방] bin-bang n. vacancy

  죄송하지만, 빈방이 없어요.
  joe-song-ha-ji-man, bin-bang-i eop-sseo-yo
  I'm sorry we're all booked up.

□ **침구** [침:구] chim-gu n. bedding

  □ **이불** [이불] i-bul n. duvet

  □ **시트** [시트] si-teu n. sheet

  □ **담요** [담:뇨] dam-nyo n. blanket

  □ **베개** [베개] be-gae n. pillow

□ **수건** [수:건] su-geon n. towel

□ **샴푸** [샴푸] syam-pu n. shampoo

  □ **린스** [린스] rin-seu n. rinse

  □ **보디 샴푸** [보디 샴푸] bo-di syam-pu body wash

□ **비누** [비누] bi-nu n. soap

□ **샤워 캡** [샤워 캡] sya-wo kaep shower cap

□ **칫솔** [치쏠/칟쏠] chi-ssol/chit-ssol n. toothbrush

  □ **치약** [치약] chi-yak n. toothpaste

□ **빗** [빋] bit n. comb

  = **머리빗** [머리빋] meo-ri-bit

□ **면도** [면:도] myeon-do n. shaving

  □ **면도기** [면:도기] myeon-do-gi n. razor, shaver

☐ **드라이어** [드라이어] deu-ra-i-eo n. blower, hair drier, hair dryer

= **헤어드라이어** [헤어드라이어] he-eo-deu-ra-i-eo

☐ **화장지** [화장지] hwa-jang-ji n. toilet paper

= **휴지** [휴지] hyu-ji

☐ **티슈** [티슈] ti-syu n. tissue

☐ **냉장고** [냉ː장고] naeng-jang-go n. refrigerator

☐ **커피포트** [커피포트] keo-pi-po-teu n. coffee pot

☐ **미니바** [미니바] mi-ni-ba n. minibar

☐ **다리미** [다리미] da-ri-mi n. iron

☐ **금고** [금고] geum-go n. safe

22. 숙소 예약

Useful Conversation

박미나   호텔 예약했니?
         ho-tel ye-ya-kaen-ni?
         Have you booked a hotel?

이준서   아직 좋은 호텔을 찾지 못했어.
         a-jik jo-eun ho-te-reul chat-jji mo-tae-sseo
         I haven't found a good hotel yet.

박미나   호텔 웹 사이트에서 평가들을 읽어 봐.
         ho-tel wep sa-i-teu-e-seo pyeong-gga-deu-reul il-geo bwa
         Check the reviews from some hotel booking sites.

이준서   그거 좋은 생각이네. 고마워.
         geu-geo jo-eun saeng-ga-gi-ne. go-ma-wo
         That's a good idea. Thank you.

Sightseeing 관광 gwan-gwang

□ **관광** [관광] gwan-gwang

n. sightseeing

□ **여행** [여행] yeo-haeng

n. trip, tour, journey

□ **크루즈** [크루즈] keu-ru-jeu

n. cruise

□ **식도락** [식또락] sik-ddo-rak

n. gourmandism

□ **안내인** [안:내인] an-nae-in

= **가이드** [가이드] ga-i-deu

n. guide

□ **관광 안내소** [관광 안:내소]

gwan-gwang an-nae-so

tourist information office

□ **지도** [지도] ji-do n. map

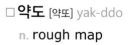

□ **약도** [약또] yak-ddo

n. rough map

□ **관광객** [관광객] gwan-gwang-gaek

n. tourist, traveler

□ **탑** [탑] tap

  n. tower, pagoda

□ **성** [성] seong n. castle

□ **궁전** [궁전] gung-jeon

  = **궁궐** [궁궐] gung-gwol

  n. palace

□ **대성당** [대:성당] dae-seong-dang

  n. cathedral

□ **절** [절] jeol

  = **사원** [사원] sa-won

  n. temple

□ **박물관** [방물관] bang-mul-gwan

  n. museum

□ **미술관** [미:술관] mi-sul-gwan

  = **갤러리** [갤러리] gael-reo-ri

  n. gallery

□ **광장** [광:장] gwang-jang

  n. plaza, square

□ **공원** [공원] gong-won

  n. park

289

□ **동물원** [동:무뤈] dong-mu-rwon

  n. zoo

□ **식물원** [싱무뤈] sing-mu-rwon

  n. botanical gardens

□ **놀이공원** [노리공원] no-ri-gong-won

= **놀이동산** [노리동산] no-ri-dong-san

  n. amusement park

□ **경로** [경노] gyeong-no

  n. route

□ **산** [산] san

  n. mountain

□ **계곡** [계곡/게곡] gye-gok/ge-gok

  n. valley

□ **강** [강] gang

  n. river

□ **호수** [호수] ho-su

  n. lake

□ **바다** [바다] ba-da

  n. sea

□ **해변** [해:변] hae-byeon

= **바닷가** [바다까/바닫까]

ba-da-gga/ba-dat-gga

  n. beach

□ **입구** [입꾸] ip-ggu n. entrance

□ **입장하다** [입짱하다] ip-jjang-ha-da
= **들어가다** [드러가다] deu-reo-ga-da
v. enter

□ **출구** [출구] chul-gu n. exit

□ **퇴장하다** [퇴:장하다/퉤:장하다]
toe-jang-ha-da/twe-jang-ha-da
= **나가다** [나가다] na-ga-da
v. go out

□ **도시** [도시] do-si
n. city

□ **시골** [시골] si-gol
n. countryside

□ **거리** [거:리] geo-ri
n. distance

□ **셀프 카메라** [셀프 카메라]
sel-peu ka-me-ra
= **셀카** [셀카] sel-ka n.
selfie

□ **선물** [선:물] seon-mul
n. present, gift

□ **기념품** [기념품] gi-nyeom-pum
n. souvenir

□ **관광** [관광] gwan-gwang n. sightseeing

관광하러 왔어요.
gwan-gwang-ha-reo wa-sseo-yo
I'm here just for sightseeing.

□ **여행** [여행] yeo-haeng n. trip, tour, journey

= **유람** [유람] yu-ram

□ **일주** [일쭈] il-jju n. traveling around

　　□ **세계 일주** [세:계 일쭈/세:게 일쭈] se-gye il-jju/se-ge il-jju

　traveling around the world

　　□ **전국 일주** [전국 일쭈] jeon-guk il-jju traveling around the country

□ **당일 여행** [당일 여행] dang-il yeo-haeng day trip

□ **크루즈** [크루즈] keu-ru-jeu n. cruise

□ **식도락** [식또락] sik-ddo-rak n. gourmandism

　　□ **미식가** [미:식까] mi-sik-gga n. gourmet

□ **안내인** [안:내인] an-nae-in n. guide

　= **가이드** [가이드] ga-i-deu

　가이드가 있어요?
　ga-i-deu-ga i-sseo-yo?
　Do you have a guide?

□ **관광 안내소** [관광 안:내소] gwan-gwang an-nae-so

tourist information office

　　□ **정보** [정보] jeong-bo n. information

　관광 안내소가 어디 있어요?
　gwan-gwang an-nae-so-ga eo-di i-sseo-yo?
　Where is the tourist information office?

□ **개인** [개ː인] gae-in n. individual

□ **단체** [단체] dan-che n. group

> 단체 할인이 돼요?
> dan-che ha-ri-ni dwae-yo?
> Do you have a group discount?

□ **지도** [지도] ji-do n. map

　　□ **약도** [약또] yak-ddo n. rough map

> 약도를 좀 그려 주시겠어요?
> yak-ddo-reul jom geu-ryeo ju-si-ge-sseo-yo?
> Could you draw me a rough map?

□ **관광객** [관광객] gwan-gwang-gaek n. tourist, traveler

　　= **여행객** [여행객] yeo-haeng-gaek

□ **방문** [방ː문] bang-mun n. visit

　　□ **방문객** [방ː문객] bang-mun-gaek n. visitor

□ **기념** [기념] gi-nyeom n. commemoration

　　□ **기념관** [기념관] gi-nyeom-gwan n. memorial hall

　　□ **기념물** [기념물] gi-nyeom-mul n. monument

　　□ **기념비** [기념비] gi-nyeom-bi n. memorial

□ **건물** [건ː물] geon-mul n. building

　　= **빌딩** [빌딩] bil-ding

□ **초고층빌딩** [초고층빌딩] cho-go-cheung-bil-ding n. skyscraper

　　= **마천루** [마철루] ma-cheol-ru

□ **탑** [탑] tap n. tower, pagoda

☐ **성** [성] seong n. castle

  ☐ **궁전** [궁전] gung-jeon n. palace

  = **궁궐** [궁궐] gung-gwol

  = **궁** [궁] gung

☐ **왕** [왕] wang n. king

  ☐ **여왕** [여왕] yeo-wang n. queen

  ☐ **왕비** [왕비] wang-bi n. queen

  ☐ **왕자** [왕자] wang-ja n. prince

  ☐ **공주** [공주] gong-ju n. princess

> **tip.** '여왕' means the female king and '왕비' is the wife of a king.

☐ **대성당** [대:성당] dae-seong-dang n. cathedral

☐ **절** [절] jeol n. temple

  = **사원** [사원] sa-won

  ☐ **대웅전** [대:웅전] dae-ung-jeon n. the main building of a temple

☐ **풍경** [풍경] pung-gyeong n. scenery

  = **경치** [경치] gyeong-chi

☐ **박물관** [방물관] bang-mul-gwan n. museum

  여기에서 박물관까지 얼마나 멀어요?
  yeo-gi-e-seo bang-mul-gwan-gga-ji eol-ma-na meo-reo-yo?
  How far is the museum from here?

☐ **미술관** [미:술관] mi-sul-gwan n. gallery

  = **갤러리** [갤러리] gael-reo-ri

  ☐ **작품** [작품] jak-pum n. work

  미술관으로 가려면 어느 쪽으로 가야 해요?
  mi-sul-gwa-neu-ro ga-ryeo-myeon eo-neu jjo-geu-ro ga-ya hae-yo?
  Which way do I go to get to the gallery?

□ **전시회** [전ː시회/전ː시훼] jeon-si-hoe/jeon-si-hwe n. exhibition

□ **과학관** [과학꽌] gwa-hak-ggwan n. science museum

□ **영화관** [영화관] yeong-hwa-gwan n. movie theater, cinema

□ **극장** [극짱] geuk-jjang n. theater

□ **개관** [개관] gae-gwan n. opening

  □ **폐관** [폐ː관/페ː관] pye-gwan/pe-gwan n. closing

□ **광장** [광ː장] gwang-jang n. plaza, square

□ **공원** [공원] gong-won n. park

□ **동물원** [동ː무뤈] dong-mu-rwon n. zoo

□ **식물원** [싱무뤈] sing-mu-rwon n. botanical gardens

□ **놀이공원** [노리공원] no-ri-gong-won n. amusement park

  = **놀이동산** [노리동산] no-ri-dong-san

  = **유원지** [유원지] yu-won-ji

  놀이공원에 가는 거 좋아하세요?
  no-ri-gong-wo-ne ga-neun geo jo-a-ha-se-yo?
  Do you like going to amusement parks?

□ **유명하다** [유ː명하다] yu-myeong-ha-da a. famous

  □ **저명하다** [저ː명하다] jeo-myeong-ha-da a. celebrated

  □ **유명인** [유ː명인] yu-myeong-in n. celebrity

□ **장엄하다** [장엄하다] jang-eom-ha-da a. majestic

□ **인상적** [인상적] in-sang-jeok n./d. impressive

□ **역사적** [역싸적] yeok-ssa-jeok n./d. historical

□ **상업적** [상업쩍] sang-eop-jjeok n./d. commercial

□ **추천** [추천] chu-cheon n. recommendation

  □ **추천하다** [추천하다] chu-cheon-ha-da v. recommend

  근처에 가 볼만한 명소를 추천해 주실래요?

  geun-cheo-e ga bol-man-han myeong-so-reul chu-cheon-hae ju-sil-rae-yo?

  Can you recommend some interesting places around here?

□ **경로** [경노] gyeong-no n. route

□ **목적지** [목쩍찌] mok-jjeok-jji n. destination

  = **행선지** [행선지] haeng-seon-ji

□ **산** [산] san n. mountain

□ **언덕** [언덕] eon-deok n. hill

□ **계곡** [계곡/게곡] gye-gok/ge-gok n. valley

□ **바다** [바다] ba-da n. sea

  □ **해변** [해:변] hae-byeon n. beach

  = **바닷가** [바다까/바닫까] ba-da-gga/ba-dat-gga

□ **강** [강] gang n. river

  □ **시내** [시:내] si-nae n. stream

  □ **개울** [개울] gae-ul n. small stream

□ **호수** [호수] ho-su n. lake

  □ **연못** [연몯] yeon-mot n. pond

□ **유적** [유적] yu-jeok n. ruins

  □ **명승고적** [명승고적] myeong-seung-go-jeok

  n. scenic spots and places of historic interest

□ **문화재** [문화재] mun-hwa-jae n. cultural properties

□ **입장** [입짱] ip-jjang n. entrance

　□ **입장하다** [입짱하다] ip-jjang-ha-da v. enter

　= **들어가다** [드러가다] deu-reo-ga-da

　□ **입구** [입꾸] ip-ggu n. entrance, gateway

□ **입장료** [입짱뇨] ip-jjang-nyo n. entrance fee, admission fee

　□ **입장권** [입짱꿘] ip-jjang-ggwon n. admission ticket

　입장료가 얼마예요?
　ip-jjang-nyo-ga eol-ma-ye-yo?
　How much is the admission fee?

□ **퇴장** [퇴:장/퉤:장] toe-jang/twe-jang n. going out

　□ **퇴장하다** [퇴:장하다/퉤:장하다] toe-jang-ha-da/twe-jang-ha-da v. go out

　= **나가다** [나가다] na-ga-da

　□ **출구** [출구] chul-gu n. exit

　출구가 어디예요?
　chul-gu-ga eo-di-ye-yo?
　Where is the exit?

□ **도시** [도시] do-si n. city

□ **지방** [지방] ji-bang n. province

□ **마을** [마을] ma-eul n. town, village

□ **시골** [시골] si-gol n. countryside

□ **도로** [도:로] do-ro n. road, street

□ **길거리** [길꺼리] gil-ggeo-ri n. street

　= **거리** [거리] geo-ri ● ⟶ **tip.** '거리' has two meanings: street and distance.

☐ **대로** [대:로] dae-ro n. avenue

   = **큰길** [큰길] keun-gil

☐ **번화가** [번화가] beon-hwa-ga n. main street

☐ **지름길** [지름낄] ji-reum-ggil n. shortcut

☐ **가깝다** [가깝따] ga-ggap-dda a. near

☐ **멀다** [멀:다] meol-da a. far

   여기에서 멀어요?
   yeo-gi-e-seo meo-reo-yo?
   Is it far from here?

☐ **사진** [사진] sa-jin n. photograph, picture, photo

   저희 사진 좀 찍어 주실래요?
   jeo-hi sa-jin jom jji-geo ju-sil-rae-yo?
   Would you take a picture of us?

☐ **셀프 카메라** [셀프 카메라] sel-peu ka-me-ra selfie

   = **셀카** [셀카] sel-ka n.   **tip.** '셀카' is short for '셀프 카메라'.

    ☐ **셀카 봉** [셀카 봉] sel-ka bong selfie stick

☐ **선물** [선:물] seon-mul n. present, gift

☐ **기념품** [기념품] gi-nyeom-pum n. souvenir

   기념품 가게는 어디 있어요?
   gi-nyeom-pum ga-ge-neun eo-di i-sseo-yo?
   Where is the souvenir shop?

☐ **엽서** [엽써] yeop-sseo n. postcard

    ☐ **그림엽서** [그:림녑써] geu-rim-nyeop-sseo n. picture postcard

□ **열쇠고리** [열:쐬고리/열:쒜고리] yeol-ssoe-go-ri/yeol-sswe-go-ri n. key ring

□ **토산품** [토산품] to-san-pum n. local production

□ **특산품** [특싼품] teuk-ssan-pum n. specialty

□ **대사관** [대:사관] dae-sa-gwan n. embassy

□ **영사관** [영사관] yeong-sa-gwan n. consulate

Useful Conversation

\# 23. 여행

이준서   난 베트남으로 여행갈 거야.
nan be-teu-na-meu-ro yeo-haeng-gal geo-ya
I'm going to travel to Vietnam.

김미나   거기에서 뭐 할 건데?
geo-gi-e-seo mwo hal ggeon-de?
What will you do there?

이준서   그냥 쉬고 싶어, 많이 관광하지 않고.
geu-nyang swi-go si-peo, ma-ni gwan-gwang-ha-ji an-ko
I just want to relax, not do a lot of sightseeing.

김미나   그럼 다낭을 추천할게. 거기는 조용하고 아름답거든.
geu-reom da-nang-eul chu-cheon-hal-gge.
geo-gi-neun jo-yong-ha-go a-reum-dap-ggeo-deun
Then I recommend you Da Nang.
There is silent and beautiful.

Cases & Accidents 사건 & 사고 sa-ggeon & sa-go

□ **사건** [사:껀] sa-ggeon n. case

□ **사고** [사:고] sa-go n. accident

□ **경찰서** [경:찰써] gyeong-chal-sseo
n. police station

□ **증거** [증거] jeung-geo
n. evidence

□ **목격자** [목껵짜] mok-ggyeok-jja
n. witness

□ **알리다** [알리다] al-ri-da
= **보고하다** [보:고하다] bo-go-ha-da
v. report

□ **범죄인** [범:죄인/범:줴인]
beom-joe-in/beom-jwe-in
= **범인** [버:민] beo-min
n. criminal

□ **도둑** [도둑] do-duk n. thief

□ **도둑질** [도둑찔] do-duk-jjil
= **절도** [절또] jeol-ddo
n. stealing

□ **강도** [강:도] gang-do
n. robber, burglar

□ **소매치기** [소매치기] so-mae-chi-gi

　　n. pickpocket

□ **사기꾼** [사기꾼] sa-gi-ggun

　　n. swindler

□ **부상** [부:상] bu-sang

　= **상처** [상처] sang-cheo

　　n. injury, wound, cut

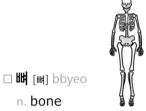

□ **뼈** [뼈] bbyeo

　　n. bone

□ **부러지다** [부러지다] bu-reo-ji-da

　　v. break

□ **화상** [화:상] hwa-sang n. burn, scald

□ **데다** [데:다] de-da v. get burnt

□ **동상** [동:상] dong-sang

　　n. frostbite

□ **피** [피] pi

　= **혈액** [혀랙] hyeo-raek

　　n. blood

□ **긴급** [긴급] gin-geup

　　n. urgency

□ **구조** [구:조] gu-jo

　　n. rescue

□ **구급상자** [구:급쌍자]

　　gu-geup-ssang-ja

　　n. first-aid kit

□ **구급차** [구:급차] gu-geup-cha

　= **앰뷸런스** [앰뷸런스]

　　aem-byul-reon-seu

　　n. ambulance

□ **심장마비** [심장마비]

　　sim-jang-ma-bi

　　heart attack

□ **심폐 소생술** [심폐 소생술/심폐 소생술]

　　sim-pye so-saeng-sul/

　　sim-pe so-saeng-sul CPR

□ **기절** [기절] gi-jeol

　= **실신** [실씬] sil-ssin

　　n. fainting

□ **치료하다** [치료하다] chi-ryo-ha-da

　= **낫다** [낟:따] nat-dda

　　v. cure

□ **회복하다** [회보카다/훼보카다]

　　hoe-bo-ka-da/hwe-bo-ka-da

　　v. recover

□ **교통사고** [교통사고]

gyo-tong-sa-go

n. traffic accident, car accident

□ **충돌** [충돌]

chung-dol

n. collision, crash

□ **견인차** [겨닌차]

gyeo-nin-cha

= **레커차** [레커차]

re-keo-cha

n. tow truck

□ **화재** [화:재] hwa-jae

= **불** [불] bul

n. fire

□ **폭발** [폭빨] pok-bbal

n. explosion

□ **소방차** [소방차]

so-bang-cha

n. fire truck

□ **소방서** [소방서]

so-bang-seo

n. fire station

□ **지진** [지진] ji-jin

n. earthquake

□ **눈사태** [눈:사태]

nun-sa-tae

n. avalanche

□ **산사태** [산사태]

san-sa-tae

n. landslide

□ **해일** [해:일] hae-il

n. tsunami

□ **홍수** [홍수] hong-su

n. flood

□ **사건** [사:껀] sa-ggeon n. case

□ **사고** [사:고] sa-go n. accident

□ **경찰** [경:찰] gyeong-chal n. police officer

　= **경찰관** [경:찰관] gyeong-chal-gwan

　　□ **경찰서** [경:찰써] gyeong-chal-sseo n. police station

　　경찰을 부르겠어요.
　　gyeong-cha-reul bu-reu-get-sseo-yo
　　I'll call the police.

□ **진술** [진:술] jin-sul n. statement

　　□ **진술하다** [진:술하다] jin-sul-ha-da v. state

□ **증언** [증언] jeung-eon n. testimony

□ **증거** [증거] jeung-geo n. evidence

□ **증인** [증인] jeung-in n. witness

　　□ **목격자** [목껵짜] mok-ggyeok-jja n. witness

□ **알리다** [알리다] al-ri-da v. report

　= **보고하다** [보:고하다] bo-go-ha-da

□ **신고하다** [신고하다] sin-go-ha-da v. declare

□ **통지하다** [통지하다] tong-ji-ha-da v. notice

□ **죄** [죄:/줴] joe/jwe n. crime

　　□ **유죄** [유:죄/유:줴] yu-joe/yu-jwe n. guilt

　　□ **무죄** [무죄/무줴] mu-joe/mu-jwe n. innocence

□ **범죄** [범:죄/범:줴] beom-joe/beom-jwe n. offense, crime

□ **죄책감** [죄:책깜/줴:책깜] joe-chaek-ggam/jwe-chaek-ggam

　n. sense of guilt

□ **책망** [챙망] chaeng-mang n. reproach

□ **가책** [가:책] ga-chaek n. scolding, blame

　□ **양심** [양심] yang-sim n. conscience, scruple

□ **범죄인** [범:죄인/범:줴인] beom-joe-in/beom-jwe-in n. criminal

　= **범인** [버:민] beo-min

　그가 범인이에요.
　geu-ga beo-mi-ni-e-yo
　He is a criminal.

□ **용의자** [용의자/용이자] yong-ui-ja/yong-i-ja n. suspect

□ **피의자** [피:의자/피:이자] pi-ui-ja/pi-i-ja n. accused

□ **가해자** [가해자] ga-hae-ja n. assailant

□ **피해자** [피:해자] pi-hae-ja n. victim

□ **도둑** [도둑] do-duk n. thief

□ **강도** [강:도] gang-do n. robber, burglar

　□ **노상강도** [노:상강도] no-sang-gang-do n. mugger

　어젯밤에 우리 집에 도둑이 들었어요.
　eo-jet-bba-me u-ri ji-be do-du-gi deu-reo-sseo-yo
　A thief broke into my house last night.

□ **도둑질** [도둑찔] do-duk-jjil n. stealing

　= **절도** [절또] jeol-ddo

□ **도난** [도난] do-nan n. robbery

□ **훔치다** [훔치다] hum-chi-da v. steal, rob

= **도둑질하다** [도둑찔하다] do-duk-jjil-ha-da

그가 내 지갑을 훔쳤어요.
geu-ga nae ji-ga-beul hum-cheo-sseo-yo
He stole my purse.

□ **소매치기** [소매치기] so-mae-chi-gi n. pickpocket

소매치기 주의하세요!
so-mae-chi-gi ju-i-ha-se-yo!
Beware of pickpockets!

□ **사기** [사기] sa-gi n. fraud, swindle

□ **사기꾼** [사기꾼] sa-gi-ggun n. swindler

□ **속이다** [소기다] so-gi-da v. trick, cheat

□ **살인** [사린] sa-rin n. murder

= **살해** [살해] sal-hae

□ **살인범** [사린범] sa-rin-beom n. murderer

= **살해범** [살해범] sal-hae-beom

□ **행방불명** [행방불명] haeng-bang-bul-myeong n. missing

□ **실종** [실쫑] sil-jjong n. disappearance

딸이 행방불명됐어요.
dda-ri haeng-bang-bul-myeong-dwae-sseo-yo
My daughter is missing.

□ **부상** [부:상] bu-sang n. injury, wound, cut

= **상처** [상처] sang-cheo

□ **타박상** [타:박쌍] ta-bak-ssang n. contusion

□ **찰과상** [찰과상] chal-gwa-sang n. abrasion

□ **멍** [멍] meong n. bruise, black-and-blue mark

　□ **피멍** [피멍] pi-meong n. bruise

□ **흉터** [흉터] hyung-teo n. scar

　= **흉** [흉] hyung

□ **다치다** [다치다] da-chi-da v. hurt

　　tip. You can also say '부상을 당하다 [부:상을 당하다 bu-sang-eul dang-ha-da]',
　　'상처를 입다 [상처를 입따 sang-cheo-reul ip-dda]' for hurt.

□ **아프다** [아프다] a-peu-da a. painful

　= **고통스럽다** [고통스럽따] go-tong-seu-reop-dda

　= **괴롭다** [괴롭따/궤롭따] goe-rop-dda/gwe-rop-dda

□ **따갑다** [따갑따] dda-gap-dda a. sore

□ **쑤시다** [쑤시다] ssu-si-da v. ache

　□ **욱신거리다** [욱씬거리다] uk-ssin-geo-ri-da v. throb, sore

□ **뻐근하다** [뻐근하다] bbeo-geun-ha-da a. stiff

□ **뼈** [뼈] bbyeo n. bone

□ **부러지다** [부러지다] bu-reo-ji-da v. break

　지난 여름에 다리가 부러졌어요.
　ji-nan yeo-reu-me da-ri-ga bu-reo-jeo-sseo-yo
　I broke my leg last summer.

□ **골절** [골쩔] gol-jjeol n. breaking a bone

□ **삐다** [삐:다] bbi-da v. sprain, wrench

　= **접질리다** [접찔리다] jeop-jjil-ri-da

□ **붓다** [붇:따] but-dda v. swell, become swollen

□ **화상** [화:상] hwa-sang n. burn, scald

   □ **데다** [데:다] de-da v. get burnt

□ **동상** [동:상] dong-sang n. frostbite

□ **베다** [베:다] be-da v. cut

   □ **베이다** [베이다] be-i-da v. be cut

□ **피** [피] pi n. blood

  = **혈액** [혀랙] hyeo-raek

□ **출혈** [출혈] chul-hyeol n. bleeding

   출혈이 멎도록 여기를 꼭 누르세요.
   chul-hyeo-ri meot-ddo-rok yeo-gi-reul ggok nu-reu-se-yo
   Press firmly here to stop the bleeding.

□ **지혈** [지혈] ji-hyeol n. hemostasis

□ **고통** [고통] go-tong n. pain, agony

  = **통증** [통:쯩] tong-jjeung

□ **두통** [두통] du-tong n. headache

□ **치통** [치통] chi-tong n. toothache

□ **의식불명** [의:식불명] ui-sik-bul-myeong unconsciousness

□ **목발** [목빨] mok-bbal n. crutch

□ **붕대** [붕대] bung-dae n. bandage

□ **깁스** [깁쓰] gip-sseu n. plaster cast

  = **석고붕대** [석꼬붕대] seok-ggo-bung-dae

□ **침착** [침착] chim-chak n. composure

　□ **침착하다** [침차카다] chim-cha-ka-da a. calm, composed

　= **차분하다** [차분하다] cha-bun-ha-da

□ **긴급** [긴급] gin-geup n. urgency

　□ **긴급하다** [긴그파다] gin-geu-pa-da a. urgent

□ **응급** [응:급] eung-geup n. emergency

　이것은 응급 상황이에요.
　i-geo-seun eung-geup sang-hwang-i-e-yo
　This is an emergency.

□ **구조** [구:조] gu-jo n. rescue

□ **응급처치** [응:급처:치] eung-geup-cheo-chi first aid

　= **응급치료** [응:급치료] eung-geup-chi-ryo

□ **구급상자** [구:급쌍자] gu-geup-ssang-ja n. first-aid kit

□ **구급차** [구:급차] gu-geup-cha n. ambulance

　= **앰뷸런스** [앰뷸런스] aem-byul-reon-seu

　구급차 좀 보내 주시겠어요?
　gu-geup-cha jom bo-nae ju-si-ge-sseo-yo?
　Could you send an ambulance?

□ **응급실** [응:급씰] eung-geup-ssil n. emergency room

　응급실이 어디예요?
　eung-geup-ssi-ri eo-di-ye-yo?
　Where's the emergency room, please?

□ **뇌졸중** [뇌졸쯩/눼졸쯩] noe-jol-jjung/nwe-jol-jjung n. stroke

　= **뇌중풍** [뇌중풍/눼중풍] noe-jung-pung/nwe-jung-pung

□ 간질 [간:질] gan-jil n. epilepsy

= 뇌전증 [뇌전쯩/눼전쯩] noe-jeon-jjeung/nwe-jeon-jjeung

□ 경련 [경년] gyeong-nyeon n. spasm

□ 경기 [경끼] gyeong-ggi n. convulsion

= 경풍 [경풍] gyeong-pung

□ 심장마비 [심장마비] sim-jang-ma-bi heart attack

□ 심폐 소생술 [심폐 소생술/심페 소생술] sim-pye so-saeng-sul/

sim-pe so-saeng-sul CPR (cardiopulmonary resuscitation)

□ 인공호흡 [인공호흡] in-gong-ho-heup n. artificial respiration

□ 질식 [질씩] jil-ssik n. asphyxiation

□ 기절 [기절] gi-jeol n. fainting

= 실신 [실씬] sil-ssin

□ 치료 [치료] chi-ryo n. treatment

□ 치료하다 [치료하다] chi-ryo-ha-da v. cure

= 낫다 [낟:따] nat-dda

□ 회복 [회복/휄복] hoe-bok/hwe-bok n. recovery

□ 회복하다 [회보카다/훼보카다] hoe-bo-ka-da/hwe-bo-ka-da v. recover

□ 분실 [분실] bun-sil n. loss

□ 분실물 [분실물] bun-sil-mul n. missing article

□ 분실물 취급소 [분실물 취:급쏘] bun-sil-mul chwi-geup-sso

Lost and Found

분실물 취급소에 확인해 보세요.
bun-sil-mul chwi-geup-sso-e hwa-gin-hae bo-se-yo
You should check the Lost and Found office.

□ **미아** [미아] mi-a n. missing child

□ **교통사고** [교통사고] gyo-tong-sa-go n. traffic accident, car accident

그 교통사고는 언제 일어난 거죠?
geu gyo-tong-sa-go-neun eon-je i-reo-nan geo-jyo?
When did the traffic accident happen?

□ **충돌** [충돌] chung-dol n. collision, crash

□ **충돌하다** [충돌하다] chung-dol-ha-da v. clash, bump

□ **정면충돌** [정:면충돌] jeong-myeon-chung-dol n. head-on collision

정면충돌이었어요.
jeong-myeon-chung-do-ri-eo-sseo-yo
It was a head-on collision.

□ **추돌** [추돌] chu-dol n. rear-end

□ **추돌하다** [추돌하다] chu-dol-ha-da v. rear-end

□ **견인차** [겨닌차] gyeo-nin-cha n. tow truck

= **레커차** [레커차] re-keo-cha

□ **도망** [도망] do-mang n. escape

= **도주** [도주] do-ju

□ **뺑소니** [뺑소니] bbaeng-so-ni n. hit-and-run

□ **미끄러지다** [미끄러지다] mi-ggeu-reo-ji-da v. slide, slip

계단에서 미끄러졌어요.
gye-da-ne-seo mi-ggeu-reo-jeo-sseo-yo
I slipped on the stairs.

□ **빙판** [빙판] bing-pan n. icy road, slippery road

□ **익사** [익싸] ik-ssa n. drowning

　□ **익사하다** [익싸하다] ik-ssa-ha-da v. drown

　　그는 수영 중에 익사할 뻔했어요.
　　geu-neun su-yeong jung-e ik-ssa-hal bbeon-hae-sseo-yo
　　He nearly drowned while swimming.

□ **안전 요원** [안전 요원] an-jeon yo-won lifeguard

□ **화재** [화:재] hwa-jae n. fire

　= **불** [불] bul

　　지난밤에 화재가 났어요.
　　ji-nan-ba-me hwa-jae-ga na-sseo-yo
　　A fire broke out last night.

□ **폭발** [폭빨] pok-bbal n. explosion

□ **소방관** [소방관] so-bang-gwan n. firefighter

□ **소방차** [소방차] so-bang-cha n. fire truck

　□ **소방서** [소방서] so-bang-seo n. fire station

□ **재난** [재난] jae-nan n. calamity

□ **천재지변** [천재지변] cheon-jae-ji-byeon n. disaster

□ **자연재해** [자연재해] ja-yeon-jae-hae n. natural disaster

□ **지진** [지진] ji-jin n. earthquake

□ **눈사태** [눈:사태] nun-sa-tae n. avalanche

□ **산사태** [산사태] san-sa-tae n. landslide

□ **해일** [해:일] hae-il n. tsunami **tip.** You can also call '쓰나미 [sseu-na-mi]' for '해일'.

□ **화산** [화:산] hwa-san n. volcano

□ **가뭄** [가뭄] ga-mum n. drought

□ **홍수** [홍수] hong-su n. flood

□ **대피소** [대:피소] dae-pi-so n. evacuation shelter

24. 미아 신고

Useful Conversation

문영주   도와주세요. 제 아들이 없어졌어요!
do-wa-ju-se-yo. je a-deu-ri eop-sseo-jeo-sseo-yo!
Please help me. My son is missing!

경찰   아드님에 대해 묘사해 주시겠어요?
a-deu-ni-me dae-hae myo-sa-hae ju-si-ge-sseo-yo?
Could you describe your son to me?

문영주   7살이고, 갈색 머리예요. 빨간 재킷을 입고 있어요.
il-gop-ssa-ri-go, gal-ssaek meo-ri-ye-yo.
bbal-gan jae-ki-seul ip-ggo i-sseo-yo
He's 7 years old and has brown hair.
He was wearing a red jacket.

경찰   걱정 마세요, 아주머니. 저희가 찾아드릴게요.
geok-jjeong ma-se-yo, a-ju-meo-ni.
jeo-hi-ga cha-ja-deu-ril-ge-yo
Don't worry ma'am. We will find him.

Exercise

Read and Match.

1. 관광 •   • accident

2. 교통 •   • accommodation

3. 구급차 •   • ambulance

4. 비행기 •   • car

5. 사건 •   • case

6. 사고 •   • driving

7. 숙소 •   • hotel

8. 여행 •   • plane, airplane

9. 예약 •   • reservation, booking

10. 운전 •   • sightseeing

11. 자동차 •   • transportation

12. 호텔 •   • trip, tour, journey

1. 관광 – sightseeing 2. 교통 – transportation 3. 구급차 – ambulance
4. 비행기 – plane, airplane 5. 사건 – case 6. 사고 – accident
7. 숙소 – accommodation 8. 여행 – trip, tour, journey
9. 예약 – reservation, booking 10. 운전 – driving 11. 자동차 – car 12. 호텔 – hotel

7장

The Others

Numbers 숫자 su-jja/sut-jja

■ **숫자** [수:짜/숟:짜] su-jja/sut-jja n. **numbers**
= **수** [수:] su

□ **소수** [소:수] so-su
 n. decimal number

 3.14 sam-jjeom-il-sa

□ **분수** [분쑤/분수] bun-ssu/bun-su
 n. fractional number, fraction

 $\frac{3}{4}$ sa-bu-ne-sam

■ **기수** [기수] gi-su n. **simple number**

□ **영** [영] yeong n. 0, zero
 = **공** [공] gong
 = **제로** [제로] je-ro

□ **일** [일] il num./d. 1, one
 = **하나** [하나] ha-na num./n.
 □ **한** [한] han d. one (thing)

□ **이** [이:] i num./d. 2, two
 = **둘** [둘:] dul num.
 □ **두** [두:] du d. two (things)

□ **삼** [삼] sam num./d. 3, three
 = **셋** [섿:] set num.
 □ **세** [세:] se d. three (things)

□ **사** [사:] sa num./d. 4, four
 = **넷** [넫:] net num.
 □ **네** [네:] ne d. four (things)

 tip. '한', '두', '세' and '네' is used with
 some measurement words.

□ **오** [오:] o num./d. 5, five
 = **다섯** [다섣] da-seot num.

□ **육** [육] yuk num./d. 6, six
 = **여섯** [여섣] yeo-seot num.

□ **칠** [칠] chil num./d. 7, seven
 = **일곱** [일곱] il-gop num.

□ **팔** [팔] pal num./d. 8, eight
 = **여덟** [여덜] yeo-deol num.

□ **구** [구] gu num./d. 9, nine
 = **아홉** [아홉] a-hop num.

□ **십** [십] sip num./d. 10, ten
 = **열** [열:] yeol num.

□ **이십** [이:십] i-sip num./d. 20, twenty

  = **스물** [스물] seu-mul num.

□ **삼십** [삼십] sam-sip num./d. 30, thirty

  = **서른** [서른] seo-reun num./d.

□ **사십** [사:십] sa-sip num./d. 40, forty

  = **마흔** [마흔] ma-heun num./d.

□ **오십** [오:십] o-sip num./d. 50, fifty

  = **쉰** [쉰:] swin num./d.

□ **육십** [육씹] yuk-ssip num./d. 60, sixty

  = **예순** [예순] ye-sun num./d.

□ **칠십** [칠씹] chil-ssip num./d. 70, seventy

  = **일흔** [일흔] il-heun num./d.

□ **팔십** [팔씹] pal-ssip num./d. 80, eighty

  = **여든** [여든] yeo-deun num./d.

□ **구십** [구십] gu-sip num./d. 90, ninety

  = **아흔** [아흔] a-heun num./d.

□ **백** [백] baek num./d. 100, one hundred

□ **천** [천] cheon num./d. 1,000, one thousand

□ **만** [만:] man num./d. 10,000, ten thousand

□ **십만** [심만] sim-man num./d. 100,000, one hundred thousand

□ **백만** [뱅만] baeng-man num./d. 1,000,000, one million

□ **천만** [천만] cheon-man num./d. 10,000,000, ten million

□ **억** [억] eok num./d. 100,000,000, one hundred million

tip. '천만' is used as a noun, it means a lot.

- **서수** [서:수] seo-su *n.* ordinal number

□ **첫째** [첟째] cheot-jjae *num./d./n.* first

□ **둘째** [둘:째] dul-jjae *num./d./n.* second

□ **셋째** [섿:째] set-jjae *num./d./n.* third

□ **넷째** [녇:째] net-jjae *num./d./n.* fourth

□ **다섯째** [다섣째] da-seot-jjae *num./d./n.* fifth

□ **여섯째** [여섣째] yeo-seot-jjae *num./d./n.* sixth

□ **일곱째** [일곱째] il-gop-jjae *num./d./n.* seventh

□ **여덟째** [여덜째] yeo-deol-jjae *num./d./n.* eighth

□ **아홉째** [아홉째] a-hop-jjae *num./d./n.* ninth

□ **열째** [열:째] yeol-jjae *num./d./n.* tenth

□ **스무째** [스무째] seu-mu-jjae *num./d./n.* twentieth

= **스물째** [스물째] seu-mul-jjae

1,234

(일)천 이백 삼십 사
(il-)cheon i-baek sam-sip sa
one thousand two hundred thirty-four

12,345

(일)만 이천 삼백 사십 오
(il-)man i-cheon sam-baek sa-sip o
twelve thousand three hundred forty-five

Korean Won 한국 돈 han-guk don

■ **동전** [동전] dong-jeon

n. coin

tip. Depending on inflation, '일 원' and '오 원' may not be used much in daily life. Thesedays, even '십 원' coins are rarely used either.

□ **일 원** [일 원]
il won **a won,**
one coin

□ **오 원** [오: 원]
o won
five won

□ **십 원** [십 원]
sip won
ten won

□ **오십 원** [오:십 원]
o-sip won
fifty won

□ **백 원** [백 원] baek won
one hundred won

□ **오백 원** [오:백 원] o-baek won
five hundred won

■ **지폐** [지폐/지페] ji-pye/ji-pe n. **bill, note**

□ **천 원** [천 원] cheon won
one thousand won

□ **오천 원** [오:천 원] o-cheon won
five thousand won

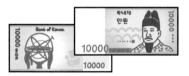

□ **만 원** [만: 원] man won
ten thousand won

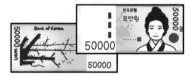

□ **오만 원** [오:만 원] o-man won
fifty thousand won

■ **수표** [수표] su-pyo n. **check, cheque**

tip. In Korea, people tend to use checks when spending more than a hundred thousand won.

Shapes 모양 mo-yang

■ **모양** [모양] mo-yang
= **꼴** [꼴] ggol
n. shape

□ **점** [점] jeom
n. point

□ **선** [선] seon
= **라인** [라인] ra-in
n. line

□ **직선** [직썬] jik-sseon
n. straight line

□ **곡선** [곡썬] gok-sseon
n. curved line

□ **사선** [사선] sa-seon
n. oblique line

□ **면** [면:] myeon
n. surface

□ **평면** [평면] pyeong-myeon
n. flat surface, plane

□ **원** [원] won
n. circle

□ **원형** [원형] won-hyeong
n. circle shape

□ **둥글다** [둥글다]
dung-geul-da
a. round
v. become round

□ **다각형** [다가켱]
da-ga-kyeong
n. polygon

□ **세모** [세:모] se-mo
= **삼각** [삼각] sam-gak
= **삼각형** [삼가켱] sam-ga-kyeong
n. triangle (shape)

□ **네모** [네:모] ne-mo
= **사각** [사:각] sa-gak
= **사각형** [사:가켱]
sa-ga-kyeong
n. quadrilateral (shape)

□ **정사각형** [정:사가켱]
jeong-sa-ga-kyeong
n. square shape

□ **직사각형** [직싸가켱]
jik-ssa-ga-kyeong
n. rectangle shape

■ **입체** [입체]
ip-che
n. solid

□ **구체(球體)** [구체]
gu-che
n. globe

□ **원뿔** [원뿔]
won-bbul
n. cone

□ **편평하다** [편평하다]
pyeon-pyeong-ha-da
a. flat

□ **수평** [수평]
su-pyeong
a. horizontal

□ **수직** [수직]
su-jik
a. perpendicular

□ **뾰족하다** [뾰조카다]
bbyo-jo-ka-da
a. pointed

□ **화살표** [화살표]
hwa-sal-pyo
n. arrow

□ **하트** [하트]
ha-teu
heart shape

Color 색깔 saek-ggal

■ **색깔** [색깔] saek-ggal
  = **색** [색] saek
  n. color, colour

□ **흰색** [흰색] hin-saek
  = **백색** [백쌕] baek-sseak
  = **하얀색** [하얀색] ha-yan-saek
  = **하양** [하양] ha-yang
  n. white •————————→

□ **검은색** [거믄색] geo-meun-saek
  = **흑색** [흑쌕] heuk-ssaek
  = **검정** [검정] geom-jeong
  n. black

tip. Add '새' to a color to express 'very'. For example, '하얀색' plus '새', is '새하얗다', which means very white. However, this only works for certain colors.

□ **회색** [회색/훼색]
  hoe-saek/hwe-saek
  n. gray

□ **빨간색** [빨간색] bbal-gan-saek
  = **홍색** [홍색] hong-saek
  = **붉은색** [불근색] bul-geun-saek
  = **빨강** [빨강] bbal-gang
  n. red

□ **주황색** [주황색] ju-hwang-saek
  = **주황** [주황] ju-hwang
  n. orange

□ **노란색** [노란색] no-ran-saek
  = **노랑** [노랑] no-rang
  n. yellow

□ **연두색** [연:두색] yeon-du-saek
  = **연두** [연:두] yeon-du
  n. yellowish green

□ **초록색** [초록쌕] cho-rok-ssaek
  = **녹색** [녹쌕] nok-ssaek
  = **초록** [초록] cho-rok
  n. green

□ **하늘색** [하늘쌕]
  ha-neul-ssaek
  n. sky blue

□ **파란색** [파란색] pa-ran-saek
  = **청색** [청색] cheong-saek
  = **파랑** [파랑] pa-rang
  n. blue

□ **남색** [남색] nam-saek
  n. indigo

tip. '푸른색 [pu-reun-saek]'
means blue color like sky
or green color like grass.

□ **보라색** [보라색] bo-ra-saek
  = **보라** [보라] bo-ra
  n. violet

□ **연보라색** [연:보라색] yeon-bo-ra-saek
  = **연보라** [연:보라] yeon-bo-ra
  n. lavender, light purple

□ **자주색** [자:주색] ja-ju-saek
  = **자색** [자:색] ja-saek
  = **자주** [자:주] ja-ju
  n. purple

□ **분홍색** [분:홍색] bun-hong-saek
  = **분홍** [분:홍] bun-hong
  = **핑크** [핑크] ping-keu
  n. pink

□ **갈색** [갈쌕] gal-ssaek

　n. brown

□ **카키색** [카키색] ka-ki-saek

　= **국방색** [국빵색] guk-bbang-saek

　n. khaki

□ **금색** [금색] geum-saek

　n. gold

□ **은색** [은색] eun-saek

　n. silver

□ **짙다** [짇따] jit-dda

　= **진하다** [진하다] jin-ha-da

　a. dark, rich, deep

□ **옅다** [엳따] yeot-dda

　= **연하다** [연:하다] yeon-ha-da

　a. light, pale

□ **다색** [다색] da-saek

　n. multicolored

□ **단색** [단색] dan-saek

　n. monochrome

Position 위치 wi-chi

□ **위** [위] wi

n. top

□ **앞** [압] ap

n. front

□ **뒤** [뒤:] dwi

n. back

□ **아래** [아래] a-rae

n. bottom

□ **안** [안] an

n. inside

□ **밖** [박] bak

= **바깥** [바깥] ba-ggat

n. outside

□ **옆** [엽] yeop

n. side

□ **왼쪽** [왼:쪽/웬:쪽] oen-jjok/wen-jjok

= **좌측** [좌:측] jwa-cheuk

n. left-side

□ **오른쪽** [오른쪽] o-reun-jjok

= **바른편** [바른편] ba-reun-pyeon

= **우측** [우:측] u-cheuk

n. right-side

□ **양쪽** [양:쪽] yang-jjok

n. both sides

□ **사이** [사이] sa-i

n. gap

□ **가운데** [가운데] ga-un-de

= **중간** [중간] jung-gan

= **중앙** [중앙] jung-ang

n. middle

□ **〜(으)로** [(으)로] (eu-)ro

p. to

tip. A word with a final consonant combines with '으로',
while a word without a final consonant combines with '로'.

□ **향하다** [향:하다] hyang-ha-da

v. head toward

Directions 방위 bang-wi

□ **북쪽** [북쫙] buk-jjok

= **북** [북] buk

n. north

□ **북서쪽** [북써쪽] buk-sseo-jjok

= **북서** [북써] buk-sseo

n. northwest

□ **북동쪽** [북똥쪽] buk-ddong-jjok

= **북동** [북똥] buk-ddong

n. northeast

□ **서쪽** [서쪽] seo-jjok

= **서** [서] seo

n. west

□ **동쪽** [동쪽] dong-jjok

= **동** [동] dong

n. east

□ **남서쪽** [남서쪽] nam-seo-jjok

= **남서** [남서] nam-seo

n. southwest

□ **남동쪽** [남동쪽] nam-dong-jjok

= **남동** [남동] nam-dong

n. southeast

□ **남쪽** [남쪽] nam-jjok

= **남** [남] nam

n. south

□ **동서남북** [동서남북] dong-seo-nam-buk n. north, west, south and east

□ **동서** [동서] dong-seo n. east and west

□ **남북** [남북] nam-buk n. north and south

> **tip.** The order of '동서남북' is different from that of English.

① 유럽 [유럽] yu-reop n. Europe

② 아시아 [아시아] a-si-a n. Asia

③ 중동 [중동] jung-dong n. the Middle East

④ 아프리카 [아프리카] a-peu-ri-ka n. Africa

⑤ 오세아니아 [오세아니아] o-se-a-ni-a n. Oceania

⑥ 북아메리카 [부가메리카] bu-ga-me-ri-ka n. North America

⑦ 중앙아메리카 [중앙아메리카] jung-ang-a-me-ri-ka n. Central America

⑧ 남아메리카 [나마메리카] na-ma-me-ri-ka n. South America

⑨ 북극 [북끅] buk-ggeuk n. North Pole

⑩ 남극 [남극] nam-geuk n. South Pole

④ 북극해

⑥ 지중해

① 태평양

③ 대서양

② 인도양

⑤ 남극해

① **태평양** [태평냥] tae-pyeong-nyang n. Pacific Ocean

② **인도양** [인도양] in-do-yang n. Indian Ocean

③ **대서양** [대:서양] dae-seo-yang n. Atlantic Ocean

④ **북극해** [북끄캐] buk-ggeu-kae n. Arctic Ocean

⑤ **남극해** [남그캐] nam-geu-kae n. Antarctic Ocean

⑥ **지중해** [지중해] ji-jung-hae n. Mediterranean Sea

Nations 국가 guk-gga

■ **아시아** [아시아] a-si-a n. Asia

■ **동북아시아** [동부가시아] dong-bu-ga-si-a n. Northeast Asia

= **동북아** [동부가] dong-bu-ga

□ **대한민국** [대:한민국] dae-han-min-guk n. Korea, Republic of Korea

= **한국** [한:국] han-guk

□ **남한** [남한] nam-han n. South Korea

□ **한국 사람** [한:국 사:람] han-guk sa-ram South Korean

> **tip.** A nation's name add '사람' or '인', it means that nation's people.
> For example, '한국' add '사람', '한국 사람' means Korean (people).
> '한국인' is same.

> **tip.** '한국' is short for '대한민국'. '남한' also means Korea.

□ **북한** [부칸] bu-kan n. North Korea

□ **북한 사람** [부칸 사:람] bu-kan sa-ram North Korean

□ **일본** [일본] il-bon n. Japan

□ **일본 사람** [일본 사:람] il-bon sa-ram Japanese

□ **중국** [중국] jung-guk n. China

□ **중국 사람** [중국 사:람] jung-guk sa-ram Chinese

□ **대만** [대만] dae-man n. Taiwan

= **타이완** [타이완] ta-i-wan

□ **대만 사람** [대만 사:람] dae-man sa-ram Taiwanese

= **타이완 사람** [타이완 사:람] ta-i-wan sa-ram

■ **동남아시아** [동나마시아] dong-na-ma-si-a n. Southeast Asia

= **동남아** [동나마] dong-na-ma

□ **말레이시아** [말레이시아] mal-re-i-si-a n. Malaysia

□ **말레이시아 사람** [말레이시아 사:람] mal-re-i-si-a sa-ram Malaysian

□ **베트남** [베트남] be-teu-nam n. Vietnam

□ **베트남 사람** [베트남 사:람] be-teu-nam sa-ram Vietnamese

□ **싱가포르** [싱가포르] sing-ga-po-reu n. Singapore

□ **싱가포르 사람** [싱가포르 사:람] sing-ga-po-reu sa-ram Singaporean

□ **인도네시아** [인도네시아] in-do-ne-si-a n. Indonesia

□ **인도네시아 사람** [인도네시아 사:람] in-do-ne-si-a sa-ram Indonesian

□ **태국** [태국] tae-guk n. Thailand

= **타이** [타이] ta-i

□ **태국 사람** [태국 사:람] tae-guk sa-ram Thai

= **타이 사람** [타이 사:람] ta-i sa-ram

□ **필리핀** [필리핀] pil-ri-pin n. the Philippines

□ **필리핀 사람** [필리핀 사:람] pil-ri-pin sa-ram Filipino

■ **남아시아** [나마시아] na-ma-si-a n. Southern Asia, South Asia

□ **네팔** [네팔] ne-pal n. Nepal

□ **네팔 사람** [네팔 사:람] ne-pal sa-ram Nepalese

□ **스리랑카** [스리랑카] seu-ri-rang-ka n. Sri Lanka

□ **스리랑카 사람** [스리랑카 사:람] seu-ri-rang-ka sa-ram Sri Lankan

□ 인도 [인도] in-do n. India

  □ 인도 사람 [인도 사:람] in-do sa-ram Indian

□ 파키스탄 [파키스탄] pa-ki-seu-tan n. Pakistan

  □ 파키스탄 사람 [파키스탄 사:람] pa-ki-seu-tan sa-ram Pakistani

■ 중동 [중동] jung-dong n. the Middle East

□ 사우디아라비아 [사우디아라비아] sa-u-di-a-ra-bi-a n. Saudi Arabia

  □ 사우디아라비아 사람 [사우디아라비아 사:람] sa-u-di-a-ra-bi-a sa-ram
  Saudi Arabian

□ 시리아 [시리아] si-ri-a n. Syria

  □ 시리아 사람 [시리아 사:람] si-ri-a sa-ram Syrian

□ 아랍에미리트 [아랍에미리트] a-rap-e-mi-ri-teu

  n. the United Arab Emirates

  □ 아랍에미리트 사람 [아랍에미리트 사:람] a-rap-e-mi-ri-teu sa-ram
  Emirati

□ 이라크 [이라크] i-ra-keu n. Iraq

  □ 이라크 사람 [이라크 사:람] i-ra-keu sa-ram Iraqi

□ 이란 [이란] i-ran n. Iran

  □ 이란 사람 [이란 사:람] i-ran sa-ram Iranian

□ 쿠웨이트 [쿠웨이트] ku-we-i-teu n. Kuwait

  □ 쿠웨이트 사람 [쿠웨이트 사:람] ku-we-i-teu sa-ram Kuwaiti

■ **아메리카** [아메리카] a-me-ri-ka n. America(North, South and Central America)

■ **북아메리카** [부가메리카] bu-ga-me-ri-ka n. North America
= **북미** [붕미] bung-mi

□ **미국** [미국] mi-guk n. America, United States of America(USA)
　□ **미국 사람** [미국 사:람] mi-guk sa-ram American

□ **캐나다** [캐나다] kae-na-da n. Canada
　□ **캐나다 사람** [캐나다 사:람] kae-na-da sa-ram Canadian

■ **중앙아메리카** [중앙아메리카] jung-ang-a-me-ri-ka n. Central America
= **중미** [중미] jung-mi

□ **과테말라** [과테말라] gwa-te-mal-ra n. Guatemala
　□ **과테말라 사람** [과테말라 사:람] gwa-te-mal-ra sa-ram Guatemalan

□ **도미니카공화국** [도미니카공화국] do-mi-ni-ka-gong-hwa-guk
n. Dominican Republic
　□ **도미니카 사람** [도미니카 사:람] do-mi-ni-ka sa-ram Dominican

□ **멕시코** [멕씨코] mek-ssi-ko n. Mexico
　□ **멕시코 사람** [멕씨코 사:람] mek-ssi-ko sa-ram Mexican

□ **쿠바** [쿠바] ku-ba n. Cuba
　□ **쿠바 사람** [쿠바 사:람] ku-ba sa-ram Cuban

■ **남아메리카** [나마메리카] na-ma-me-ri-ka n. South America
= **남미** [남미] nam-mi

□ **브라질** [브라질] beu-ra-jil n. Brazil

   □ **브라질 사람** [브라질 사:람] beu-ra-jil sa-ram Brazilian

□ **아르헨티나** [아르헨티나] a-reu-hen-ti-na n. Argentina

   □ **아르헨티나 사람** [아르헨티나 사:람] a-reu-hen-ti-na sa-ram Argentine

□ **에콰도르** [에콰도르] e-kwa-do-reu n. Ecuador

   □ **에콰도르 사람** [에콰도르 사:람] e-kwa-do-reu sa-ram Ecuadorian

□ **우루과이** [우루과이] u-ru-gwa-i n. Uruguay

   □ **우루과이 사람** [우루과이 사:람] u-ru-gwa-i sa-ram Uruguayan

□ **칠레** [칠레] chil-re n. Chile

   □ **칠레 사람** [칠레 사:람] chil-re sa-ram Chilean

□ **콜롬비아** [콜롬비아] kol-rom-bi-a n. Colombia

   □ **콜롬비아 사람** [콜롬비아 사:람] kol-rom-bi-a sa-ram Colombian

□ **페루** [페루] pe-ru n. Peru

   □ **페루 사람** [페루 사:람] pe-ru sa-ram Peruvian

■ **유럽** [유럽] yu-reop n. Europe

□ **그리스** [그리스] geu-ri-seu n. Greece

   □ **그리스 사람** [그리스 사:람] geu-ri-seu sa-ram Greek

□ **네덜란드** [네덜란드] ne-deol-ran-deu n. the Netherlands

   □ **네덜란드 사람** [네덜란드 사:람] ne-deol-ran-deu sa-ram
Dutchman/Dutchwoman

☐ **노르웨이** [노르웨이] no-reu-we-i n. Norway

   ☐ **노르웨이 사람** [노르웨이 사:람] no-reu-we-i sa-ram Norwegian

☐ **덴마크** [덴마크] den-ma-keu n. Denmark

   ☐ **덴마크 사람** [덴마크 사:람] den-ma-keu sa-ram Dane

☐ **독일** [도길] do-gil n. Germany

   ☐ **독일 사람** [도길 사:람] do-gil sa-ram German

☐ **러시아** [러시아] reo-si-a n. Russia

   ☐ **러시아 사람** [러시아 사:람] reo-si-a sa-ram Russian

☐ **루마니아** [루마니아] ru-ma-ni-a n. Romania

   ☐ **루마니아 사람** [루마니아 사:람] ru-ma-ni-a sa-ram Romanian

☐ **벨기에** [벨기에] bel-gi-e n. Belgium

   ☐ **벨기에 사람** [벨기에 사:람] bel-gi-e sa-ram Belgian

☐ **스웨덴** [스웨덴] seu-we-den n. Sweden

   ☐ **스웨덴 사람** [스웨덴 사:람] seu-we-den sa-ram Swede

☐ **스위스** [스위스] seu-wi-seu n. Switzerland

   ☐ **스위스 사람** [스위스 사:람] seu-wi-seu sa-ram Swiss

☐ **스페인** [스페인] seu-pe-in n. Spain

   = **에스파냐** [에스파냐] e-seu-pa-nya

   ☐ **스페인 사람** [스페인 사:람] seu-pe-in sa-ram Spaniard

   = **에스파냐 사람** [에스파냐 사:람] e-seu-pa-nya sa-ram

☐ **영국** [영국] yeong-guk n. England

   ☐ **영국 사람** [영국 사:람] yeong-guk sa-ram Englishman/Englishwoman

□ **오스트리아** [오스트리아] o-seu-teu-ri-a n. Austria

　□ **오스트리아 사람** [오스트리아 사:람] o-seu-teu-ri-a sa-ram Austrian

□ **이탈리아** [이탈리아] i-tal-ri-a n. Italy

　□ **이탈리아 사람** [이탈리아 사:람] i-tal-ri-a sa-ram Italian

□ **튀르키예** [튀르키예] twi-reu-ki-ye n. Turkey

　□ **튀르키예 사람** [튀르키예 사:람] twi-reu-ki-ye sa-ram Turk

　　tip. Turkey's national name was changed to Turkiye with the UN approval in June
　　2022, but both are in use.

□ **폴란드** [폴란드] pol-ran-deu n. Poland

　□ **폴란드 사람** [폴란드 사:람] pol-ran-deu sa-ram Pole

□ **프랑스** [프랑스] peu-rang-seu n. France

　□ **프랑스 사람** [프랑스 사:람] peu-rang-seu sa-ram French

□ **핀란드** [필란드] pil-ran-deu n. Finland

　□ **핀란드 사람** [필란드 사:람] pil-ran-deu sa-ram Finn

□ **헝가리** [헝가리] heong-ga-ri n. Hungary

　□ **헝가리 사람** [헝가리 사:람] heong-ga-ri sa-ram Hungarian

■ **오세아니아** [오세아니아] o-se-a-ni-a n. Oceania

　= **대양주** [대:양주] dae-yang-ju

□ **뉴질랜드** [뉴질랜드] nyu-jil-raen-deu n. New Zealand

　□ **뉴질랜드 사람** [뉴질랜드 사:람] nyu-jil-raen-deu sa-ram New Zealander

□ **호주** [호주] ho-ju n. Australia

　= **오스트레일리아** [오스트레일리아] o-seu-teu-re-il-ri-a

□ **호주 사람** [호주 사:람] ho-ju sa-ram Australian

= **오스트레일리아 사람** [오스트레일리아 사:람] o-seu-teu-re-il-ri-a sa-ram

■ **아프리카** [아프리카] a-peu-ri-ka n. Africa

□ **가나** [가나] ga-na n. Ghana

　□ **가나 사람** [가나 사:람] ga-na sa-ram Ghanaian, Ghanian

□ **나이지리아** [나이지리아] na-i-ji-ri-a n. Nigeria

　□ **나이지리아 사람** [나이지리아 사:람] na-i-ji-ri-a sa-ram Nigerian

□ **남아프리카공화국** [나마프리카공화국] na-ma-peu-ri-ka-gong-hwa-guk
n. the Republic of South Africa

= **남아공** [나마공] na-ma-gong

　□ **남아공 사람** [나마공 사:람] na-ma-gong sa-ram South African

□ **모로코** [모로코] mo-ro-ko n. Morocco

　□ **모로코 사람** [모로코 사:람] mo-ro-ko sa-ram Moroccan

□ **수단** [수단] su-dan n. Sudan

　□ **수단 사람** [수단 사:람] su-dan sa-ram Sudanese

□ **에티오피아** [에티오피아] e-ti-o-pi-a n. Ethiopia

　□ **에티오피아 사람** [에티오피아 사:람] e-ti-o-pi-a sa-ram Ethiopian

□ **이집트** [이집트] i-jip-teu n. Egypt

　□ **이집트 사람** [이집트 사:람] i-jip-teu sa-ram Egyptian

□ **케냐** [케냐] ke-nya n. Kenya

　□ **케냐 사람** [케냐 사:람] ke-nya sa-ram Kenyan

Korean Parts of Speech 한국어 품사

체언	noun	명사 myeong-sa	a word (other than a pronoun) used to identify any of a class of people, places, or things (common noun,) or to name a particular one of these (proper noun)
			가방 ga-bang (bag) 서울 seo-ul (Seoul) 것 geot (thing) 한국인 han-gu-gin (Korean)
	pronoun	대명사 dae-myeong-sa	a word that replaces a noun that has been mentioned before or that is already known. Pronouns can be used in place of people (e.g. I, you) or things (e.g. it, this)
			나 na (I) 너희 neo-hi (you) 이것 i-geot (this) 저기 jeo-gi (there)
	numeral	수사 su-sa	number
			하나 ha-na (one) 첫째 cheot-jjae (the first)

관계언	postpositional particle	조사 jo-sa	Korean postpositions, or particles, are suffixes or short words in Korean grammar that immediately follow a noun or pronoun
			tip. Some postposition particles in Korean are used as prepositions in English.

가 ga /이 i (subject's particle)
를 reul /을 eul (object's particle)
과 gwa /와 wa (with)
로 ro /으로 eu-ro (to)
에 e (at/in/on)

ending, suffix	어미 eo-mi	a letter(s) added to the end of a word to change its meaning

습니다 seum-ni-da /어요 eo-yo
(the final ending)
니? ni /나요? na-yo
(the interrogative ending)
고 go (the conjunctive ending)

용언	verb	동사 dong-sa	a word used to describe an action, state, or occurrence, and forming the main part of the predicate of a sentence

tip. A noun add '이다 [i-da]' is used as a verb.

놀다 nol-da (to play)
사람이다 sa-ra-mi-da (to be a person)

	adjective	형용사 hyeong-yong-sa	a word naming an attribute of a noun, but an adjective in Korean can be used in the predicate

tip. Korean adjectives function as verbs. These are called '상태동사 [상태동:사 sang-tae-dong-sa], stative or descriptive verbs.'

귀엽다 gwi-yeop-dda (to be cute)
춥다 chup-dda (to be cold)

수식언	determiner	관형사 gwan- hyeong-sa	a word that is placed in front of a noun or noun group to modify/describe it
			tip. Determiners can describe quality (new, old,) quantity (each, some) or show which object is being referred to (this, that.)
			순 sun (pure) 한 han (one)
	adverb	부사 bu-sa	a word or phrase that modifies the meaning of an adjective, verb, or other adverb, expressing manner, place, time, or degree
			매우 mae-u (very) 많이 ma-ni (a lot of) 늘 neul (always)
독립언	interjection	감탄사 gam-tan-sa	an abrupt remark, especially as an aside or interruption
			아 a (ah) 아이구 a-i-gu (ouch) 어머 eo-meo (oh my)

Korean Word Order 한국어 어순

Korean's basic word order is 'SOV(subject + object + verb).'
There are many subject's particles, object's particles and
the others' particles in Korean.

1. **s**ubject + **v**erb(predicate)

    s   **v**
나는 산다.
na-neun san-da
I buy.

2. **s**ubject + **o**bject + **v**erb

  s   **o**   **v**
나는 책을 산다.
na-neun chae-geul san-da
I buy a book.

3. **d**eterminer + **n**oun

  d **n**
나는 저 책을 산다.
na-neun jeo chae-geul san-da
I buy that book.

4. **a**dverb + **v**erb

  ad **v**
나는 책을 많이 산다.
na-neun chae-geul ma-ni san-da
I buy a lot of books.

Honorifics 존댓말

The Korean language observes a speaker or writer's relationships with both the subject of the sentence and the audience. Due to Korean traditional culture, honorifics are a very important part of the Korean language.

1. Honorific Nouns 존대 체언 jon-dae che-eon

meaning	basic word	honorific
meal	밥 bap	진지 jin-ji
home, house	집 jip	댁 daek
saying	말 mal	말씀 mal-sseum
age	나이 na-i	연세 yeon-se
honorific suffix	씨 ssi /님 nim	**tip.** '님' is the highest form of honorific, even above '씨'.
teacher	선생 seon-saeng	선생님 seon-saeng-nim
father	아버지 a-beo-ji	아버님 a-beo-nim
mother	어머니 eo-meo-ni	어머님 eo-meo-nim
elder brother	형 hyeong	형님 hyeong-nim
particle (to someone)	에게 e-ge	께 gge
subject particle	가 ga /이 i	께서 gge-seo

tip. There are ways a speaker with a lower status can express honor.
For example, use '저 [jeo]' instead of '나 [na] (I).'
'저는 학생입니다. [저는 학생입니다 jeo-neun hak-ssaeng-im-ni-da] (I am a student.)'
This sentence shows respect to the listener.

2. **Honorific Verbs** 존대 용언 jon-dae yong-eon

All verbs and adjectives can be converted into an honorific form by adding the infix '–시 si–' or '–으시 eu-si–' after the stem and before the ending.

meaning	basic verb	honorific
to go	가다 ga-da	가시다 ga-si-da
to receive	받다 bat-dda	받으시다 ba-deu-si-da
to be	있다 it-dda	계시다 gye-si-da
to drink	마시다 ma-si-da	드시다 deu-si-da
to eat	먹다 meok-dda	드시다 deu-si-da, 잡수시다 jap-ssu-si-da
to sleep	자다 ja-da	주무시다 ju-mu-si-da
to be hungry	배고프다 bae-go-peu-da	시장하시다 si-jang-ha-si-da

Ending Sentences 문장 종결법

1. Declarative Sentence 서술문 seo-sul-mun

tip. When you read declarative sentences, you should lower your tone at the end.

	It's raining.
formal polite style	비가 옵니다. bi-ga om-ni-da
formal style(written)	비가 온다. bi-ga on-da
familiar style	비가 오네. bi-ga o-ne
intimate polite style	비가 와요. bi-ga wa-yo
intimate style	비가 와. bi-ga wa

2. Interrogative Sentence 의문문 ui-mun-mun

tip. When you read/say interrogative sentences, you should raise your tone at the end.

	Is it raining?
formal polite style	비가 옵니까? bi-ga om-ni-gga?
familiar style	비가 오니? bi-ga o-ni?
intimate polite style	비가 와요? bi-ga wa-yo?
intimate style	비가 와? bi-ga wa?

tip. When you read/say wh-questions, you should lower your tone at the end unless the question is being asked to clarify something already discussed (Where did you say we are going?). There are some questions in English that don't necessarily require a specific answer but one is given anyway (Are you going somewhere? Yes, I'm going to the park.). In Korean, however, a more simple answer can be given (Yes, I'm going somewhere.). Although this might sound strange in English, it's accepted in Korean.

345

3. **Imperative Sentence** 명령문 myeong-nyeong-mun

tip. In imperative sentences, the subject is 'you' but it is not written or said.

	Go there.
formal polite style	저리로 **가십시오.** jeo-ri-ro ga-sip-si-o
formal style(written)	저리로 **가라.** jeo-ri-ro ga-ra
familiar style	저리로 **가게.** jeo-ri-ro ga-ge
intimate polite style	저리로 **가세요.** jeo-ri-ro ga-se-yo
intimate style	저리로 **가.** jeo-ri-ro ga

Conjugating Verbs 동사의 활용

Verbs in the Korean language come at the end of a clause. Verbs are the most complex part of speech, and a properly conjugated verb may stand on its own as a complete sentence.

Korean verbs are conjugated. Every verb form in Korean has two parts: a verb stem, simple or expanded, plus a sequence of inflectional suffixes. A Korean verb stem is bound, meaning that it never occurs without at least one suffix.

active or processive verb		stative or descriptive verb		copulative verb	
stem	suffix	stem	suffix	stem	suffix
to eat		to be a lot		to be (a bag)	
먹	는다	많	다	(가방)이	다
	느냐?		으냐?		냐?
	습니다		습니다		ㅂ니다
	고		고		고
	어서		아서		어서
	는		은		ㄴ
	기		기		기

< Examples of Irregular Verbs >

1. **Stems are Changed** 어간 변화 <small>eo-gan byeon-hwa</small>

ㄹ irregular	알	다	to know		
		는	알는	**아는**	
		ㅂ니다		**압니다**	
		세요	알세요	**아세요**	
으 irregular	기쁘	다	to be happy		
		어서	기쁘어서	**기뻐서**	
ㄷ irregular	듣	다	to hear, to listen to		
		으면	듣으면	**들으면**	
ㅂ irregular	돕	다	to help		
		아서	돕아서	도오아서	**도와서**
ㅅ irregular	낫	다	to heal, to cure		
		으면	낫으면	**나으면**	
르 irregular	부르	다	to sing, to be full		
		어요	부르어요	불ㄹ어요	**불러요**

2. **Stems and Suffixes are Changed**

어간과 어미 변화 eo-gan-gwa eo-mi byeon-hwa

ㅎ irregular	빨갛	다	red	
		으면	빨갛으면	**빨가면**
		아서	빨갛아서	**빨개서**

3. **Combining Special Suffixes**

특정 어미와 결합 teuk-jjeong eo-mi-wa gyeol-hap

하다 irregular	노래하	다	to sing a song	
		여	노래하여	**노래해**

tip. Some nouns, adverbs and roots of verbs add '하다' to become verbs.

< The Examples of Verb Conjugation >

verb	meaning	ㅂ(습)니다	었(았/였)습니다	고
가볍다 ga-byeop-dda	to be light	가볍습니다	가벼웠습니다	가볍고
걷다 geot-dda	to walk	걷습니다	걸었습니다	걷고
고맙다 go-map-dda	to appreciate	고맙습니다	고마웠습니다	고맙고
낫다 nat-dda	to be better	낫습니다	나았습니다	낫고
놓다 no-ta	to put	놓습니다	놓았습니다	놓고
다르다 da-reu-da	to be different	다릅니다	달랐습니다	다르고
닫다 dat-dda	to close	닫습니다	닫았습니다	닫고
돕다 dop-dda	to help	돕습니다	도왔습니다	돕고
멀다 meol-da	to be far	멉니다	멀었습니다	멀고
모르다 mo-reu-da	not to know	모릅니다	몰랐습니다	모르고
무겁다 mu-geop-dda	to be heavy	무겁습니다	무거웠습니다	무겁고
받다 bat-dda	to receive	받습니다	받았습니다	받고
부르다 bu-reu-da	to call	부릅니다	불렀습니다	부르고
살다 sal-da	to live	삽니다	살았습니다	살고
씹다 ssip-dda	to chew	씹습니다	씹었습니다	씹고
아프다 a-peu-da	to be hurt	아픕니다	아팠습니다	아프고
웃다 ut-dda	to laugh	웃습니다	웃었습니다	웃고
입다 ip-dda	to wear	입습니다	입었습니다	입고
잡다 jap-dda	to catch, to take	잡습니다	잡았습니다	잡고
춥다 chup-dda	to be cold	춥습니다	추웠습니다	춥고

는/(으)ㄴ/(으)ㄹ	(으)니까	더니	(으)면	어/아/여서	어/아/여야	어/아/여요
가벼운	가벼우니까	가볍더니	가벼우면	가벼워서	가벼워야	가벼워요
걷는	걸으니까	걷더니	걸으면	걸어서	걸어야	걸어요
고마운	고마우니까	고맙더니	고마우면	고마워서	고마워야	고마워요
나은	나으니까	낫더니	나으면	나아서	나아야	나아요
놓는	놓으니까	놓더니	놓으면	놓아서	놓아야	놓아요
다른	다르니까	다르더니	다르면	달라서	달라야	달라요
닫는	닫으니까	닫더니	닫으면	닫아서	닫아야	닫아요
돕는	도우니까	돕더니	도우면	도와서	도와야	도와요
먼	머니까	멀더니	멀면	멀어서	멀어야	멀어요
모르는	모르니까	모르더니	모르면	몰라서	몰라야	몰라요
무거운	무거우니까	무겁더니	무거우면	무거워서	무거워야	무거워요
받는	받으니까	받더니	받으면	받아서	받아야	받아요
부르는	부르니까	부르더니	부르면	불러서	불러야	불러요
사는	사니까	살더니	살면	살아서	살아야	살아요
씹는	씹으니까	씹더니	씹으면	씹어서	씹어야	씹어요
아픈	아프니까	아프더니	아프면	아파서	아파야	아파요
웃는	웃으니까	웃더니	웃으면	웃어서	웃어야	웃어요
입는	입으니까	입더니	입으면	입어서	입어야	입어요
잡는	잡으니까	잡더니	잡으면	잡아서	잡아야	잡아요
추운	추우니까	춥더니	추우면	추워서	추워야	추워요

ㅅ

ㅌ

기타

408

411

412

416

G

J

O

437

443

445

W